Alternative Scriptwriting

Second Edition

Alternative Scriptwriting

Second Edition

Ken Dancyger and Jeff Rush

Focal Press

Boston Oxford Melbourne Singapore Toronto Munich New Delhi Tokyo

Focal Press is an imprint of Butterworth-Heinemann
Copyright © 1995 by Butterworth-Heinemann
& A member of Reed Elsevier group
All rights reserved.

Recognizing the importance of preserving what has been written, Butterworth-Heinemann prints its books on acid-free paper whenever possible.

Library of Congress Cataloging-in-Publication Data

Dancyger, Ken.
    Alternative scriptwriting : writing beyond the rules / Ken
Dancyger and Jeff Rush. — 2nd ed.
        p.   cm.
    Includes index.
    ISBN 0-240-80218-7 (pbk. ; acid-free paper)
    1. Motion picture authorship. 2. Motion picture plays—Technique.
I. Title.
PN1996.D36   1995
808.2'3—dc20   95-7237
                                                                    CIP

British Library Cataloguing-in-Publication Data
A catalogue record for this book is available from the British Library.

The publisher offers discounts on bulk orders of this book.
For information, please write:

Manager of Special Sales
Butterworth-Heinemann
313 Washington Street
Newton, MA 02158-1626

10 9 8 7 6 5 4 3 2 1

Printed in the United States of America

For Ida *For Ilene*

Contents

Preface

Alternative Scriptwriting: Writing Beyond the Rules celebrates a multitude of approaches to screenwriting and filmmaking. Beginning with a reevaluation of the much-discussed issue of three-act structure, this book proceeds to encourage the writer to consider alternative approaches to both conventional and offbeat film stories.

Alternative Scriptwriting takes a mixed-genre approach not only to its content, but to its form. Theory and practice are intentionally intermingled to suggest the mixture of intellectual context and inchoate intuition with which the writer works. Key issues, exceptions, case studies, and exercises are included and designed to encourage the writer to come to a personal accommodation with the broad range of narrative and dramatic practices that make up our long history of storytelling.

Finally, because this is a book about differences in writing, the co-authors have not smoothed over the occasional, minor divergences between their perspectives and writing styles. Rather than detract from the text, these differences serve to reinforce their beliefs that there can be no single, right approach to an art form that, like all art forms, thrives on exception rather than rule.

Introduction to the Second Edition

Since it was published in 1991, *Alternative Scriptwriting* has generated much reaction and discussion which convinced us of the value of a second edition. Many of the reactions came from the readers for whom we had originally written the book, but others proved to be a pleasant surprise.

We discovered that the book has reached two distinct audiences. The first of those readers who have already determined they are interested in alternative approaches to writing and thinking about narrative film.

The second audience has been the surprise—those readers who are fully committed to mainstream film, but who nonetheless find *Alternative Scriptwriting* to be valuable precisely because it is unlike any other book on screenwriting. They have told us that it offers a cogent analysis of mainstream forms even as these forms are contrasted to the alternatives. And these readers find the notion of writing from the inside out, of building from one's own conflict and needs, to be useful in writing mainstream scripts that distinguish themselves by their passion and originality.

We are delighted to welcome these readers and have added two chapters that speak specifically to this edge—"Personal Scriptwriting—The Edge" and "Personal Scriptwriting—Beyond the Edge." Our goal, as in the original, is to continue to be as inclusive about narrative options as possible.

We also realized that many of the ideas in *Alternative Scriptwriting* about genre, character, structure, and voice need more consideration, and so we have included many more examples in each of these areas, which we consider the beginning rather than the definitive end. We look forward to our colleagues around the world deepening the work in each of these areas.

Additional questions have arisen since the original book's publication. Do European—or, more specifically, non-American—films conform to the strategies suggested in *Alternative Scriptwriting*? Do women write scripts with the same narrative intentions as male writers? Do challenges to genre motifs assure better scripts? Does mixed genre storytelling imply originality but guarantee commercial failure? These are some of the issues that we will address in this new edition.

The original goals of *Alternative Scriptwriting: Writing Beyond the Rules* remain the same: to link scriptwriting to other forms of storytelling and to suggest that a strictly formulaic approach to scriptwriting—whether about character, structure, or form—is too limiting. Every script needs a mix of narrative strategies to best tell its story effectively.

Acknowledgments

By Ken Dancyger:

I have taught screenwriting for 15 years and would like to thank all of my students at York University who, in their questions and screenplays, helped me to refine my ideas about writing for film.

I'd also like to thank Harvey Markowitz, Bill Peters, Stu Robinson, Richard Curtis, and Andre Stein, whose professional support at crucial points in my career helped me to continue to write.

At Focal Press, I'd like to thank Karen Speerstra for accepting our concept of *Alternative Scriptwriting,* and Marie Lee and Sharon Falter for working carefully with two writers to create one book.

I'd like to thank my colleagues, in a unique group of screenwriting teachers, who have come together twice to share ideas and approaches to teaching screenwriting. This group catalyzed the idea that there is much to learn from one another about the art and craft of screenwriting. I'm sure all of us will hear a great deal from these twenty creative teachers and their students.

At York University, I would like to thank Michael Stokes and George Robinson for their help in preparing the manuscript. A second thanks is extended to George for helping me make that first screenwriting conference at York such a success, that I had no choice but to write a book about the issues raised at that conference!

Above all, I'd like to thank my colleague and collaborator, Jeff Rush. Our association has been a pleasurable, stimulating experience. Jeff's persistent intelligence and high standards have pushed me to expect more of myself and to produce a standard of work commensurate with his own.

Reprinted with permission of the University of California Press and MCA, are script excerpts from *The Lady Eve* and *Sullivan's Travels* from *Five Screenplays,* by Preston Sturges, edited By B. Henderson, 1985.

By Jeff Rush:

I would like to thank all those who have joined us in helping to broaden the discussion of screenwriting over the last few years. The organizations with which we've had productive exchanges include the Symposium for Screenwriting and the Academy, SCRIPT, the University Film and Video Association, the Florida State Conference on Literature and Film, the Ohio University Film Conference, and the Society for Cinema Studies.

I am particularly indebted to Bill Miller, Director of SCRIPT; Yvette Biro of NYU; Milena Jelinek of Columbia; Mary Gage and Dorn Hetzel of Penn State; Erin Preis of Purdue; Michael Jacot of York; Jim Ambandos and Warren Bass of Temple; Andrew Horton of Loyola; Marilyn Beker of Loyola Marymount; Paul Lucey of USC; and Richard Walter of UCLA. I thank you all for your support, interest, and passionate argument.

In addition, I would like to thank my critical colleagues Lisa Henderson, Roberta Pearson, Bill Urrichio, and Brian Winston of Penn State, and Jeanne Allen and Paul Swann of Temple for countless discussions on theory and practice.

Of course, I want to mention my students at Iowa, Penn State, and Temple who have put up with me over the last ten years and whose questions have taught me so much. From what I've learned over that time, I worry what my first students had to suffer.

I echo Ken's thanks to Karen Speerstra, Marie Lee, and Sharon Falter at Focal Press. A more supportive pair of editors would be hard to imagine.

Most importantly, I would like to thank my colleague and collaborator, Ken Dancyger, whose steadiness, vast film knowledge, and insight always brought me down to earth. Our work has been the beginning of a collaboration that will extend far beyond this one document.

Most profoundly, I would like to thank my wife, Ilene Raymond, whose love and support has helped me to understand just how subtle and precious are those moments that most define and sustain us. It is to express such nuances that I undertook the explorations in this book.

And finally, I'd like to thank my parents, Frank and Renee Rush, whose never-ending curiosity and openness to the world have been such an inspiration to me. And who, along with my grandfather, Max Carol, so deeply instilled the notion that there is music in everything if you only listen for it.

With some modifications, Chapter 11 first appeared as the article, "Internalizing History: The Limits of Transforming Documentary into Fiction," in the Fall 1990 Special Screenwriting Issue of the *Journal of Film and Video* (42:3).

1

. . . .

Beyond the Rules

There are many views about what is important for you to know to become a better screenwriter. Before we explain our versions of what you need to know, we'll state our biases at the outset.

First, we think of the screenwriter as a storyteller who happens to write for film. Many screenwriters write for more than one medium. Steve Tesich *(Breaking Away)* and Harold Pinter *(The Handmaid's Tale)* write for theater and film. David Hare *(Strapless)*, William Goldman *(Butch Cassidy and the Sundance Kid)*, and John Sayles *(Baby, It's You)* write fiction and screenplays, as do many others. You, as the scriptwriter, are part of a broad storytelling tradition. To disregard other forms of writing or to view scriptwriting as an exclusive art form is to cut yourself off from a large cultural community with which you have more in common than you might realize.

Our second bias is that a screenplay should be more than merely structurally sound. How often has the screenwriter been referred to as a technician—the equivalent to the draftsman in architecture? Although there are screenwriters who are content to be technicians, many are not. Nor should you be. This book suggests ways to move beyond conventional structure.

Third, you have to know about structure in order to move beyond it. It isn't possible to reinvent the process without knowing it in detail. Consequently, much of what we say highlights the conventions of screenwriting developed to date.

Now that you know our biases, we can state our fairly simple approach. We outline conventions and then suggest practical ways to undermine or alter those conventions. We use specific examples, often to illustrate the points we're trying to make. Ultimately, we will help you develop better screenplays.

To help you reach this goal, we talk about form and content, character, and language, while pressing you to develop alternative narrative strategies that prompt you to write the best screenplay you can write. Melanie Griffith, recognizing that people aren't always what they appear to be, says to the conventional Jeff Daniels in Max Frye's *Something Wild*, "I know you, you're a closet rebel." Just as she sees beyond his superficial characteristics, we want you to look beyond the surface of scriptwriting, beyond form. You'll be surprised at what you'll find.

Conventions

There are some fundamental story devices that remain constant regardless of your scriptwriting approach. All screen stories use plots in which the premise is expressed in terms of conflict. The focus on conflict is so central to storytelling that its use can be traced from the original Ten Commandments to the two film versions of the story. Discovery and reversal are other conventional storytelling devices. Surprise is important to all stories; without it, the story is flat and becomes a report of a series of events, rather than a story that invites the viewer to get involved and stay involved. A turning point is another device that is typically used in storytelling. The number of turning points varies from screen story to screen story, but their usefulness is critical. All of these elements—conflict, discovery, reversal, and turning point—are the technical devices you use to involve the reader in your story. Beyond these devices, however, your choices are limited only by your willingness and your imagination.

Structure

In the past 10 years, *structure* as applied to film has come to mean Act One, Act Two, Act Three. Each act has its own characteristics—Act One: introduction of character and premise; Act Two: confrontation and struggle; Act Three: resolution of the crisis introduced in the premise. Operating in each act are various plot devices intended to intensify conflict, characterize, and propel the plot forward. Structure is discussed in more detail in Chapter 2.

Noteworthy, however, is the difference of scriptwriting structure from other structured forms of storytelling. Most plays have two acts and most books have more than three chapters. Although many operas do have three acts, the unfolding of the narrative to suggest the greater importance of subtext over text indicates how far removed opera is from film (but here, too, the screenwriter can learn something from another medium).

Premise

The *premise*, sometimes referred to as the concept, central concept, or central idea, is what the screenplay is about. Usually, it is presented in terms of the central character's dilemma at a particular point in her life (the point at which the screen story begins). For example, the premise in *All About Eve* is: What happens to a great actress (Bette Davis) when age threatens her physical beauty and her career? In *Inside Moves*, a story about a young man, played by John Savage, the premise is: What happens when this young man decides to kill himself and fails?

Premise is usually presented in terms of conflict. In *All About Eve*, the conflict offers two options—to accept aging with whatever amorous and career consequences that suggests or to struggle for relationships and roles beyond natural reason. This struggle and its outcome are the basis of the script. When Bette Davis makes her decision, the screen story is over.

In *Inside Moves*, Rory, John Savage's character, attempts suicide but fails. Consequently, he has two options—to try again or to find a way to make a life he can live with, even enjoy. Life or death is the basis of this screen story. Once he makes his decision and commits to one option, the screen story is over. The premise, then, is central to the screen story and is best posited in terms of the central conflict for the main character.

A variation worth mentioning is the existence of two types of premises. We mention them because they are discussed in other books and they have become part of industry parlance. The two variations are *high concept* and *low (or soft) concept*. High concept refers to a plot-oriented premise and implies excitement. Low concept refers to a premise that is softer on the plot and consequently relies more on the strength of the characters. A simple way to describe the difference is to view a high-concept premise as a plot-intensive story and a low-concept premise as a character-intensive story. During the 1980s, films with high-concept premises were more desirable because that type was more successful and thus more likely to be produced.

The Role of Conflict

Conflict is a central feature of the screen story. Man against man, man against environment, and man against himself are the classic versions found in the screen story. Variations of sex, age, religion, and culture provide variety to the conflict, while polarities (i.e., extreme opposites) make screen conflict operational. In the Western, the most obvious polarity was the white horse and clothing of the hero, and the black horse and clothing of the villain. Policeman/criminal, lawyer/accused, rich/poor, hero/villain—all are polarities that exemplify the character conflicts featured in different screen stories.

All screen characters are developed using polarities—opposites in physical appearance as well as in behavioral characteristics. In *On the Waterfront*, the main character is the only character who is physically fit. His brother, a criminal, looks older, dresses differently, and speaks differently. The main character is dark; the young woman he falls in love with is a blonde. It should come as no surprise that she speaks better and behaves more intensely than the main character. When she is committed to a decision, the main character hedges. The polarities go on and on. When we look at all the other characters' physical variations (slim and heavy), age variations (young and old), aggression variations (violent and meek), we see that they permeate the screen story. Polarities are the most obvious, useful devices for instilling conflict in your story.

Character

The main *character* of the screen story is the primary means for the audience to experience the story, for the audience will be involved to the extent that it identifies with the character and his dilemma. On the surface, the character may be recognizable via a dominant physical or behavioral characteristic. However, during a moment of private revelation or a moment when the character allows himself to appear foolish or vulnerable, our sense of fellow feeling for that character is realized and our identification with the character is secured.

Generally, the main character is energetic and is exposed to sufficient conflict to propel her through the story. The main character differs from secondary characters in a variety of ways. The primary difference is that she undergoes a metamorphosis during the course of the story. On the other hand, the secondary characters not only don't change, they serve as a source of contrast to the main character. Through this interaction, secondary characters help to move the story along.

All the characters (main and secondary) have distinct goals in the screen story. Generally, these goals parallel the premise. Secondary characters take each side of the issue and the main character is faced with the conflict. In *On the Waterfront*, Marlon Brando's character is faced with this question: Can he, a washed-up boxer, be a more moral person than his brother, the criminal? Should he be a criminal or a saint? Actors Lee J. Cobb and Rod Steiger, who play gangsters in the film, are important secondary characters, along with Eva Marie Saint and Karl Malden, who play the roles of saints. Each secondary character prods Brando to join his side. The screen story moves to its conclusion once Brando has made his choice.

Dialogue

Since 1927, films have had sound, comprised of dialogue, sound effects, and music. *Dialogue* in film fulfills three roles. First, it characterizes. How one speaks tells us whether or not the character is educated, as well as the character's origins, profession, approximate age, and emotional state. Second, dialogue helps define the plot. What the character says depends on the role of the character in the story. Louis, in *Four Friends*, is a dying man who loves life, as opposed to the central character's tentative approach to life. Louis's function is to highlight, through dialogue, his joy of living, his enthusiasm for science and for sex, and all those elements absent from the life of the main character. Dialogue's third function is to relieve tension, through humor, when it occurs in a script (an inevitable state given the writer's attention to conflict). Humor puts us at ease about the characters; we like people more readily after we've had a laugh.

In a more general sense, dialogue has an additional purpose—to create believability about the characters in the screenplay. The first line of defense for the writer is whether the audience believes the story, or more specifically, the characters in the story. If the dialogue is working, the audience should believe that the words, their specificity, creates an aura of believability about the characters. When dialogue does not work, it tends to be because the characters who speak it are not believable. Consequently, dialogue plays an important role in the creation of credibility about character.

Atmosphere

When a reader reads a screenplay, she is confronted with a good deal of description and then dialogue. So how can the writer create *atmosphere?* Doesn't it come from visualization when the screenplay is filmed? Not entirely. Atmosphere, in a screenplay, is the accumulation of details that creates the illusion of believability in the character, place, and situation.

The writer creates a spatial or three-dimensional sense of believability when the dialogue is credible and when the accretion of detail about time and place are so convincing that the reader says, "I know that person. I've been in that place or situation." Meaningful, particular detail is the key here. When there is enough detail, the atmosphere of the screenplay moves from generic to particular, from mechanical to meaningful.

Action Line

Action line is frequently referred to as the story line or the plot. The term, however, is most appropriate for film, because the visual nature of the medium suggests visual action as the preferred form of characterization. Also, action line is occasionally referred to as the foreground story or the major story line, as opposed to the *background story* or the secondary story line.

Foreground story implies the more important aspects of the story, which isn't always true. Indeed, in many stories the more subtle background (or minor story line) involves the deeper relationship elements of the story as opposed to the larger events that drive the story. For an audience, these relationship elements are frequently the most meaningful emotional link to the screen story. Consequently, the background story can be just as, if not more, important for the audience.

Often, the action line, although more sensational, is more superficial in its meaning for the audience. For simplicity, the action line can be viewed as the exterior action of the story and is definitely conflict-oriented. The background story can be viewed as the interior (main character) action of the screen story. Background story is identification-oriented.

Rising Action

Rising action carries the action line from the beginning to the end and implies that the level of conflict that confronts the major character increases as we move through the screen story. The level of conflict is greatest in Act Three. There is a dip in the rising action at the beginning of Act Two and Act Three. The illustration indicates the levels of action during Acts One through Three in a screenplay.

Subtext

Subtext is the background story or the interior struggle of the main character to choose the most appropriate solution to his interior con-

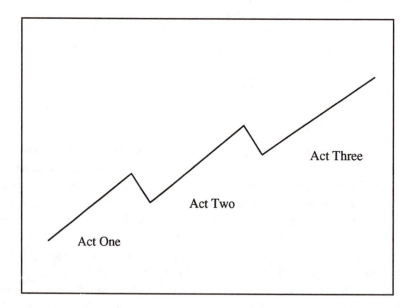

Act Three

Act Two

Act One

flict. Subtext is often expressed in terms of general human emotional states: love-hate or life-death. Not every screen story deals with such primal feelings, but the memorable films have these dimensions to their stories. At the deepest level, subtext can reach the audience in a more complex and gripping manner than action. The screen stories you most likely remember have a strong subtext.

Discovery

The presence of surprise is important in the screenplay. Whether it refers to plot or character, an unexpected revelation, no matter how trivial, maintains our interest. *Discoveries* made later in the screen story must be greater in scale than those found earlier in the screen story.

Reversal

Plot twists manifest a *reversal* of fortune for the main character. Such setbacks create tension and heightened concern for the fate of the character, but should be used more sparingly than other plot devices. Too many reversals in a screen story tend to depreciate their impact. Deploy them with care to create for maximum impact.

Turning Point

Turning points, sometimes referred to as plot points, yield surprise, anticipation, and tension, and help maintain our interest in the screen story. Turning points are classified as minor or major, while *reversals* tend to be major turning points. Minor turning points take place frequently throughout the screen story. Early major turning points open up the story and provide a broader spectrum of options for the main character. Late major turning points help to focus the story by pointing the main character toward the resolution of his crisis.

Going Against Structure

Structure is such an important characteristic of the screenplay that we devote Chapters 2 through 6 to discussing structure, counterstructure, genre, and working against genre. As previously mentioned, the structured approach uses three acts to tell your screen story, and, if you choose, the use of a particular genre to deliver your three acts.

The central question you face if you don't wish to use the conventional three-act structure is: What is available to you? Can you, for example, tell a story in one act? Probably not. Can you tell a story in two acts? Yes, as evidenced in *Full Metal Jacket.* In four acts? Yes, as shown in *Mo' Better Blues.*

Although the setup-confrontation-resolution approach to structure remains the predominant form, the absence of resolution in *Full Metal Jacket* and the addition of a second optional resolution in the fourth act of *Mo' Better Blues* adds a dimension to those films that is not present in the classic case. The potential benefit of the fresh addition of a second resolution is to alter the meaning of the film.

A limitation of scriptwriting is that a screen story must be set up and must have some level of conflict or confrontation. Consequently, a story that is all setup, or all confrontation with no setup (the one-act option), is too limiting and too similar to a fragment of a larger story, rather than a feature-length screen story.

One qualification to this argument about going against structure poses another question. When Julie Dash wrote *Daughters of the Dust*, was the circularity of the story going against conventional structure or was she opting to tell the story in a manner most sensible to her? Similarly, is she opting for a group of characters over a single goal-oriented main character and does that choice imply working against convention, or, is it a case of a woman telling a story in a manner most sensible to her? This issue of the manner in which men and women tell stories is not easily captured, but for those interested we refer you to a fascinating book that does imply gender difference. The title is *Women's Ways of Knowing* (Basic Books, 1986) and the authors (Mary Field Belenky, Blythe McVicker Clinchy, Nancy Rule Goldberger, and Jill Mattock Tarule) make a persuasive argument that women are less interested in linear storytelling and are far more empathetic with the circular approach used by Julie Dash.

With genre, the scriptwriter's options increase. Genres, or particular types of films such as gangster or horror, have certain identifiable characteristics. For example, audiences identify the monster-antagonist with the horror film and the urban setting with the gangster film. You can use a particular genre as the envelope for your structural choice or you can challenge a particular genre motif. For example, in a Western, the protagonist is generally positive, moral, and faces his challenges alone. However, in *The Wild Bunch*, the scriptwriter challenged the genre motif of the positive protagonist by making the main character an outlaw and a murderer and surrounding him with people who were worse.

The violation of genre can relate to any motif, not just to character. A scriptwriter can vary the presentation of the antagonist, the nature of the confrontation, or the resolution. For example, the unseen enemy in the war film *Full Metal Jacket* robs the viewer of a classical view of the antagonist. In fact, the antagonist becomes a fellow American in the first half of the film.

Another challenge to genre is the use of mixed genres to alter meaning. This particular scriptwriting option became quite popular in the 1980s. Given the number of genres, many options are available to the scriptwriter, and while not all genres mix with success, attempts to mix even the most unlikely have yielded interesting results. For example, by mixing the musical and *film noir* genres, *Diva* is fresher than it would have been as a straight musical or *film noir* screen story.

The ultimate challenge to conventions has been met by Woody Allen in his film *Crimes and Misdemeanors*. Not only does Allen alter structure (he presents two three-act stories in one film), he also mixes genres and challenges particular motifs in each of the genres. The result is a startling screen story during which the shifts in our expectations and moods are so rapid, that we are left dazed and dazzled by his audacity. *Crimes and Misdemeanors* suggests audiences will tolerate a good deal of experimentation and are sufficiently film-experienced to know what to expect from conventional structure and genres. Allen challenges these expectations on as many bases as he feels are manageable.

Character Alternatives

If the classic main character is active, likable, and central to the story, alternative approaches challenge each of these qualities. These character alternatives are explored in detail in Chapters 7 through 9.

What happens to your screen story when the main character is more passive, more voyeur than participant? What happens when your main character is not admirable or even likable? What happens when your main character is overshadowed by one or more secondary characters? Do these initiatives undermine the effectiveness of your screen story? The answers to these questions yield a new range of possibilities. They can weaken your story or they can alter the experience of your story in new and interesting ways. In all likelihood, you will have to adjust your treatment of all the characters and of the amount of narrative necessary to tell your story. This is especially true for the role of the antagonist.

Taking up the issue of the unconventional main character, we can find examples throughout the history of film.

Aiello (James Mason), the main character in Michael Wilson's *Five Fingers*, is a spy trying to sell secrets to the Nazis, including the time and place of the Allies' planned Normandy invasion of Europe. Hardly a person to admire, Aiello is, nevertheless, a fascinating and involving character. Travis Bickle (Robert De Niro) in Paul Schrader's *Taxi Driver* is an alienated, highly disturbed war veteran. He is sufficiently antisocial and prone to violence to have little appeal as a main character. Rupert Popkin (Robert De Niro) in Paul Zimmerman's *King of Comedy* is even less appealing. Delusional and desperate, Popkin wants to be a television celebrity.

In each of these cases, the scriptwriter presented characters and action in a way that allowed the viewer to identify with the main character. In *Taxi Driver*, the uncaring, callous nature of the majority of characters makes Travis Bickle seem more sensitive, and he becomes a victim rather than a perpetrator. The consequence is that, in spite of his neurotic behavior, we identify with Travis Bickle. This is the sort of adjustment the writer makes if she wants to move away from the classic presentation of the main character.

Another character alternative is the ironic character, who promotes distance between us and the character. This allows us not only to sympathize with the character's plight but also to wonder why events and people seem to conspire against him. Often, the ironic character is portrayed as an innocent victim of a person or system. This type of character is very useful when you feel that the ideas are more important than the people in your screen story.

Dialogue Alternatives

Dialogue in a screen story enhances the particular credibility of the character. Whether it's used to advance the plot or to characterize, audiences expect film dialogue to be believable, in keeping with film's illusion of realism. Film looks real, and when behavior and appearance of performers help support that illusion, it is easier for us to relate emotionally to the story we see and the people portrayed.

What if the screenwriter wants to use dialogue to undermine credibility or to supercede the sense of realism? Then, the quality and function of the dialogue in the screenplay broadens considerably and invites the influence of other storytelling forms—the play, the performance, the burlesque—all of which are dependent on dialogue in more elaborate ways.

Dialogue can be more highly charged and more emotional than conventional movie dialogue. Paddy Chayefsky uses this approach in his screenplay *Network*. The old-time producer (William Holden) and the new-style programming executive (Faye Dunaway) argue eloquently about their conflicting philosophies in dialogue that illustrates the conflict. Dialogue can also be stripped of feeling and abstracted so that the viewer relates to it as a metaphor for his state of mind rather than a sense of plausibility. David Hare uses this approach in his screenplays *Plenty* and *Strapless*.

A third option for dialogue is to use language ironically in order to destroy the most literal meaning of the language. This type of dialogue is often associated with the Marx Brothers; Groucho was constantly trying to undermine meaning. For example, Groucho plays Rufus T. Firefly in Bert Kalmar and Harry Ruby's *Duck Soup* (1933). Firefly is the new leader of Freedonia, a fictional middle European state. Fanfare announces the arrival of the leader.

In the palace he is greeted by Mrs. Teasdale. The regal guests eagerly await his arrival. The exchange of dialogue follows.

```
                    MRS. TEASDALE
          We've been expecting you.
                    (She gives him her hand; pompously.)
          As Chairwoman of the reception
          committee, I extend the good
          wishes of every man, woman and
          child of Freedonia.

                    FIREFLY
          Never mind that stuff. Take a
          card.
                    (he fans out a pack of cards)

                    MRS. TEASDALE
          A card? What'll I do with a
          card?
                    (she takes it)

                    FIREFLY
          You can keep it. I've got
          fifty-one left. Now, what were
          you saying?[1]
```

Another dialogue alternative is used in screen stories that have very little action and thus may be subject to a loss of screen energy. This situation may be compensated for through the use of energized dialogue, which is sufficiently charged so that the dynamism of the story is brought out. This alternative necessitates a great deal more dialogue because it then becomes considerably more important than in the conventional screen story. Spike Lee's *She's Gotta Have It* is a recent example of the use of this type of dialogue. Budget limitations can also promote the use of excessive, energized dialogue in order to avoid costly action sequences.

Atmosphere Alternatives

Atmosphere is created by visual detail and lends visual credibility to your screen story. If your goal is to challenge credibility or to add another level of meaning to your story, manipulation of environmental details becomes your most direct tool to alter atmosphere.

---

[1] The Marx Brothers, *Monkey Business, Duck Soup, and A Day at the Races.* Faber and Faber, London, 1953.

In *Local Hero*, Bill Forsyth uses detail to subvert and alter the original direction of the narrative. *Local Hero* is the story of a Texas oilman's efforts to buy land in Scotland for the purpose of exploiting offshore oil. To underscore the corporate dimension of the story line, we would expect offices, oil rigs, and the material benefits of the exploiters and the exploited. Forsyth has little interest in this type of detail. Instead, we are presented with a sensual otherworldly presentation of the land and its hypnotic effect on the would-be exploiters. The result is that the oilmen, by the end of the narrative, don't get what they came for, but they don't seem to mind. The owner of the company, a mystic portrayed by Burt Lancaster, and his salesman, portrayed by Peter Riegert, have been changed by their exposure to this mystical landscape. They are sensually enriched, but materially worse off.

Francis Ford Coppola and Michael Herr use the atmosphere of *Apocalypse Now* to move that story from a realistic treatment of the Vietnam War to a metaphor of war and Vietnam as hell. In his screenplay for *The Untouchables*, David Mamet, moves his gangster film about Al Capone and Elliot Ness to a story about the struggle of good and evil. The metaphor moves us away from the events of the story toward the subtext of good and evil.

Finally, the scriptwriter has the option of altering atmosphere by using details that undermine the sense of place developed from preceding details. A good example is in David Lynch's *Blue Velvet*. A tranquil, pastoral town is presented—beautiful flowers, content inhabitants, and, of course, rosy-cheeked children. Then, suddenly, Lynch shows us the ants and insects that inhabit the ground under the grass. Soon after this shot, the surface impression of the town is shattered when the main character finds a severed ear. The tranquility is broken and we can't trust our expectations for the balance of the screen story.

Foreground and Background Story Alternatives

The scriptwriter has broad options in the area of foreground and background stories. Film stories have been long divided between personal interest stories and adventure (action) stories. Often, the personal interest story is more literary and the action story is linear. Today, the action story is called the high-concept premise and the personal interest story is called the low-concept premise. The high-concept film, particularly since *Star Wars*, has become the dominant type of screen story. Foreground stories are the prevalent form, and the resulting schism has screenwriters scurrying to maintain their positions in the marketplace. In spite of the market, screen stories benefit from having both strong foreground and background stories, as described in Chapter 10.

It should be noted that the current remarkable level of dominance of the American film internationally is attributable to the success of the foreground story, plot-oriented film. Films such as *The Terminator* series and the *Lethal Weapon* series, as well as the earlier *Indiana Jones* series and the *Star Wars* series, deploy stars, special effects, and production values but at heart all are linear stories with memorable set pieces of action. When European films such as *La Femme Nikita* or Australian films such as *The Road Warrior* deploy a similar narrative strategy they too are great international successes. This does not mean, however, that writers should now all devote themselves to the action genre. Indeed, the success of films such as *Sleepless in Seattle* and *Forrest Gump* demonstrates that audiences also want low concept or character-driven stories.

For the scriptwriter, alternatives begin to develop when you work with the balance of foreground and background. The key ingredient in creating that balance is the main character. If the scriptwriter positions her in a deeply personal dilemma, the outcome of the story is less predictable. Background stories, which dwell on the interior life of the main character, tend to be less predictable because interior life is not linear.

Although foreground stories are the current dominant form, much attention has been paid to background stories, as evidenced in *Moonstruck*. Background story-oriented screen plays tend to have particular characteristics beyond their character orientation. Often, dialogue moves away from realism toward a more literary quality and is distinctive and eccentric. Playwrights are accustomed to using dialogue—literary, charged dialogue— because there is less action on stage. Feeling levels intensify through language and dialogue. The dialogue in *Moonstruck* shouldn't come as a surprise since the scriptwriter, John Patrick Shanley, is a playwright. So, too, are Sam Shepard, Ted Talby, Steve Tesich, Hanif Kureishi, David Hare, and David Mamet, all interesting playwrights who also happen to write screenplays with strong background stories.

In spite of the commercial trend toward foreground stories, many options arise from the deployment of a strong background story or using a mix of foreground and background stories. Foreground stories may be sensational to watch, but they present the central character superficially. When the writer uses the background story, the main character becomes more personal to us and more open-ended. The result invites a deeper involvement from the viewer.

Rising Action Alternatives

When writers deploy a stronger background story, they open up possibilities in varying the convention of rising action. Generally, the action of the screen story gradually rises to a climax, except for a brief pause at the beginnings of Act Two and Act Three, which allow the writer to set up the parameters for the acts that follow. When using a background story, the scriptwriter can devote more time to the characters, although this does not necessarily advance the plot or move the story toward the climax. A good example of this alternative approach to rising action is found in Louis Malle's *My Dinner with Andre*. Less extreme, but no less interesting, is Jean-Claude Carrière and Louis Malle's *May Fools*. In these films, the shift from rising action affords the audience a greater opportunity to know the characters.

As we mention in Chapter 4, moving away from three-act structure results in a more open-ended sense of character and structure. A similar result occurs when the scriptwriter moves away from rising action. In order to make this step effective, however, the screenwriter must make the visitation with the characters worthwhile. They must be interesting and the dialogue has to be as involving as new plot developments would be. This means charged, witty, and surprising dialogue. Without these characteristics, the viewer will experience a flatness that does not serve the interests of the screen story.

This idea of modulating rising action applies only to Act Two of the screenplay. The screen story still needs the rise in action during the setup in Act One and the continued rise in action to the resolution in Act Three, unless you choose not to use an Act Three.

Developing Narrative Strategies

There are more ways to tell a screen story than the conventions of screenwriting suggest. This message is the central theme of this book. In order to tell your story you need to develop a narrative strategy that is best suited to your idea. First, you need to answer these questions: Who is your main character? What is the premise of your story? What is the most exciting action line for this story? Does the action line best highlight your main character's dilemma? Is your main character's dilemma situational or is it deeply rooted in her personality?

The choices you make when answering these questions are inherently dramatic choices and will influence the effectiveness of your screen story. You, as a screenwriter, must make the best dramatic choice, bearing in mind that the most interesting choice is not necessarily the most obvious.

A central issue for all scriptwriters is the creation of a story that invites the viewer to identify with the main character or with that character's situation. If your narrative strategy employs characters who don't invite identification, you can't guarantee that the viewer will stay with you for the length of your story.

What narrative strategies are available to the writer? There are many, and you have options with every factor in the screenplay, including character, language, atmosphere, action line, background story, and structure. In regard to the main character, for example, you can opt for an active, energetic main character, a more passive one, or a less likable one. Your choice depends on the type of character that best elicits the dramatic results you seek. In dialogue, you need not be limited by character function, and in terms of structure, you can vary or mix genres, challenge the convention of three-act structure, or vary the foreground-background mix. In all cases, exploring alternative strategies to develop your narrative strategy yields a fresher approach to your story and more open-ended characters.

The scriptwriter must be flexible to ensure that what he takes away from one area of the screenplay is compensated for elsewhere. If we don't like your main character and the challenge is to create a situation in which we identify with that character (in spite of our reservations about him), there are certain steps you must take. You may have to shift your approach to the other characters, your dialogue may have to be more emotionally charged and more intense, and you'll need a more elaborate plot. Alfred Hitchcock, in his work with writers Ben Hecht and Raymond Chandler, exemplifies the ability to capture viewer identification in spite of the use of less-than-admirable main characters. In *Psycho*, *The Birds*, and *North by Northwest*, it's the situation, rather than the character, that brings us into the story. In *Notorious* and *Strangers on a Train*, the unsympathetic main characters are offset by extreme antagonists, people we like to hate.

A scriptwriter also has to concern herself with the issue of stimulation for the viewer. Audiences go to movies to enjoy themselves. Whether stimulation comes from the elaborations of the plot or the wit of the dialogue, the charm-stimulation element is necessary to link the screenwriter to the audience. What happens to this element when you begin to challenge screenwriting conventions? It begins to fade. Therefore, you have to include stimulation in some other form. Spike Lee challenges conventional structure in *She's Gotta Have It*, but his additional charm comes from the dialogue. Whatever narrative strategy you use, audience identification and stimulation are critical factors in determining the success of your screenplay. If you select an alternative strategy, these factors will still have to be present.

Conclusion

In this chapter, we discussed conventions and counter-conventions to scriptwriting. Conventions are critical building blocks to tell your story. Counter-conventions can make that story fresh and more exciting. In order to use new strategies, however, you have to know the conventions of scriptwriting. Throughout this book we highlight the creative opportunities that lie between those conventions and counter-conventions.

2

......

Structure

Consider the story line of a mainstream film. In *The Verdict*, Galvin, an alcoholic lawyer who has lost faith in the law, is given a lucrative open-and shut-case to settle out of court. But finding himself moved by its injustice and seeing an opportunity to redeem himself, he decides to bring the case to trial. We know this is crazy and sure enough, he runs it into the ground. At this point, there's nothing left and the script may as well end with Galvin's return to his dissolute life. But now Galvin digs down and seizes the story. He finds "something in himself" and when everyone else wants to quit, he keeps on. At the "darkest moment," Galvin comes up with the clue that leads him to the critical witness. He wins the case and achieves personal redemption.

Now contrast this story line with that of *She's Gotta Have It*. Nola Darling, speaking directly to the camera, tells us she is consenting to this film in order to clear her name. We are then taken back into her past where, in a series of interviews and documentary-like scenes, we learn that Nola refuses to choose between her lovers. She insists that she wants them all. The lovers, however, aren't so understanding and Jamie, the one she most cares about, finally dumps her. This event throws Nola into a period of despair. Her desire for freedom has backfired and the cost is loneliness and bitterness. To escape this, she decides to drop her other lovers and return to Jamie. However, at the last moment, we are brought back to the present and learn that her attempt at monogamy was a mistake. "I'm not a one-man woman," she says.[1]

During the next three chapters, we're going to analyze the contrast between the approaches to narrative structure illustrated by these two stories. Before we do, however, we want to stop for a moment and consider their differences. In the first story, there is a clear progression, a developing connection between acts. The end of the story is a consequence of all that has taken place before. In the second story, the end seems to contradict the loneliness and bitterness that precedes it (although, actually, it makes perfect sense and may seem more believable than the change in *The Verdict*). In the first story, Galvin changes; he overcomes his past humiliation and regains his self-respect. In the second story, Nola seems to be the same person at the end of the film as she is at the beginning, only more so. In the first story, the structure is linear; in the second story the structure is coiled. The events in *The Verdict* are transparent; they are expressions of and serve to articulate character change. The events in *She's Gotta Have It* are more opaque; they seem arbitrary and open to conflicting interpretations. In *The Verdict*, recognition of failure leads to new strength and redemption. In *She's Gotta Have It*, the notion of failure is revealed as a success.

Both of these stories are structured, but the structure works in opposing ways. In *The Verdict*, the structure contains the line and the meaning of the story. Because Galvin reaches into himself when events look hopeless, he finds an inner strength that allows him to overcome injustice and find personal redemption. Everything in the script works to develop this movement. In *She's Gotta Have It*, the structure does not contain the line and the meaning of the story. While Nola reaches into herself after she loses Jamie, her self-examination does not have the outcome we expect—her taking one lover and accepting domestic life. Instead, the expected connection is blatantly violated and we are invited to look elsewhere for the meaning of the film—to the documentary style, the flatness of the image, the picaresque quality of the scenes. While *She's Gotta Have It* is clearly structured, the film does not reveal its meaning through structure in the same way as *The Verdict* does. These differences are critical and profoundly affect the way we respond to the two films.

Understanding how structure works and the options it offers greatly expands our potential as scriptwriters. To start our exploration of the alternative screenplay, we are going to look at variations in structure by distinguishing between scripts that foreground structure (as seen in *The Verdict*) and those that challenge, undermine, or underplay structure (as in *She's Gotta Have It*). In this chapter, we look closely at the most common articulation of the structural model—a version of the traditional three-act form that we call *restorative three-act form*. In Chapter 3, we examine the fictional world that the restorative three-act structure tends to create, and in Chapter 4, we examine alternative ways of structuring screen stories.

Restorative Three-Act Structure

Basic screenwriting texts introduce some variation of the three-act form that is claimed as the basis for every mainstream American screenplay. Three-act form is derived from Aristotle's broad notion that all dramas have a beginning, a middle, and an end and that these parts are in some proportion to one another. Unfortunately, this formulation is so general, it tells us very little. (Was Aristotle all that serious when he said, "A middle is that which is itself after some other thing and after which there is something else"?[2])

A more specific variant of three-act form, derived from the well-made play developed by the French playwright Eugene Scribe in the 1820s, has become the dominant model for mainstream films. Characterized by a clear and logical denouement, this conservative model of storytelling was the most popular dramatic form of the newly dominant French and English middle class that emerged in the "safe" Europe after the Napoleonic wars. By requiring a return to complete order, the well-made play allows us to act out our fantasies of breaking the rules without in any way threatening the structural framework of society. In *Romantic Quest and Modern Query, A History of the Modern Theatre*, Tom F. Driver notes, "It is not supposed to have any 'remainder' or unsolved quotient to puzzle the audience."[3] Hence, its name of restorative three-act structure.

Before we examine this structure, let's first review the basic foundation of three-act structure as it is presented in the textbooks.

- A 120-page feature script is divided into three acts. The first act is roughly 30 pages long, the second is 60, and the third is 30.
- Each act rises to a point of crisis, or greatest intensity, called the *act curtain scene* or the *plot point.* The resolution of this plot point throws the story into the following act.
- The plot point "hooks into the action and spins the story around in another direction."[4]
- The first act is concerned with setup, the second act with confrontation, and the third act with resolution.
- There is a period of relaxation at the start of each act before the act begins to build. Each act builds to a greater intensity than the previous act.

Let's apply this outline to *The Verdict.*

- *The Verdict is* a 123-page script. The first act is 28 pages long, the second 60, the third 35.
- Each act rises to a plot point.

The first-act plot point occurs when Galvin chooses to turn down the out-of-court settlement and bring the case to trial. While holding the settlement check in his hand, he says, "If I take that money I'm lost. If I take it I'm just going to be a rich ambulance chaser."[5]

The second-act plot point occurs when, after Galvin has mishandled the defendant on the stand, he walks out of the courtroom in despair and the case seems doomed.

Once Galvin decides to take the case (end of first act) everything changes. Instead of wandering dreamily, Galvin strides determinedly, aggressively putting together his attack. But the change is still superficial and he's in over his head. His witness drops out; he tries to settle his case again, but this time he cannot; someone seems to be protecting a possible critical witness. His new expert witness is limited and Galvin's court manner is rusty. Meanwhile, the defense anticipates his every move, waiting for him to fail; finally, he does.

But after the case seems lost (end of second act), Galvin refuses to give up. Now in another turn, he discovers a new sense of purpose. Through sheer perseverance, he finds the critical witness. Galvin also learns of the duplicity of his lover and refuses to go back to her. He regains his self-respect and wins his case.

- The first act is concerned with setup, the second act with confrontation, and the third act with resolution.

In the first act, we meet all the principal characters except the surprise witness (who is being held for Act Three) and the new expert witness who is not needed until Galvin's first act witness drops out. This drop-out witness is the only character set up in the first act who does not appear later in the film. As Galvin ponders whether to bring the case to trial, we learn the essential expository information about it. The first act ends with the confrontation drawn, but not yet developed.

The second act follows the playing out of that confrontation until it appears to defeat Galvin. With the exposition out of the way, complication may be piled on top of complication. There is no way out. If we ended the film at the end of Act Two, the resolution would feature the total defeat of Galvin.

In the third act, Galvin, having come to terms with himself, is able to move the case toward resolution. Once he engages in his quest for the critical witness and comes to terms with his false lover, we sense that he holds his fate in his hands. All he has to do is follow his instincts and we are sure he will prevail.

- There is a period of relaxation at the start of each act before the act begins to build. Each act builds to a greater intensity than the previous act.

After Galvin decides to take the case (end of Act One), there is a period of relaxation where he is quite confident that he will win. Only when his expert witness drops out does he start to have doubts and only then does the act tension begin to build. After Galvin appears to lose the case (end of Act Two), there is a period of relaxation where he lets himself be taken over by his doubts. Only when he decides to press on and seek out the missing critical witness does the story begin to move toward its climax.

Act Two (Galvin's apparent failure) has much greater dramatic impact than his decision to take the case at the end of Act One. And of course, the climatic third act victory in the courtroom dwarfs all that goes before it.

The Verdict is a textbook example of the three-act structure. The clear-cut pattern of transgression and recognition (the Act One and Act Two plot points) is followed by sufficient opportunity for the character's redemption and restoration. Galvin figures things out just in time to fit his life back together. Also, *The Verdict is* straightforward and lacks irony or any other narrative device that undercuts the significance of this structure. These two elements—sufficient time for restoration and lack of irony—characterize restorative three-act structure. As we see in later chapters, alternative screenplays, along with many other narrative forms, challenge both of these elements.

We have stated that different structures have distinct and characteristic forms that affect how we respond to them. To understand how structure determines our response in restorative three-act structure, we need to look at the way acts are used to structure not only the action, but also character development and the progression of our viewing experience.

Character Change

Restorative three-act stories are character-driven. They are not about action alone, nor about characters incidentally caught up in events. Rather, they are about the intersection of a particular action and a particular character so that the working out of the action is a simultaneous working out of the character. One of the most difficult challenges in writing a three-act, character-driven story is to devise plot points that not only feed into the action, but also articulate character development.

This is true even in most generic action films. Take *Jurassic Park*. At first glance, it appears to be structured entirely around the dinosaur attack. However, such a structure would so minimize our investment in character that even the T. Rex would not faze us. To gain our investment, a simple but still essential character line is laid down that both involves us in the characters and uses the wonder/fear of the dinosaurs to develop this. In the first act, Grant rejects children and the whole notion of parenting while at the same time he inadvertently demonstrates, through his affection for the newly born dinosaur, his fundamental caring. The second act brings him to the realization of how important the children are to him. The third act plays out this caring, giving him any number of opportunities to put himself on the line for the children and suggests that this dry man of the past has discovered a hitherto unknown life force in himself. We can see this character development if we compare the strained smile of his partner/lover Ellie at the end of the first act as she watches his contempt when he meets the children and her loving smile at the end when both children lean gratefully against Grant in the helicopter.

The three acts thus structure the character change by articulating a series of progressive stages of character development.

The Central Character

By definition, restorative three-act stories are structured around one central character. While there may be many characters of interest, there is only one character who carries us through the act breaks. *Bull Durham* is a good example of how act structure focuses on a single character. Even though the film opens with Annie's long voice-over and then moves to the ball park where we meet Nuke, Crash Davis is the central character because the act breaks turn on him. When Crash walks out (after Annie brings the two men home to audition as lovers), leaving Annie with Nuke and himself estranged from the woman he clearly desires, this action leads to the end of the act.

During the entire second act, Crash fights his pride and eventually loses. The second act ends at the low point—the moment when, after guiding Nuke to the major leagues, Crash is released from baseball.

The stimulus that starts the third act also comes from Crash; he decides to go to Annie and the movement through the act comes from his need to prove himself. The story ends only after he hits his record home run, reconciles himself to becoming a manager, and returns to Annie. Thus, although Annie provides a running voice-over throughout the script and Nuke is the only character who breaks out of the minors, Crash is the character whose movement defines the dramatic spine of the story. All other action is ultimately subordinated to his change.

Relating Internal and External Conflict

In restorative three-act stories, the action is designed specifically to highlight a particular form of character psychology presented in a stark, either/or form of conflict. We can see this if we watch how act breaks chart the character's development.

Bud, the central character in *Wall Street*, is torn between respect for his father and his values, and overwhelming greed and a desire to escape from his father's life. In the first act, greed seems to win and Bud worms his way into the graces of takeover king Gordon Gekko by selling inside information that Bud obtained from his father. His success gives him a taste of the good life. However, Gekko is not interested in a one-shot deal; he wants Bud to make a career out of gathering and using insider information. Bud agonizes over this career choice and then agrees to support Gekko.

Thus, the first act of *Wall Street* is a victory for one side of Bud's character. But this is meaningful only if we see that Bud has another side, the one represented by his father, because only then will we know how much his pact with Gekko is costing him.

The second act follows Bud's rise in the financial world. He pulls off deals, buys a fancy East Side apartment, and gets the girl who, as anyone except Bud can see, is just along for the money. There are a few glitches in his new life, but nothing he can't overcome. He doesn't even hear his father's warning that he's become Gekko's whore until his new world comes crashing down. When Gekko decides to take over the airline that Bud's father worked for all his life, Gekko's actions are too much for Bud. He destroys his fancy apartment and lets his girlfriend walk out the door—end of Act Two.

Now the other side of Bud's character asserts itself. By helping to save the airline, Bud's character is redeemed in the third act, even though we leave him on the courthouse steps awaiting sentencing.

A critical technique in restorative structure is building the plot so that self realization can come before external payback. Although the Stock Watch investigation brings the whole swindle down in the third act of *Wall Street*, Bud's fall in the second act comes not from external intervention, but from his realization that he's lost himself. This makes redemption possible. In *Rookie of the Year*, the twelve-year old Henry becomes an all-star major league pitcher by virtue of the mysterious strength he gains in his pitching arm after it heals from a break. We know that something will happen to Henry to cause him to lose this magical strength. However, if the film's resolution were to turn on this alone, if the loss of his strength ended the second act, the story would have a degree of arbitrariness we don't usually accept in a mainstream film. The story's motivational force would be medical rather than dramatic. Instead, the second act ends when, after losing his friends and his childhood, Henry decides to retire from professional baseball so he can experience a normal life. His arm has to be returned to normal for the story to end. But that happens in the third act, well after the key second act character decision has been made.

Either/or character tension is central to restorative three-act structure. Gekko, without this binary character tension (or possibly with more complex tension), would never destroy himself in this way. If *Wall Street* were Gekko's story, the structure would be two acts—he succeeds and he gets caught. Restorative three-act structure allows for character realization, which leads to character redemption and restoration. A character may not escape the law in a restorative three-act story, but he will have opportunity to redeem himself before he is arrested, to show that the real punishment came from within himself.

Not all restorative three-act stories are as blatant as *Wall Street*, but all pose this kind of decision. Crash must give up his pride to succeed with Annie. Galvin must give up his naive notion of justice and get his hands dirty to win his case. Henry must give up his major league career in order to have his life.

First Act Characteristics

The Point of No Return.   Unlike picaresque, slice-of-life, or other flatter forms of storytelling discussed in the next few chapters, restorative three-act stories seize a particular period of time and call it the single defining moment in the character's life. The first act curtain functions as a one-way gate. Once the character moves through the gate, he has entered a unique situation and can never return to the way things were. The gate is different for each picture and is given significance by the difficulty the character has in passing through it and by the role it plays later in the story. For example, once Benjamin makes love to Mrs. Robinson in *The Graduate*, he becomes the vulnerable character in the second act. He could have made love to Mrs. Johnson, who does not have any daughters, and it would not have mattered. The importance of this turning point is underscored, because it takes him most of the first act to get up the nerve to make love to Mrs. Robinson and, later, because his action appears to doom his affair with Elaine.

False Solution.   The first act plot point is a solution to the central character's dilemma, because it seems to answer the dramatic problem raised in the first part of the film. Will Crash Davis become Annie's lover? Will Galvin take the case? Will Bud work for Gekko? However, the solutions are false; if they weren't, the story would be over. The false solution splits the character's intimate perspective of "It's my life. I've got things under control" from the audience's long-term perspective of "The movie's not over yet. Don't do that. You're going to get in trouble." The first act curtain scene, while appearing to solve the crisis, opens up a whole new set of problems.

The false solution can be an obvious wrong turn, such as Benjamin sleeping with Mrs. Robinson, Bud working for Gekko, and Crash walking out on Annie. Or it can be a turn in the right direction with insufficient understanding or preparation, such as Galvin deciding to bring his case to trial without coming to terms with his rustiness, his drinking, and his innocent belief that the injustice in his case is so obvious it will speak for itself.

Second Act Characteristics

Moving Ahead of the Character.   One of the surprising elements of restorative three-act structure is that for much of the story we are ahead of the character. This is particularly true during the second act when the character seems oblivious to fate. It is as if the character is running away from her history, her background, and her circumstances with a rubber band tied to her waist. She doesn't see the rubber band, but we do. We wait for the band to reach the point of greatest elasticity and snap her back.

In some screen stories, the central character's obliviousness in the second act is overt and the internal conflict seems to vanish. For most of the second act in *Wall Street,* Bud does not question his actions. In fact, the one scene in which he wonders what is happening to him, calls attention to itself precisely because it comes out of nowhere. In other stories, the character is not so much oblivious to his fate as he is working to deny it. Crash Davis's bitterness seems to evolve from a growing awareness that his playing days are numbered and he will never again make the big leagues. However far ahead of the character we are, the tension works the same way. We wait for things to go bad and we wait for the moment when the character is forced to face what he has done to himself.

Act of Consequence.   The second act is the act of consequence—when the character finally catches up to the viewer. Act Two reaches its climax when the character finally has to face the implications of the false solution at the end of Act One. This recognition provides the opportunity for insight, which leads in Act Three to resolution and restoration.

The second-act curtain scene is given particular impact by a kind of double resolution. The character finally realizes her mistake, while we, the viewers, are finally satisfied that the character has come back to us. Frequently, this is the moment of highest identification. We are in sync with the character.

Character Assertion.   The end of the first act tends to thrust a decision upon the central character. In many cases, the structure leads us to believe that if the character had made a different decision, the story would be over. All of our sample stories would end if the characters had decided differently—Bud would turn down Gekko, Galvin would settle out of court, Crash would win over Annie the first night, and Benjamin would refuse Mrs. Robinson's advances.

The feeling at the end of the second act is quite different. The story appears to recede and leave the character beached. Although we are with the character, our momentum is exhausted because we have just seen the character defeated by the events we knew would defeat him. The cost of the character's earliest mistakes is not so much punishment as it is indifference.

Therefore, the character needs to re-assert his importance to the story, and the willingness to do this propels us into the third act. Now the character leads us, amazes us with resourcefulness, connects insight to success, and proves that once he has faced himself, he will triumph. Although this connection of self-realization with success has been given its most obvious expression in *sex, lies, and videotape,* where self-knowledge overcomes impotence and fear, it underlies most restorative three-act stories. Bud's success in pulling off the deal that challenges Gekko comes only as a result of the righteousness of his motivation—to help his father's airline.

Third Act Characteristics

Recognition and Restoration.   A restorative three-act story has an upbeat ending. Having recognized his failure, the character is able to rise and overcome internal tension and story conflict. Usually, the resolution of internal conflict comes first. The force of the recognition is sufficient to allow Crash finally to overcome his pride and make love with Annie, to allow Galvin to recognize that innocence alone won't win a case, and to allow Bud to reunite with his father in the hospital room.

The remainder of the third act is the playing out of the external conflict, which is now approached with a single-minded purpose. For Crash, this event is simple—he must hit his record home run. But for Bud and Galvin, the rest of the third act is melodramatic. Will Bud succeed in freeing Blue Star Airlines from Gekko and saving his father's job? Will Galvin overcome a corrupt judge and the discovery that his lover is the spy, and win his case?

Once internally resolved and armed with an external goal, the character is given the chance to triumph over the odds. The external events of Act Two have led to recognition, not irredeemable disaster. Recognition comes in time to stave off tragedy; this is the key to the feel of restorative three-act stories—there is a second chance, personal redemption and restoration are more significant than events, and actions are less important than motives.

Restorative three-act structure is a gentle form of storytelling. Characters are expected to make mistakes—that's part of life. The real test comes when the mistakes are laid bare, when the character realizes what we, as viewers, have already figured out—how false the character has been to himself. Out of this understanding comes the character's chance to prove himself and earn redemption.

Working It Out—Restorative Three-Act Structure in Practice

Before we go on, we will look at a few hints for working with restorative three-act structure.

Three-Act Skeleton

One of the major advantages to working in any three-act structure is that it breaks down a two-hour story into more manageable units. You will find this story breakdown most useful if you think about it as an ongoing process, rather than something you do only once. Writing is anything but a step-by-step process; the breakdown of acts is continually refined and rethought.

Here are some useful ways to conceptualize three-act structure.

- Summarize the first and last scene in each act, and then write a connecting paragraph.
- Write a paragraph for each act.
- Write the whole story in a paragraph using one sentence for each act.
- Convey the whole thematic movement implied by the acts in one sentence. For instance, for *Wall Street* we could write, "The realization that one's greed has caused the loss of one's identity and the destruction of loved ones' lives leads to a rethinking of values and the knowledge that self-awareness and love are more important than money."

Notice how the thematic sentence reveals the dynamic of restorative three-act structure. The active verb, *leads,* is placed between the second and third act, connecting realization to restoration.

Build

Acts must build progressively. Unless you are purposely trying to thwart the viewer's expectations, you are committed to topping your first act. If your story goes flat in the second and third acts, it may be from lack of progressive development or it may be that you are giving too much away in the first act. If you find you cannot top your first act, then pull it back and see if you cannot hold your build until later in the story.

Focus

Act structure demands focus. Each dramatic scene must do at least two things. The first thing is a variable—each scene can develop character, provide texture, and cause us to laugh or cry. The second thing is a must—each scene must move the plot. Specifically, the scene must refocus the act's tension and move us toward resolving that tension. Benjamin's inviting Mrs. Robinson to the hotel refocuses the question of whether Benjamin will sleep with Mrs. Robinson at the same time it moves toward resolving the tension.

Align Action with Character

The most difficult thing about restorative three-act structure is to align the act breaks demanded by the action with the stages of development needed for clear characterization. Once this has been done, the progress of events will be inevitable. There are many ways to separate Bud from Gekko other than by the potential destruction of his father's airline. The most obvious is to move the Stock Watch investigation into the second act. However, only the potential destruction of his father's airline would trigger that one line of vulnerability in Bud and cause him to bring himself down.

As you work to align character with action, you may find it helpful to use one of the three-act structure conceptual aids previously listed to chart act development. Make two parallel breakdowns—one for the development of the action, one for the development of the character. At first, you may find that there is little correspondence between the breakdowns, but as you work with the story, you should find that they eventually align. When they are aligned, you will find that a three-sentence summary of the action of the story also summarizes character development and change.

Relationship of the First Act to the Third Act

When a story goes bad in the third act, usually the problem can be traced to the first act. Restorative three-act stories are not about surprises; rather, they are about the playing out of events that have already been set up. Frequently, an inexperienced scriptwriter will reach the end of the second act (the point of recognition) and get stuck, unable to make a believable character change. The potential for character change must be planted in the first act. We have to see Bud's love for his father early in the story in order to know how that love is being compromised in the second act. The energy that comes from recognizing the compromise causes the character to change.

Directionality

In restorative three-act structure, the acts tend to move in opposite directions. In most cases, the climax of the first act frantically pushes the story upward and outward, and the climax of the second act is downward and inward. The story ends with a consolidation—an upward and outward push that is no longer frantic.

If you find that your acts are all going in the same direction, you have effectively written a one-act story. We discuss what you can do with a one-act story later in this book. However, if this is the case, you have most likely removed the interim victories and disappointments of restorative three-act structure and your story will be unrelenting. Go back and see if you can modulate the act breaks. Give us something at the end of the first act before you take it away.

Conclusion

The restorative three-act form that organizes most mainstream American screenplays is one of many means to structure a screen story. Most restorative stories share certain characteristics, such as a central, sympathetic character who drives a story line that clearly relates external conflict to internal tension. Each act provides the impetus for the next act; the story moves forward, with the first and second acts building tension toward the ultimate restoration in the third act.

Because restorative three-act structure gives maximum opportunity for character redemption and restoration, this form of storytelling is very positive. Typically, the first act sets up the conflict and allows the character to find a solution to her problems. During most of the second act, the audience is ahead of the central character, waiting for her to fall as a result of her poor first-act solution. This is the act of consequence because at the very end, when the character finally recognizes the false solution and catches up with the audience's awareness, she usually reaches her lowest level in the story. This recognition leads into the third act where she has the opportunity to redeem herself.

In the next chapter, we need to look deeper, at the kind of fictional world restorative three-act structure tends to create. Then we'll move on to the alternatives.

References

1. Spike Lee, *She's Gotta Have It* (New York: Simon & Schuster, 1987), p. 361.
2. Aristotle, *Poetics* (Chicago: Henry Regnery, 1967), p. 15.
3. Tom F. Driver, *Romantic Quest and Modern Query, A History of the Modern Theatre*, 1st ed. (New York: Delacorte 1970), p. 48.
4. Syd Field, *Screenplay: The Foundations of Screenwriting* (New York: Dell, 1982), p. 9.
5. David Mamet, *The Verdict*, (20th Century-Fox, 1982), p. 28.

3

Critique of Restorative Three-Act Form

In restorative three-act stories, there is an implied contract between viewer and filmmaker, a tacit agreement that, although the characters will err, we are never to lose sight of the costs. Although part of us may wish that the heroine will get away with something, we need the satisfaction of payback to fulfill our sense of dramatic completion.

But this need for payback is not inevitable; there are many stories that satisfy precisely because the character is not governed by such a fixed moral system and its consequent need for retribution. Rather, we seek payback in most mainstream films because of the way that restorative three-act structure organizes our expectations. Because we are invited to identify with the transgressing character, while at the same time the transgression is so clearly exposed at the end of the first act, we are positioned both to understand the character's motivation and to see her mistakes.

This helps explain that familiar feeling of sitting in a theater and begging the character on the screen not to do something. She always does, and the thing she does always comes back to haunt her. Thus, in the broadest sense, the premise of most restorative three-act stories is that crime doesn't pay, that good will triumph over evil, and that there is no confusion over which is which.

But suppose this simple morality is foreign to us? Suppose the world we know is more likely to be marked by small missteps, unexpected tenderness, and, most of all, a lack of overriding predetermined purpose or clarity? Suppose we realize that the corruption of money and power is much more subtle than that portrayed in *Wall Street?* Suppose we know that situations are rarely as unambiguously unjust as the one faced by Galvin in *The Verdict*, and that good deeds are frequently tainted with blurred motivations? Forget corporate raiders and do-good lawyers. Suppose we find ourselves asking such questions as: Why do our lives seem to slip by in a succession of little details that appear so unimportant? How do we reconcile material success with personal malaise? Are we free of values long considered traditional or do they haunt us in unexpected ways? How do we respond to the call of the larger world?

The creative screenwriter may not find it possible to answer these questions in a restorative three-act script. Although many restorative three-act films have less naked and foregrounded act breaks than do *Wall Street* and *The Verdict*, still that structure, like all forms of storytelling, suggests a point of view. No matter how we disguise it, a story with a clear violation followed by recognition and redemption seems like a moral tale, a reaffirmation of a preexisting, commonly understood ethic.

Are we saying that to write a thought-provoking script you have to abandon restorative three-act structure? Absolutely not. The purpose of this book is not to prescribe, but to explore. No one can tell you in which style to write. If you allow someone to do so, you are ceding your power as a writer. We can, however, look at the things that are communicated by different styles and different approaches and invite you to consider whether these correspond to the way you see the world.

You can go even further and ask: Is the form of the story really that important? Is there such thing as a neutral form, one into which we can pour any story? The answer is No and is the focus of this chapter. Nothing is neutral; form is inextricably linked to content. There is no single way to tell a story, no right way, because the choice of form is a creative decision. The scriptwriter's choice of form communicates a basic feel and point of view that fundamentally determines how we understand the story.

Before we look at alternative structures, we need to examine in more detail the point of view suggested by restorative three-act form. When we make our choice of how to tell our stories, we need to know what comes along for the ride and whether we want it or not. We will see how restorative three-act structure implies broad perspectives on issues of free will, the relationship of character to society, our ability to change ourselves, and the transparency of motivation.

Story over Texture

In the beginning of the last chapter, we stated that restorative three-act stories disclose their essential meanings through the playing out of their structure. While all stories reveal their meanings over time, restorative three-act stories are particularly horizontal in design, if we halt their forward plot movement, we have little left to organize the story.

To create the forward movement, each major scene must push the story toward the plot point that, with its own circular logic, gains its significance because it is the moment toward which the story so carefully builds. This progression leads to a clear hierarchy of values for the viewer—we understand what is important (that which brings us closer to the plot point) and what is merely background (texture and detail). In a restorative three-act script, forward movement comes at the expense of texture, of resonance, and of ambiguity.

One of the fundamental problems in grasping real-life experiences is that these experiences have no inherent focus. A million things compete for our attention. How do we know what is important? Once we find what's important, how do we maintain the clarity to follow it? If we are to write scripts that reflect this ambiguity, we have to go beyond the clear-cut order of restorative three-act structure to suggest the sheer overabundance of detail, of stimuli in contemporary life.

But the scriptwriter should be cautioned. When we talk about writing from the complexity of experience, we are not talking about transcribing reality. If you attempt merely to copy the disorder of direct experience, if you write with a million things competing for your attention—shaving, washing the dishes, tying shoes, feeding the cat—then all you'll create is disorder. Reproducing disorder is not a matter of writing in a disorderly fashion. The trick to writing about the complexity of reality is to find a way to put the problem of focus and confusion in the foreground. Although the meaning points in a different direction, this approach requires as much control as restorative three-act structure.

Consistency of Tone

To be intelligible, all stories must have some form of tonal consistency. As in a game, the rules can be arbitrary, but once they are established they must be maintained. Otherwise, events and actions will have no meaning.

In a restorative three-act story, however, tonal experimentation is particularly limited by the need to serve the progression of the act breaks. The film *Heathers* provides an example of this limitation. An apparent black comedy, the first act of *Heathers* ends with Veronica and her devilish boyfriend, J. D., killing her tormentor Heather (one of the high school's three most popular girls with the same name) and then covering up the crime with a fake suicide. This is outrageous stuff and it cries out to be pushed further. But by the end of the second act, after two more sets of killings, Veronica's had enough. She breaks off her relationship with J. D. and, in the third act, seeks revenge. The movie ends with her finally killing J.D., who has been the driving force behind her rage. Simple morality takes over; Veronica is redeemed. She has killed the evil force and now accepts the least popular person in the school, her old friend Martha Dumptruck. The chaos suggested in the first act, the outrageous acting out of the impulses of teenage rivalry, is tamped down and made tame in the same way that the more freewheeling tone early in the movie has been contained to service the plot.

Decision-Making Space

Acts tend to start out loosely structured and then gradually focus, constricting the character and forcing some decision. As we reach the act climax, we get the feeling that all action would stop and the movie would end if the character did not make the decision that moves the story into the next act.

It is impossible to mistake the fact that a decision is being made or the importance of that decision. The overall structure of the script builds to and is dependent on the decision-making moment. Often, the moment is slowed down, exaggerated, or frozen. This clear-cut articulation can be thought of as a decision-making space, a moment that is emptied of any distractions aside from the decision.

In *Wall Street*, Gekko and Bud are riding in a limousine when Gekko proposes that Bud work for him. As the car stops, Bud has just a moment to make up his mind before the limousine pulls away, leaving him alone on the street corner and the promise of Gekko's wealth literally disappearing in front of him. There is no mistaking what Gekko is asking nor that Bud will have any later chance to accept it. Thus, Bud and the viewer are both fully aware of the one-way gate we are passing through.

Rarely do we experience decisions in these clear-cut moments where we can isolate and weigh the consequences, and then decide our fate. By decisions, we are referring to the millions of things that define us (the kind of people we like, what we enjoy doing) that are so fundamental to our character that we rarely think of them as decisions at all. If we think of decisions in this way then Bud would not stand outside his experience enough to weigh the pros and cons of this choice. Rather, all his small actions, his step-by-step revelation of himself that led to his getting involved with Gekko, would serve to make the decision for him. If he did later become aware of what he had gotten into, he would not be able to point to one single moment where that had happened. Of course, if we imagine Bud's character drawn this way, then reversing his fate would be that much more difficult. To write a film that acknowledges the unconscious flow of moments that makes up the patterns of our lives, we have to rethink our articulation of decisions and recognize how limited are our options to change.

Understanding Motivation

Restorative three-act stories are character-driven: The action turns on character decision and the motivations that underlie the decision are made accessible to the audience. In fact, the essence of restorative three-act structure is that action is an expression of motives, of character conflict.

Clearly, if we are to write a story about human actions, we must have some way to read motivation. However, the manner in which motivation is portrayed is variable.

In restorative three-act stories, it is very rare for the central character to make a decision that hasn't been carefully prepared for the viewer. The first act breaks of all the films we've discussed—*Wall Street, The Verdict, Bull Durham, The Graduate*—have been calculated so that we understand the conflicting forces underlying the decision being made. The fact that we weigh the options as we wait for the character to decide, gives us a feeling of participating in the decision-making process.

By contrast, in *She's Gotta Have It*, Nola's final decision to abandon Jamie appears, at least initially, to come out of the blue. Her decision makes sense only when we look back on the rest of the film and put things together. Our understanding is not instantaneous. We are supplied with clues not only from the movement of the story, but from the texture, the details, and most importantly from the ellipses, the things not there. Our understanding is more reflective and its full impact may not hit until the film is over.

Binary Character Psychology

In order to be distinct, acts tend to inflict extreme choices. Bud is either with Gekko or he is not; Crash is either with Annie or he isn't; there is no middle ground. Since the strength of restorative three-act structure is its use of the acts to chart a progression of character, we see the either/or quality transposed onto character. To side with Gekko, Bud has to turn on his family and their values. To reject Annie, Crash, overtaken by his pride, rejects his romanticism.

In some restorative three-act stories, the third act represents a return to innocence, as in Bud's return to his family at the end of *Wall Street*. However, this shedding of all that happens to him during the course of the film may seem unsatisfactory. To return to his family, Bud rejects the greed and ambition that drove his actions for most of the film. The residue of this ambition is never accounted for: How did he come to terms with it? Where did it all go?

In other restorative three-act stories, the third act represents a compromise between the extremes of the first two acts, and we feel that the character's experiences are more satisfactorily accounted for. In *The Verdict*, Galvin attempts to defend a case based solely on justice. In the second act, his cocoon-like innocence is shattered. It is only when he is willing to misrepresent himself, to lie, to open other people's mail, that he gets to the one witness who will help him win the case. At the end of the film, the two sides of Galvin's character have been integrated. While he still seeks justice, Galvin can now play the game.

The force of restorative three-act structure comes from a certain willful blindness on the part of the character. In the second act, the character does not see his mistakes like we do, which allows the second act to build while we wait for the character to fall. This obliviousness generates dramatic force at the expense of self-awareness. The character develops precisely because he does not notice what is perfectly plain to us. When he does, the character tends not to adjust by making small accommodations, but rather to snap back into place.

At first glance, restorative three-act structure appears to bring us closer to the characters. Its paradox is that upon closer examination, the comfortable awareness of the first act transgression places us safely outside of the story. As discussed in the next chapter, other forms of stories, those that don't have such a clear-cut first-act climax, tend to leave the viewer much less certain about the circumstances and the morality of the situation in which the character finds herself. Since we are not pre-positioned, we have to work constantly to reassess the meaning and the relative morality of the character's actions. In fact, these kinds of screen stories tend to do away with the larger ethical questions and suggest less the affirmation of general morality than the struggle to deal with an ambiguity as problematic to the viewer as it is to the character.

History as Backdrop

The underlying assumption in a restorative three-act script is that the character is restrained by her conflict, her flaw, her psychology. Even though the conflict is externalized (i.e., there is a real dramatic problem), the problem expresses an internal conflict. Once the character stops fighting herself (usually in the beginning of the third act), she tips the plot in her favor and eventually triumphs.

So what is the problem with this? Nothing. Except that this form of scriptwriting doesn't account for the particular historical, social, political, economic, gender, and familial circumstances that also condition fate. History, as an event or impersonal force, serves merely as a vehicle for psychological development. The film scholar David Bordwell cites an example of the appropriation of history as a plot device. "As an old Russian emigre says at the end of *Balalaika (1939):* 'And to think that it took the Revolution to bring us together.' ''[1]

We see this even in films without an apparent political perspective. Consider *Jurassic Park.* Ellie's role as professional woman who treats an ailing stegosaurus and her braving the raptors to switch on the power would seem to suggest a much more progressive view of women than is traditionally presented in mainstream films. This is quickly dispelled, however, when we look at Ellie's dramatic function in the film. She has no doubts, no hesitation, and no conflict or growth so that her actions indicate nothing about her internal life. Instead, her dramatic function is to smile knowingly at Grant when he is around children, thus serving merely to mark his progress through the acts. While she is portrayed with the mannerisms of a feminist, her dramatic role is that of a static signpost against which we measure the male character's growth. It is worth nothing that even though *Jurassic Park* is not advertised or thought of as a political film, it conveys, as do all films, a political meaning nonetheless.

While the use of history as a backdrop to psychological development is not always as obvious, barriers of race, gender, class, and history are still presented as secondary to the transcendence of individual will. If we find ourselves suspicious of this world-view, if we feel our history has shown us the limitations and corruptions that underlie our illusion of free will, then we must be leery of restorative three-act structure. If we are not, we may find ourselves reinforcing, through the structure of our screenplays, the very conservative notions we wish to challenge in our stories.

Motives Outweigh Events

Action in restorative three-act stories services and gains importance as expression of character conflict. The physical world and the force of history are subordinate to their roles as reflections of the character's personal redemption. The effect of this subordination is to coddle the character, to make the consequences of action less important than motives. Redemption is not only spiritual, but is also a literal reconstruction of the circumstances of the character's predicament. The character is never allowed to get in so deep that he can't get out.

To understand this coddled form of storytelling, compare restorative three-act structure to classical tragedy. In *King Lear,* Lear falsely condemns his one true daughter, Cordelia, in the first act. The rest of the play is a depiction of the consequences of that condemnation. His recognition of his wrong, wrought by four acts of hardship and disintegration, leads him to kneel when he finally meets Cordelia again. Yet, such recognition is too late. Although he is finally about to see, he cannot transform the world into a reflection of his own psychology. Forces larger than his motives and desires have been set into motion. He may recognize them, but it is too late to stop the tragedy of his death and the destruction of his kingdom.

In contemporary literature, stories often work the other way. Instead of being faced with the destruction of a whole kingdom, characters confront the stone cold indifference of the material world. In the short stories of contemporary American writers, such as Raymond Carver, Bobbie Anne Mason, and Annie Beattie, the most remarkable elements are the limit of human expression and the lack of a clear-cut ethical imperative in a world that is so resistant to universal meaning.

Restorative three-act structure doesn't work that way. It is a moralistic form of storytelling whose basic premise is that good motives triumph, and the world is understandable, consistent, manageable, and responsive to goodness and truth. As a result, external events are rarely arbitrary—instead, they are earned. In a three-act structure script, not only is your fate in your hands, but as long as you are willing to admit to your mistakes, the consequences of your actions can be eradicated.

The Effaced Narrator

One of the dominant aspects of mainstream film is the extent to which it seeks to erase the evidence of a storyteller and to imply that what takes place on the screen would take place whether a camera were recording it or not. The screenwriter should be aware of this distinction between showing and telling, dramatizing and narrating. Aristotle makes a distinction between the poet "imitating everyone as acting" and the poet narrating "by being himself and not changing."[2] The poet imitating everyone stands effaced and presents himself as an ideal, invisible agent that reproduces, without comment, events that have happened. The poet being himself and not changing presents himself as a storyteller who stands between us and the events, and consciously interprets them. In the first instance, the story is understood to be transparent; the subject is the event. In the second, the story is understood to be a vague, indeterminate interaction between the events and the narration. The events may be so minimized that the story is largely about the voice recounting them.

Clearly, there is no such thing as a story without a storyteller. No matter how much the storyteller seeks to disappear, there is always an interpreting sensibility or point of view that structures the action for us. Yet, restorative three-act structure is based on a conventional structure designed to divert our attention from narration and suggest that the story tells itself.

In a novel, we expect to find a narrator, a voice that speaks directly to us. Unlike the more omniscient narration used by 19th-century writers, such as George Elliot, most 20th-century literary fiction implicates this voice in the story. Thus, we have degrees of unreliable, first-person narrators or third-person narrators inflected with the voice and emotional charge of characters within the story. We will talk about this in Chapter 15. In fact, this overt narrative shaping is one of the reasons novels can frequently turn on events that have less obvious import than those in films.

In most plays and films, there is no overt narrator who speaks directly to the camera and interprets events. However, this does not mean there is no narrator. Rather the narrator is implied, in large part, through dramatic structure. This is why we say that restorative three-act films reveal themselves through their structure—the structure itself functions as the narrator. It modulates our interest and gives significance and meaning to events without calling attention to itself, as though the story just happened, as though the characters really control their own fates.

It is critical that we understand the narrative role of restorative three-act structure. All stories need a narrative voice. If we want to work with other forms of stories, we have to find other means to serve this function. As we see in the next chapter, one of the things that happens when we break out of restorative three-act form is that the effaced narrator becomes increasingly visible.

Conclusion

The pattern of transgression, recognition, and redemption makes restorative three-act structure a very comforting form. It allows us to identify with characters who have gone beyond acceptable behavior, while at the same time remaining aware that they will be forced to confront their behavior. Three-act structure eases the individual over any social, historical, economic, and familial limitations. While this may be underplayed, we cannot avoid the implications of the form altogether. If the feeling of transgression, recognition, and redemption is what we want, there is no better way to express this than with restorative three-act structure. But to create a different feel, to find a way to respond to the arbitrariness and indifference of the contemporary world, we have to look elsewhere.

References

1. David Bordwell, Janet Staiger, and Kristin Thompson, *The Classical Hollywood Cinema. Film Style & Mode of Production to 1960* (New York: Columbia University Press, 1985), p. 13.
2. Aristotle, *Poetics* (Chicago: Henry Regnery, 1967), p. 5.

4

. . . .

Counter-Structure

As we have seen, stories cast in restorative three-act form tend to be conservative, suggesting an orderly, clear-cut world in which characters control their own fates and action is redeemable by motive. These stories don't speak to the more ephemeral sense of experience we mentioned in the last chapter. To express a more disjointed world, changing content is not enough—structure too must function in more ambiguous ways. Sometimes, it is placed in the foreground and made very obvious. By calling attention to itself, structure suggests the artificiality of form over the chaos of day-to-day experience. At other times, structure becomes flattened and apparently minimized, creating the illusion of documentary randomness.

We can comfortably define restorative three-act structure because it provides a framework that tends to promote the story, or, as Syd Field says, if you know the three-act paradigm, "you can simply 'pour' your story into it."[1] However, counter-structures, which evolve organically from less preplanned needs, are as open-ended and various as the stories from which they grow.

The following examples are not meant to indicate preexisting categories or a definitive list but to demonstrate some of the options open to the scriptwriter.

Structure in the Foreground

We will start by looking at a central paradox that governs all art. By definition, art demands some shaping to give it meaning. The problem, then, is how to represent a world whose organization seems elusive at best. One way is by making structure very obvious. By calling attention to itself as the fundamental organizing principle, this use of structure exaggerates its artificiality. Because it is shown to be artificial, it organizes the story without reducing the feeling of chaos underneath.

Ironic Three-Act Structure

In *Chinatown*, Syd Field clearly demonstrates how acts function. The first act ends when the real Mrs. Mulwray shows up at Gittes's office. As Field points out, this spins the plot around: "If she is the real Mrs.

Mulwray, who hired lack Nicholson? And who hired the phony Mrs. Mulwray, and why?"[2] Gittes must find out who set him up. The second act ends with the discovery of the eyeglasses in Mrs. Mulwray's salt water pool, apparently implicating her in the death of her husband. Having shielded her from the police inquiry and then becoming her lover, Gittes now realizes his mistake.

The act structure clearly delineates the development of Gittes's character from the cool outsider to the emotionally involved lover. By the time he makes love to Mrs. Mulwray, we know that he's tied up with the same personal demons that drove him out of Chinatown in the first place. We can speculate on those demons—an unwillingness to take orders, the inability to separate personal commitment from professional judgment—whatever they are, his super-cool indifference in the first scene, during which he gloats as his client studies pictures of his wife's adultery, has changed into a personal entanglement that goes beyond simple justice in the second act.

We believe that Gittes will overcome this personal entanglement because of the self-conscious detective story-genre connections that *Chinatown* plays on. We know that the detective will spurn love in favor of justice, will destroy highly placed criminals, precisely because he lives on the margin of society and will be most dangerous when apparently defeated.

However, while evoking the classic detective genre, *Chinatown* also distorts it, setting up another line of expectation. Unlike the classic detective whose failure to fit into the domestic world is presented as heroic, Gittes is portrayed as somewhat incomplete. We sense a sorrow under his glibness and a loss we will later learn is connected with Chinatown. Unlike the classic detective whose life, but not emotions, turns on the working out of the plot, Gittes's whole personality is threatened by his growing involvement with Mrs. Mulwray. We don't expect him to be sitting calmly at his desk the day after Mrs. Mulwray is shot, waiting for whoever comes through the door, the way we do with Sam Spade at the end of *The Maltese Falcon.* Despite the evidence of the sequel, at the end of this movie, we believe Gittes is emotionally destroyed.

Chinatown evokes not only the detective genre but also the restorative three-act genre in which a character's vulnerability is exposed, addressed, and then overcome. This double expectation of triumph—justice will be done by the detective and he will overcome his vulnerability—is turned topsy-turvy when the criminal, Noah Cross, defeats the detective by getting away with his crimes and Mrs. Mulwray, the only person to have touched Gittes since his last fling in Chinatown, is shot. The story gains its power precisely because of the extent to which it invites us to believe that our expectation of a happy ending will triumph over a darker reality. When our expectations are not met, the darker reality seems all that much more oppressive, because it has penetrated the apparently safe frame of the story.

Ironic three-act structure, then, involves setting up the expectation raised by coherently developed act breaks, then foiling it at the end. The extent of the unexpected turn of events is tricky, because even though it breaks the logic of the acts, it must conform to a deeper story logic to satisfy us.

For instance, while Buck Henry's screenplay of *The Graduate* follows the restorative form (with Ben busing off triumphantly with Elaine), Mike Nichols's film adds a twist to this ending. Nichols focuses on the lovers in the back of the bus for what seems to be an uncomfortably long time, allowing them to reveal themselves. At first, they look at one another apparently with joy, then they stare forward without a word until we become uncomfortable. Have they triumphed, or are they condemned to the same unfulfilling life that Mr. and Mrs. Robinson started in the back of their Ford?

The ending works because the ironic reading keeps us close enough to restorative expectations to satisfy ourselves, while at the same time teasing us with something more. Although we had expected both Benjamin and Gittes to triumph, we can reconstruct the logic of their failures by rethinking what has gone on before. The fact that Ben seems to have nothing to say to Elaine is consistent with the circumstances of their courtship. Thus, ironic three-act stories don't break the structural logic, so much as they turn it in other directions.

Exaggerated Ironic Three-Act Structure

By contrast, at the conclusion of *Blue Velvet*, Sandy and Jeffrey regard mechanical robins as though they were real and buy into a notion of small-town happiness without ever addressing the implied voyeuristic perversity that earlier involved Jeffrey with Dorothy. Nothing quite adds up, yet because we are aware of this from the beginning (by the exaggerated small-town images), the film still somehow satisfies us. Unlike *Chinatown*, which lets us believe the story might all work out, *Blue Velvet* never ceases to remind us of its ironic distance.

From the opening credit sequence, we are teased with the multiple meaning of images. The highlighted icons of innocence—the white picket fence, the yellow tulips, the slow-motion fire truck—set against Jeffrey's father's stroke both suggest and parody small-town harmony. The presence of evil is constantly overstated, so that everything from the heavily underscored pan shot of the Lincoln street sign (after Jeffrey had been warned to stay away from that neighborhood) to Frank's gratuitous use of the word "fuck," serves to make us suspicious of, rather than to accept, the simple good/evil dichotomy.

Despite the multiple meaning of its images, *Blue Velvet* relies on three-act structure to drive the story. The tension between the restorative organization and the exaggerated representation of small-town life gives the film its particular irony.

The first act comes to a close when, determined to pursue the mystery of Dorothy and the disembodied ear, Jeffrey breaks into her apartment and steals her key. The long second act follows Jeffrey's growing involvement with both Dorothy and Sandy up to the point that he is warned off the case by Sandy's father. His impotence is underscored at the act break when, powerless, he watches a man he knows to be criminally implicated visit Sandy's father. The final act kicks toward resolution when Dorothy shows up at Jeffrey's house naked and beaten. This event leads to the final showdown, after which order is restored to Timberton, but it is an order as artificial as the mechanical birds.

Does *Blue Velvet* rely on three-act structure? Yes. But set against the exaggerated representation of good and evil, the stagy meetings in the malt shop and the dreams of robins coming home, the three-act structure seems equally artificial. The undeveloped decision to go after Dorothy, the coincidence of the toilet flushing that covers the honking of the car's horn, the banality of the evil, all exemplify and parody the structure and its happy ending. Like *Chinatown*, *Blue Velvet* uses three-act structure, but where *Chinatown* teases us with the possibility of a restorative ending, *Blue Velvet*, by making both its structure and the world it represents into a cliche, mocks even the aims of restoration. Restore what? A small town myth that existed only in the movies?

One of the classics in film history uses a similar technique. Jean Renoir produced *Rules of the Game* in the spring of 1939, and it opened in Paris just weeks before the outbreak of World War II. The film is structured around a hunting party on the grounds of a magnificent chateau outside of Paris and it turns on the introduction of a bourgeois "hero," the aviator Andre Jurieu, into its aristocratic company. After a number of misadventures involving confusion of identity and motive, and after Andre is killed, the film ends with the guests all filing back into the chateau in response to its owner's invitation to put all this unpleasantness behind them.

Rules of the Game borrows liberally from French farce. The butler is named Corneille, the hijacks upstairs are matched with the amorous misadventures downstairs, and both the conflict and its resolution is infused with a Mozartian delight. However, it doesn't all quite fit. By both evoking a genre from the past, by mining its innocent tendernesses while exposing its incongruity, Renoir is able to suggest that the closure the film achieves comes from the artifice of art, of genre, rather than any order in the lives being portrayed. We are invited to appreciate the magnificent symmetry of the form while also recognizing the impotence, rot and isolation of the particular social world which that form represents. Less than nine months after its release, the German army tore through France in ten days and that impotence was revealed to the rest of the world. The film is simultaneously exquisitely beautiful and starkly terrifying.

Filmmaker as Antagonist

We don't watch *After Hours* for very long before we are aware that something is off center here, too. But, unlike *Blue Velvet*, where the characters do not know that the birds are mechanical, in *After Hours*, Paul gradually becomes aware that he is being affected by something that exists outside of the story. At a climactic moment, as the camera pulls up and away, Paul gets on his knees and yells into the lens, "Why are you doing this to me?" This action breaks down the fundamental assumption of realism—that no one in the story is aware of being observed. Once this happens, the whole notion of a structure that organizes the story for a viewer, but is not apparent to the characters, is undercut. Instead of the structure being concealed behind the actions of character, it becomes the exact opposite—both obvious and antagonistic to character. The character becomes aware that something is controlling his life and, in this way, must face how limited his freedom is. He is forced to fight something that is so deeply embedded in his existence that he can't step outside and confront it. As we will see in Chapter 15, this tension between character and narrator can be a way to express the tension between our illusion of complete freedom and the subtle ways that, unbeknown to us, the outside pressure of society, class, gender, and history condition our choices.

Documentary Randomness

In contrast to the previous examples, other scripts flatten and minimize structure, creating the illusion of documentary randomness.

Indifferent Three-Act Structure

Badlands has two distinct turning points that resemble act breaks—the moment when 14-year-old Holly runs off with her boyfriend, Kit, who has just killed her father, and the moment when, several murders later, Holly finally decides to leave Kit. Certainly, these two decisions would function very well in a redemptive mode, suggesting a story about an adolescent's mistake and the realization of its costs. The difference in *Badlands* is that Holly, who provides the blank, emotionless voice-over narration, does not seem to learn anything.

Let's look, in detail, at the treatment of Holly's decision to run off with Kit. In the script (page 19), Kit shoots Holly's father in the back. Holly kneels by her father, then goes into the kitchen followed by Kit. Then Kit, followed by Holly, comes back into the living room, feels Holly's father's heart, and says, "He don't need a doctor."[3]

Cut to Kit dragging Holly's father into the basement—script page 20. An indefinite period of time has passed. Kit picks up a toaster and brings it up to the kitchen where Holly slaps him. She walks into the living room. He follows, then decides to leave for a while. She sinks down on the couch.

Cut to the exterior of the house at night—script page 21. More time has passed. Cut back to the interior. Holly comes up the stairs and looks through the bedroom window at two boys playing outside.

Cut to the train station—script page 21. Same time period. Kit puts a coin in a slot of a gramophone booth and makes a record on which he confesses that Holly and he plan to kill themselves. Kit leaves the booth.

Cut to gasoline being poured over the piano—script page 22. Leaving the record playing, Holly and Kit set the house on fire and run to the car. The camera focuses on Cut to Holly collecting her books from her locker at dawn—script page 23. In a voice-over, she tells us she could have snuck away, but her destiny now lies with Kit, for better or for worse.

What has been carefully cut out of this sequence is the moment when Holly decides that her destiny lies with Kit. In place of this moment, we have static, almost tableau-like scenes that seem inappropriate to what is happening. Since we do not see them as transitions or attempts to come to terms with the killing, we can only try to make sense of them by attributing our own emotions to them and assume that Holly is mourning her father. However, our assumptions of Holly's mourning are confused when, inexplicably, she runs away with Kit. When her voice-over expresses no feeling for her father at all, we realize that we have no way to penetrate the images. Why is everything photographed so beautifully? Why does the main character have such limited reactions? We don't know. But what better way to convey the coldness we associate with a mass killing spree than that eerie, inexplicable distance?

To understand the power of this oblique structure, we can look at a film like *Bonnie and Clyde*. Despite the bullet holes, the violence in *Bonnie and Clyde* feels like abstract movie violence, while the killing in *Badlands* casts an unrelenting oppressiveness over the viewer that lingers long after the end of the film.

Badlands uses another technique worth noting. As we watch, we struggle to relate the time of the voice-over to the time of the events in the movie. Because the voice-over seems so immature and so undisturbed by the violence it is describing and because it seeks to cast Holly's actions as adventures in a romance novel, we tend to place it very close to the time of the images. However, as the movie draws to a close, we learn that Holly is speaking from a position a number of years distant from the events on the screen.

This makes the perspective of the movie even more chilling. Although this much time has past and she has thought about what she has done, she is still unable to recount the horror or even the unromanticized dreariness of what she has gone through.

Ironic Two-Act Structure

She's Gotta Have It makes no attempt to answer restorative expectations. In fact, the film ends with a deliberate flouting of our expectations. We expect Nola Darling, having lost the man she seemed to love, to abandon her free-spirited life-style, but she does not. Yet, we find Nola's declaration of indifference satisfying. That is quite unlike our response to *Chinatown*, in which we would be lost if Gittes declared himself no longer interested in Mrs. Mulwray.

In *Chinatown* we move through a clear first-act transition when Gittes, threatened by Mrs. Mulwray, decides to take her on. This transition engages us and draws us into the second act; our participation commits us to its playing out. *She's Gotta Have It* has no such first-act turning point. In fact, its flashback structure discourages a linear, three-act reading. Nola moves ahead of us throughout the film. Although we first assume that she has a monogamous relationship with Jamie, we are not explicitly told this. When we later learn about her other lovers, we are learning about something that has already been decided, rather than participating in a newly made decision. Thus, unlike Gittes in *Chinatown*, we are not implicated in the shaping of a life; we are presented with Nola's life-style as a given.

She's Gotta Have It does have something akin to an act break. After Jamie leaves her, Nola decides to drop her other two lovers and go back to him. However, because we have not been involved in Nola's initial decision to have three lovers and are not positioned to see the taking of the three lovers as a first-act mistake, we do not feel this break serves as a consequence of some earlier misdirection. We have no sense of her coming back into sync with us as we would with a traditional second-act break. Rather, we stand outside and watch, wondering what she is going to do without being able to prejudge her actions. When she does not stay with Jamie, we are left trying to piece together the story to figure out why.

One-Act Structure

While *She's Gotta Have It* is structured in two acts, Martin Scorsese's *Mean Streets* has no act breaks at all. *Mean Streets* follows one line—Charlie's attempt to find salvation in the streets by backing Johnny-Boy. Within the first ten minutes of the film, we learn that Charlie has guaranteed Michael's loan to Johnny. When Johnny throws away what little money he has, Charlie pulls him aside to get it sorted out. This scene has all the makings of a first-act curtain. We know, even though Charlie does his best not to notice, that Johnny is a disastrous credit risk. Yet, since Charlie's decision has already been made, all this scene does is affirm and deepen action that began in the back story.

At the beginning of the film, Charlie is warned by Michael against guaranteeing Johnny's loans. This is essentially a second-act scene, one that heightens the cost of the decision traditionally made at the end of Act One and that the rest of the film continues to develop. For the rest of the movie, Charlie is repeatedly warned off Johnny-Boy, while at the same time Johnny becomes the source of Charlie's salvation—a cross he has chosen to bear. This pressure slowly builds until Charlie, fleeing with Johnny and Teresa, is shot by Michael.

Without plot turns, without small victories or misdirections, a one-act script is extremely difficult to sustain for two hours. But when it succeeds, it carries a relentless accumulation of power that is hard to achieve in a more segmented story. Such a story starts with a conflict that is already well engaged and runs through a long, slow, arch. Frequently, the conflict is so intense and fundamental it is beyond a defining, third-act character resolution. For example, Charlie's struggle between salvation and family is no closer to a resolution at the end of *Mean Streets*.

Although divided into thirds, *Stranger Than Paradise* provides a similar example. Each of its three parts moves in the same direction and gives us the same single-minded directionality we see in *Mean Streets*. Whatever itch Eddie is seeking to scratch, his trips to Cleveland, Florida, and finally Budapest propose the same kind of solution. Eddie will feel displaced wherever he is, which we knew from the beginning of the film. Thus, rather than reveal or expose character, flattened structure tends to confirm and deepen what we already know.

It also tends to cast doubt on any possibility of change. What will Eddie discover in Budapest? We don't know but would be surprised if he finds it any different than Cleveland. In Lizzie Borden's *Working Girls*, the central character, after spending a dull, grueling day and night as a prostitute, decides to quit. Because we are never invited to ask why she's become a prostitute in the first place, because this has been predetermined before the film starts, we regard her decision with skepticism.

Mixed Modes

We have artificially separated forms into those that put structure in the foreground and those that flatten it. In practice, most alternative screenplays use both tendencies. We generally avoid concentrating on non-American films because we believe that the best work comes from and acknowledges the traditions native to us. However, Jean-Luc Godard's *Masculine/Feminine* is a perfect illustration of playing out the tension between opposite ways of approaching structure.

Masculine/Feminine, which follows Paul's involvement with the rising pop singer Madeline, is subtitled "15 Precise Acts." The action is punctuated with numerical intertitles, which progress erratically toward number 15. For instance, we see no number titles for a time, and when we do, we see 4, then 4A, then nothing, then 7 and 8 in the middle of other titles. These numbers, however erratic, provide an obvious and self-conscious structure. We know the film will be over by the time we reach 15.

By contrast, the scenes are flat, underlit, highly documentary in style. They are structured like imperfect interviews, with the suggestion that the most important information is always that which cannot be said. Words are a poor approximation of what is meant; the world appears heavy, opaque, uninterpretable, and impervious to emotion. Characters are observed at a distance. There are few transitions and no unambiguous point-of-view shots.

The film plays on this paradox between the artifical and the documentary. By providing an explicit, overt, narrating structure (the progressive numbers), the script acknowledges its artificiality, freeing it from hiding the coincidences that determine all narrative structure. We cannot miss this sense of external control, the implication that the characters are not controlling their own lives. They seem lost in a world that provides them only with advertising slogans. Paul speaks to Madeline through a record machine, unable to find his own words to express his feelings for her.

At the same time, this narrative presence is rendered suspect by the documentary style. No matter how many interview questions are asked and how hard the camera seeks to penetrate, the flat, opaque surface of the world reveals very little, either to the characters or to the narrator.

One of the functions of narration is to signal the end of a film. In a mainstream film, the story ends without calling attention to whatever actually structures a sense of ending. The questions raised by that structure seem to resolve themselves. In *Masculine/Feminine,* by contrast, the end is intentionally arbitrary—the title, 15, flashes on the screen. Madeline and one of her roommates sit in a police station, answering routine questions. Everything is emotionless. We learn that Paul came into some money, bought an apartment, and, when showing it to Madeline, stepped back too far and fell to his death. The film ends. Self-consciously structured to the point of overt manipulation, *Masculine/Feminine* becomes a reflection of larger elements—advertising, culture, class, history—that affect our lives. At the same time, it seeks, like Paul, to find meaning in a world that has lost emotion or connection.

Some Additional Examples

We conclude with a few brief examples of alternative structures. We will return to many of these films later.

Julie Dash's *Daughters of the Dust* takes place in 1902 on the day the Peazant family is to leave the South Carolina island of Ebo Landing to head north. The opening title leaves no doubt that they will in fact go, and so the forward narrative tension is diverted into a circular meditation on the departure's meaning. The timelessness of this moment is rendered with particular perspective because one of the two voice-over narrators is the great-grandmother Nana Peazant looking back, while the other is an unborn child looking forward.

Swoon is based on the famous 1924 case involving Nathan Leopold and Richard Loeb's gratuitous murder of a young boy. Rather than presenting this event as though we are there, the film gives us perspective by using a number of anachronisms that emphasize the tension between then and now. Because we never forget we are watching these events from today's viewpoint, our attention is turned from the event itself to the treatment of homosexual love in the 1920s and today, as well as to the need to declare oneself through violent, defining actions.

Both *Nashville* and *Slacker* make a city and its culture—Nashville, Tennessee, and Austin, Texas—respectively, their central focus. They do this by introducing a large cast of characters whose relationship to one another seems so tangential that we feel the only unifying story factor is the place itself. *Nashville*, however, repeatedly returns to the same groups of characters and finally brings the pieces together in an ending that seems either coincidental or so intentionally manipulated as to call attention to itself. *Slacker* remains serial throughout, moving from incident to incident without returning to any of them. This flattens our building expectations and, as we watch each incident, we struggle to make connections between it and the others. The film seems to be structured around a random train of alternative lives whose very lack of direction defines a cross-section of this city.

To Sleep With Anger is structured around an ambiguity of genre. Harry, a trickster/storyteller, visits a middle-class family of old friends in Los Angeles and overstays his welcome. At one level, the conflict is between the old and the new, about a past catching up to characters, about personalities and how they change. Underneath, however, the story has a hint of magic realism and, for most of the film, we are never quite sure whether we are watching a family melodrama or a mythic confrontation. Only in the last ten minutes does the film declare itself in favor of the mythic. The celebration over Harry's dead body that marks the end pulls us out of the limited perspective of the family story and makes us understand that we cannot respond to these characters only through their individual histories but that we must also confront the larger culture forces that inform their world.

Conclusion

We have demonstrated two contrasting alternatives to restorative three-act structure. Sometimes, structure is emphasized and made very obvious. Then, it calls attention to itself, suggesting the artificiality of form over the chaos of day-to-day experience. Ironic three-act structure twists the standard form, turning it in unexpected directions, while exaggerated three-act structure parodies the norm and undercuts the value of restoration. At other times, structure may be flattened and minimized, creating the illusion of documentary randomness. For example, indifferent three-act structure creates a sense of inevitability by not providing the standard insight into character motivations or the meaning of their actions. One- and two-act structures narrow the screenplay's focus to just one conflict or goal and tend to confirm what we already know about the character or situation.

Many alternative screenplays mix structural emphasis and structural minimalization, playing on the tension between the two impulses. Alternative structures should grow organically out of the needs of the individual work. The possibilities are infinite. In the following chapter, we detail the specifics of creating the stories themselves.

References

1. Syd Field, *The Foundations of Screenwriting* (New York: Delacorte, 1982), p. 11.
2. Ibid., p. 9.
3. Terrence Malick, *Badlands*, (Warner Brothers, 1973), p. 20.

5

Working With Genre

One of the most observable characteristics of American film is the continuing strength of genres, or story forms. The Western, the gangster film, and the musical are forms synonymous with Hollywood. *Film noir* and the horror film, although originating in Europe, have proved to be enduring in North America. The popularity of genres over time means that most scriptwriters, during the course of their careers, will have to work with genre and consequently should understand genres and how to work with them. Genres are, in effect, a shorthand to structured types of stories. Knowing that shortcut, the scriptwriter is free to explore aspects that have particular relevance for him.

Genre is more than formula. More often it is a type of story that has a visceral appeal to its audience. The scriptwriter who ignores the strength of that appeal does so at considerable cost.

Genre and the Audience

Film sociologists have long probed the relationship between movies and the audience. But the most insightful views of genres and their relationship to the audience have come from a less scientific perspective. Such writers as Susan Sontag, Paul Schrader, and Robert Warshow have examined particular genres and found complex relationships between the fears and aspirations of audiences and the genres that speak to these feelings. Warshow, for example, examines the hero in the gangster and Western genres and suggests that the gangster is the same as most other citizens.[1] He is a new arrival, an immigrant who wants to succeed in this society. He differs from most of us in the means by which he chooses to succeed—criminality. Warshow suggests that all of us want to succeed, but in the modern milieu of the city, many fail. The gangster's failure leads to the ultimate failure, his death, and there lies the tragedy.

The more optimistic view of the hero is present in the Western genre, where the hero functions on a plane of morality unavailable to the modern gangster. In the idealized world of the Western, simpler resolutions to conflict and to ethical aspirations give an audience the kind of wish-fulfillment associated with a simpler, pastoral time. Warshow is careful to underline that neither genre is about history. Facts are not as important as dreams in genres, which are dreamscapes for their audiences.

Dreams and nightmares are the emotional baselines for storytelling via the genre approach. The world of the nightmare is central to the horror film and to *film noir*. A world where dreams come true is central to the Western, the adventure film, and the musical; and, of course, more recognizable people, situations, and behavior are the basis of the more realistic genres—the documentary, the melodrama, and the situation comedy.

The writer, however, should be aware that just as audiences change over time, so to do genres in order to tell classic stories in a new guise. One could not make a classic Western without taking in the events that have affected audiences' views about Western heroes, villains, Indians, the land, and civilizing forces. The nuclear age and space, our new frontier, also have an impact on the Western set as it is on the old frontier. In the past 15 years, we have seen at least three Westerns set in space—*Outland*, *Star Wars*, and *Aliens*—which have many characteristics of the classic Western. Their frontier, however, is space, rather than the land called The West.

Genres

It is not our intention to tell the history of genres in this chapter, but some sense of both the classic genre and its contemporary equivalent is valuable to the development of your genre shorthand.

We deal with the following genres in detail:

- The Western
- The Gangster Film
- The *Film Noir*
- The Screwball Comedy
- The Melodrama
- The Situation Comedy
- The Horror Film
- The Science Fiction Film
- The War Film
- The Adventure Film
- The Epic Film
- The Sports Film
- The Biographical Film
- The Satire Film

In terms of understanding genres and using dramatic components in writing them, it's best to consider their particular common features. These are:

1. The nature of the protagonist
2. The nature of the antagonist
3. The shape of the dramatic action
4. The catalytic event
5. The resolution
6. The narrative style
7. The narrative shape
8. The tone

Each genre has its own distinct characteristics, which differ from one genre to another. For example, the protagonist or main character in the horror film tends to be a victim while the main character in the Western is a hero. By highlighting some of the differences among genres, we will show how the writer can use these features best in writing genre stories and then in working against expectation to make a story seem fresh.

1. The Nature of the Protagonist. The main character and the character's goal are the primary focus of the story in any genre. While the main character in the Western is heroic and tends to be romanticized and the main character in the horror film is a victim, the main characters in the war film tend to be far more realistic. In the musical, the main character tends to be presented energetically while in *film noir* he is constricted and desperate. The qualities of the main character within a particular genre tend to be consistent, which makes the shorthand dimensions of that character readily available for the writer.

2. The Nature of the Antagonist. The importance of the antagonist is constant across genres, but the nature of the antagonist depends on the level of realism associated with particular genres. Where the presentation of the main character exclusive of realism is heroic, the adventure film or the Western, for example, the antagonist becomes more evil, more powerful, sometimes more than human. Where the genre is nightmarish, as in the horror film and *film noir*, the antagonist is equally extreme.

Only in the realistic genres, such as the war film, the melodrama and the gangster film, does the antagonist take on more human rather than superhuman qualities. In these genres the goal of the main character is more understandable, more realistic; consequently the antagonist, although important, takes on a more human dimension.

3. The Shape of the Dramatic Action. Gangster stories tend to be shaped around the rise and fall of a gangster. Police stories are shaped around the perpetration of a crime, its investigation and its successful conclusion, which is the apprehension of the perpetrator. All genre films have a very particular dramatic shape. And all begin with the expected opening: A soldier is inducted into the army to fight in a foreign war; a cowboy dreams of acquiring land and a cattle herd; a poor boy from the Midwest wants to improve his life in the industrial Northeast.

In the course of the dramatic action, we will find out if the soldier survives, what personal sacrifice is necessary for the cowboy to improve himself, and what transgressions are necessary for the young Midwesterner to get ahead.

In each case, the fate of the character will differ in accordance with genre expectations. And in each case the characters' attempts to fulfill their goals will dictate the shape of the dramatic action.

4. Catalytic Event. Stolen cattle, a friend's death, the end of the Civil War, an Indian raid—all are the catalytic events in different Westerns. Each propels the main character to find and resolve the consequences of the action resulting from that event.

Every genre has its own kind of catalytic event. A crime is the catalytic event of the police story. In a horror film, a young family moves into a reputedly haunted New England home. The critical catalytic event should occur quickly or the dramatic vitality of the story form, the genre, is dissipated. The audience expects a quick start.

5. The Resolution. Dramatic action of course leads us to the resolution. But not every genre leads us to the same kind of resolution. Although the fate of our Midwesterner in the melodrama tends toward the tragic, this is not the case in the classic Western or in the war film. In the Western, although the main character pays a price for his ambition, he does tend to succeed and be experienced as a hero in the effort. That effort requires a ritualized demonstration of heroism—the climactic gunfight. In the war film, although there is a climactic battle, the character's fate may not be determined by his individual actions but because of the superior forces of the protagonist's side. Or the resolution may come through superior air power, or through the simple action that allows the character to survive the battle. Whatever the reason, it does not come from the individual action of the main character and consequently the sense of him as a hero is less apparent than in the Western, where individual action is central to the resolution.

6. Narrative Style. Every genre has a particular narrative style that the audience expects and enjoys. Westerns, for example, tend to be punctuated by gunfights, deployment of weaponry, expertise in horsemanship, and use of survival skills in what is essentially a rural primitive wilderness. Violence and violent resolution to conflict characterize the genre.

This is not the case in melodrama, where relationships, their evolution, and their outcome are central. Although there may be a tragic outcome in melo-drama, the violence is emotional rather than physical.

7. Narrative Shape.   Different genres exhibit different shapes. Although Westerns such as *High Noon* take place in a single day, this is not at all typical of the Western, many of which have an expansive time frame—years in the case of *Red River* and *The Searchers*. This is unusual, however, in *film noir* where the character is running out of time; this is his last chance. Consequently, *film noir* stories tend to have a far more intense narrative shape. The time frame collapses, as does the accelerated presentation of a desperate relationship for the main character.

Time is critical in the adventure film and in the thriller; it is far less important in the situation comedy and the war film. Consequently, the narrative shape in each of these genres differs considerably.

The primary consideration here is the level of intensity the genre requires to be in tune with the goals of the main character. In *film noir* the main character is desperate, trying to survive his tragic fate. In the adventure film, the level of threat to the main character has to be constant so that the audience stays with the plot. In the Western and the situation comedy, the relationship with the main character is relatively more relaxed, and consequently the narrative shape is also more relaxed.

8. Tone.   Although tone will be discussed in detail in a later chapter, it is important to consider it here as an element of genre.

Tone can range from the fantastic (the adventure film and the musical) to realistic (the war film and the melodrama), from ironic (the screwball comedy and the satire) to totally involving (the thriller and the horror film).

As with all the elements mentioned in this section, the clarity of these elements, whether tone or dramatic shape or the nature of the protagonist, offers the writer clear opportunities to alter or challenge these conventions in order to make the story seem different or fresh. But for the purposes of this chapter we will assume constancy within genres. We turn now to the genres themselves.

The Western

The Western genre has an elaborate, rich history. Its central themes, which play themselves out in the classic Western, the predominant western form until 1950, are these:

- The hero, a man alone, functions with a world view that is both moral and decent.

- The hero has a distinct skill with guns and horses.
- The antagonist has mercantile goals—the accumulation of money, land, cattle—and will recognize no person or ethic that stands in his way.
- The land plays a pastoral, but critical, role. It represents not only freedom but also the primitivism of all natural phenomena.
- Civilization is represented by those forces of an organizing influence on life—the town, the army, married life, children.
- The struggle between the forces of primitivism (the land, the Indians) and those of civilization (the army, the town) forms a particular dilemma for the Western hero. In which world will he reside? His classic conflict exists because his heart sides with the forces of primitivism, but his head sides with civilization.
- The drama plays itself out in a ritualized form—gunfights, cattle drives—and individual conflicts are acted out rather than negotiated.

Having characterized the classic Western, we should also recognize how the Western has changed since 1950. Revisions to the classic Western have attempted, as their primary goal, to make it less innocent. In *The Gunfighter*, Gregory Peck as the hero is demystified by being made a victim of his reputation. Demystification also occurs in *Winchester '73*, in which James Stewart portrays a neurotic hero; and in *The Wild Bunch*, in which William Holden is a killer without a hint of the tenderness of the classic hero.

Other Westerns have focused on the issue of the civilizing forces. Armies have been presented as more primitive than the primitives (i.e., the Indians)—Apache, The Outlaw Josey Wales—and towns have been hell rather than heaven—*High Plains Drifter*. The central character's struggle has come to make him seem much more jaded and much less idealistic. Indeed, both *The Culpepper Cattle Company* and *Heaven's Gate* are about the loss of idealism.

More recently, there has been a resurgence in the Western, and here too, we see subtle and not-so-subtle shifts in the genre. The idealism of the classic Western is again challenged in *Wyatt Earp*, where the myth of Wyatt Earp is as much the writers' target as the historical events or the dramatic opportunities provided by the gunfight at the OK Corral. *Tombstone*, released the same year, 1994, conforms more closely to the typical Western, but here too the struggle is less about primitivism against civilization than it is about opposing material goals. This theme of the materialism of the main character is particularly notable in David Webb Peoples's *Unforgiven*. It seems that the Western hero is less a hero and more a man of the 1980s than of the 1880s!

So, the Western has changed, but the dreamscape—a frontier where the struggle between primitivism and civilization unfolds—has not. Western film stories have just moved to another frontier.

The Gangster Film

The classic gangster film, like the Western, concerns itself with a very particular story—the rise and fall of a man who has no patience for progress through the ranks. The gangster is a man in a hurry; his time is running out. The motifs of the classic gangster film are:

- The hero is an immigrant who is low in status but desires higher status.
- The city is the gangster's home; it is the location for his struggle to move up in the social order.
- Power comes from the willingness to take power. This means courage, cunning, and a willingness to murder those who object to sharing power. This is the law of the jungle.
- The hero is loyal to his immigrant roots.
- The antagonist is the society that cannot tolerate the law of the jungle. The representatives of the society are the police and the F.B.I., which act as the front line of combat against the law of the jungle.
- The symbols of success are material—guns, cars, and women.
- Getting ahead is everything and the ends justify the means.

The classic gangster film is an ongoing dimension of American film; *The Godfather* and *The Untouchables* are recent examples. However, the genre has been too important a representation of modern life to limit itself to the character of the gangster. The gangster has been joined by the central character—the cop *(Dirty Harry)*, the detective *(The Big Sleep)*, and, on the international level, the spy *(The Spy Who Came In From the Cold)*. All of these characters seek to find a way of succeeding in their particular jungles. As with the gangster, the struggle for position involves pushing out the other spy or killer who challenges the existing order. In all cases, the struggle is to the death. Their worlds will be subverted under any other outcome.

Recently gangster films have added an existential dimension to the struggle. It is as if hope has dimmed and a kind of nihilistic death wish pervades the gangster and his fate. Whether focused on the individual *(The King of New York)* or a gang *(Reservoir Dogs)*, betrayal has become the focus for the fate of the gangster. This dramatic shift crosses ethnic barriers, and we see the gangster's fate more tragically magnified in the Puerto Rican ghetto *(Carlito's Way)*, in the black ghetto *(Clockers)*, and in the Irish ghetto *(State of Grace)*. Whether it is the encroaching effectiveness of the law or the feeling that there is overpopulation in the urban jungle and Malthus's law of population control has come into effect, these stories portray a less hopeful, more desperate gangster hero, less heroic and more violent; his struggle is the last act of a condemned man who knows he is condemned.

As to the setting, Harry Callahan lives in San Francisco, Phillip Marlowe works in Los Angeles, Elliot Ness lives in Chicago, and Don Corleone lives and works in New York City. The identifiable locale gives a particular credibility to the gangster film, but make no mistake: The subject matter of the gangster film is not a documentary on urban life, but like the Western is a dreamscape and nightmare of that life. Gangster films are psychodramas, the equivalent of modernized tales of gladiators and Christians. For all of these characters in this genre, there is nothing less at stake than their lives.

Because these stories are primal and male, there is little scope in this genre for male-female relationships. The genre does have memorable women— Bonnie in *Bonnie and Clyde*, James Cagney's mother in *White Heat*, and Gloria Grahame in *The Big Heat*—but in each case, the role of the woman is catalytic to the action of the gangster. In no case is the woman a stand-alone character functioning in an interesting way in her own world. Whether they be sibling, mother, virgin, or whore, women play supporting roles in gangster films.

A final word. If fiction prose foreshadows genre activity in film, in the near future we will soon see detectives who are Indians working on reservations (Tony Hillerman) and Eskimos working in the Arctic (Scott Young). We will see rural cops (Ted Wood) and more international manifestations of the gangster genre (David Thompson). All of these authors have portrayed detectives in different or unusual settings that have struck a cord with the public. Hollywood producers have taken note, particularly in telling stories of international gangsters (e.g., *Red Heat, The Russia House*).

The classic gangster film's search for success is taking on an international dimension and the world is beginning to look like an oversized jungle in which the stakes of human drama grow increasingly dangerous. The gangster genre has never had more material with which to work.

The Film Noir

Beginning in the pessimistic 1920s in Germany, *film noir* as a genre appealed to the darker fears of an increasingly urbanized population. *Film noir* could be subtitled "the genre of betrayal"—personal betrayal, national betrayal, and international betrayal. Its characteristics are as follows:

- The desperate central character lives on the edge; he merely exists. We can't call him the hero, as in the gangster and Western genres, because the behavior of the central character in the *film noir* is anything but heroic.

- The central character thinks that his chance at a better, richer, more vital life can only be found in another character—usually a woman. This may be his last chance and he certainly acts as if it is.
- The relationship between the central character and his savior is a highly charged, sexual relationship.
- The central character will be betrayed in this relationship.
- A by-product of the relationship is violence.
- The key root of the problem with the relationship is the city, the stand-in symbol for modern life. The city saps the generosity out of the relationship. All that is left is deception and betrayal.
- There are no children in *film noir*. Children represent hope and there is no hope in any relationship, nor in the future.
- Sexuality and violence coexist and seem to be cause-and-effect.
- The sense of aloneness in the central character is palpable. It represents an existential state.

Needless to say, *film noir* is a genre that symbolizes our nightmares. The classic of the genre is represented by Billy Wilder's *Double Indemnity*, a film of murder for the promise of love and the discovery that there is no love, only more murder. More recent representations of *film noir* are *Body Heat, Chinatown, Raging Bull, Basic Instinct,* and *Romeo is Bleeding*. For such a pessimistic genre, *film noir* seems to elicit many creative films. As a genre that depicts the worst in human beings, it brings out the best in writers and directors. An interesting irony.

The Screwball Comedy

The screwball comedy is funny *film noir* that has a happy ending. The characteristics of this genre are quite similar to *film noir:*

- The central character is an isolated male.
- He looks desperately for a female to overcome his isolation or anxiety.
- The premise of the film is about the struggle in their relationship.
- During the course of the struggle, which is highly sexually charged, the maleness of the central character is challenged. The female is the dominant character in the relationship. This role reversal is central to the screwball comedy.
- Whereas the outcome of *film noir* is tragic, the outcome of the screwball comedy is happy.
- The urban setting of the genre is as much a jungle in screwball comedy as it is in *film noir.*
- There are no children and only troubled married couples in the screwball comedy.

- The aggression in this genre is the source of the humor, rather than the violence it evokes in *film noir.*

The screwball comedy is a genre that requires more risk and more aggression than the situation comedy. Consequently, few screwball comedies are made. *Shampoo* and *Something Wild* are recent examples of this genre, but few writers are developing scripts such as *Bringing Up Baby* and *Monkey Business*. Screwball comedies make most male writers very nervous because they threaten their masculinity and dominance or wished-for dominance in their relationships. The genre is, however, very lively and energetic.

Both *Tootsie* and *Mrs. Doubtfire* borrow the dynamic from screwball comedies but neither follows through in the classic screwball comedy sense. Both work with the masculine–feminine side of their main characters, and *Tootsie* particularly characterizes the male side as the antagonist of the story. This New Age approach moves both films into the safer realm of the situation comedy and away from the dangerous shoals of the screwball comedy.

The Melodrama

The melodrama is frequently associated with soap operas, an unfair generalization, because the genre of melodrama is closest to the people, issues, and events of our times. This is not to say that it is a dramatized documentary of our own lives. Melodrama may be better classified as the dramatized lives of our neighbors. The genre's characteristics are these:

- The central character is more often female than in many other genres. However, the central character can be male.
- The presence of a distinct social order is a barrier to the central character and indicates the power structure in the city, region, town, or country.
- The central character transgresses the power structure. This is usually attempted through a relationship with someone from within the power structure.
- Beauty and intelligence are not equivalent to the symbols of power—money and social or political connections.
- The central character's behavior while transgressing the power structure is as much a threat to her own family as it is to the powerful family of which she and they would become a part if the new relationship is a success. The central character is unsupported in her goal.
- The conviction of the central character is fueled by the belief that life must be and can be improved. The status quo (e.g., original family or unsuccessful marriage) is an insult to her sense of self.

- The vitality of the melodrama is, in part, supported by its modernity. Period melodramas are less successful because they are too distant from the audience. More successful melodramas reflect the people, lives, and issues of the audience that attends the film.
- Idealism, cynicism, sexuality, and aggression reflect the attitudes of the characters and, more important, support the central characteristic of the melodrama—a story of power and powerlessness set against an inflexible power structure.

Perhaps the most important power struggle of the 1980s was the battle of the sexes. The sexual revolution and the rise of feminism together with rapid economic change has fueled a redefinition of the male–female relationship. Attitudes toward career, childrearing, and marriage are all in flux. Yet, the male–female relationship, as it has been for centuries, is a central dimension of our existence. It is no surprise that *Thirtysomething* was one of the most successful television shows of the decade. Some of the most memorable films of the period—*Kramer vs. Kramer, Independence Day, My Beautiful Laundrette, Breaking Away*—are melodramas. Societal change has unleashed a torrent of films about power relationships at all ages and stages. *Fast Times at Ridgemont High, Crossing Delancey,* and *Beaches* have much in common. They are all melodramas—only the ages of the central characters differ—and each film has a woman as its central character.

Melodrama can also be examined as a reflection of the structure of political power in a society. Within this framework, the male–female dynamic is just one axis of a larger political construct. Another is the politics of the family. Here the struggles of fathers and sons are reflected in films such as *East of Eden* and *A River Runs Through It.* The rebellious son was made an archetype of the era in *Rebel Without a Cause.* The daughter who dared to be different was the focus of *Peyton Place.*

The framework of politics itself is the theme of Rossen's famous *All the King's Men* and the not-so-famous but equally interesting John Sayles take on urban politics, *City of Hope.* Add race and we have Euzhan Palcy and Colin Welland's *A Dry White Season.* In this complex melodrama, it is the liberal white man, portrayed by Donald Sutherland, who challenges the laws of his own country, South Africa, to defend the dignity of his black gardener. His punishment, death, is the classic consequence for the main character in melodrama.

In *Lorenzo's Oil,* death is challenged by Susan Sarandon and Nick Nolte as parents who are told their son has an incurable disease. These parents do not accept the conventional wisdom of the medical power structure. They spend time, money, and energy to find a cure for their son's illness. And they do find one in George Miller and Nick Enright's *Lorenzo's Oil.* This melodrama about the politics of health and medicine is a victory for the parents, but the screen story highlights the power of the melodrama to take us realistically to the darkness and tragedy that is part of life.

The Situation Comedy

The situation comedy is very similar to the melodrama, although the outcome differs. The outcome in a melodrama is often tragic or has a dimension of tragedy. The mother leaving the family at the end of *Ordinary People* is a good example of a tragic melodrama. In situation comedy, the tragic potential dissipates and a more satisfying outcome results. A good example of the situation comedy is in *Ruthless People* when Bette Midler's character kicks her husband, played by Danny DeVito, into the ocean at the end of the film. Of course, humor is the result of all the character conflict in the situation comedy, whose characteristics are:

- The central character is more often male than female. Examples of central characters in recent situation comedies are Dudley Moore in *10* and *Arthur*, John Ritter in *Skin Deep*, and Michael Caine in *Blame It On Rio*.
- The setting is contemporary.
- The central character transgresses not the power structure but the values of the power structure.
- Money and social connections are not enough. The central character needs to recapture values he feels are lost (e.g., idealism, vitality).
- As in the melodrama, the central character's transgressions isolate him from everyone—friend and foe.
- The situation comedy readily embraces current issues, uses them to the disadvantage of the central character, and promotes a search for new values. *An Unmarried Woman* and *Moscow on the Hudson* are examples of quality situation comedies.

Just as *The Apartment* was the situation comedy that heralded the end of the '50s, so too do the filmic meditations of Woody Allen on urban life, in *Crimes and Misdemeanors*, reflect the end of the affluent '80s. *Forrest Gump* may prove to be the quintessential situation comedy of the '90s. Acknowledging the limits and the cruelty of the surrounding society, this mentally limited character has the emotional capacity to transcend that society. As he did in *Big*, Tom Hanks captures a sensibility at odds with everyone around him, and by doing so teaches them.

This dissonance between character and society is also the theme of two other important situation comedies, *Dave* and *Groundhog Day*. In *Dave*, the presidency of the United States is the focus, while *Groundhog Day* focuses on the media. In each, the transcendence of the individual characters over deficiencies affirms hopefulness in a bleak time. These films differ from the populist comedies of Frank Capra, which fused the transcendence of the individual to the potential for good in American society. These '90s comedies are less optimistic about the society as a whole; their focus is on the individual as his own salvation. The society itself is portrayed as the source of the problem, whereas for Capra it was the true source of strength for the individual.

The dysfunctional family and dissonant characters are important sources for the situation comedies of the '90s. *Mrs. Doubtfire* focuses on a dysfunctional husband. *Home Alone* focuses on one of the children accidentally left at home by hurried parents. *It Could Happen to You* tells what happens when an unhappily married couple wins the lottery.

The Horror Film

The horror film, originating from the 19th-century literature of Robert Louis Stevenson, Edgar Allen Poe, and Mary Shelley, is principally a reaction (as was the literature) to the veneer of civilization that comes with the material successes of modern life. Monsters, unbridled aggression, and sexuality—the inhabitants of our nightmare world—have a continuing popularity, particularly with young people, who are so much less inhibited than their parents. The world of our unconscious is the central source of material for the horror film, whose characteristics are:

- The central character is a victim, rather than a hero.
- The antagonist is often manifested from a technological aberration (e.g., Frankenstein's monster) or a social aberration (e.g., Freddy Krueger).
- Unbridled aggression and sexuality play an important role. Cruelty knows no relative form; this is a genre of absolutes.
- Technology, science, and scientific activity often unleash the antagonist. Fears about the future are as important as fears about the past.
- Religion is viewed as an intermediary that can influence the outcome of events. The central conflict is often portrayed as a struggle between God and Satan *(The Exorcist, Rosemary's Baby, The Seventh Sign).*
- Children have special powers, exhibiting vision, insight, and tolerance. The opposite traits are exhibited by adults.
- Relationships can't save the central character. Very often, the victimizer is a member of the family.
- The location (house, village, archaeological find) has a special significance that influences the outcome of events for the central character.

- The supernatural has a significant role in the horror film; most events can't be explained rationally. Since the genre dwells on the irrational, some form of understanding devolves from a supernatural explanation.
- In the '90s, the horror film has returned to a key dimension of the horror novel: the humanity of the monster. James V. Hart's screenplay of *Bram Stoker's Dracula* focuses on the historical evolution of Count Dracula and poignantly suggests that immortal love has created Dracula and that compassion rather than cruelty will do him in. Similarly, Amanda Silver focuses on the creation of a nanny as the monster in *The Hand That Rocked the Cradle*. Recent films depict more empathy for and understanding of the monster than the horror films of the previous two decades.

The Science Fiction Film

The science fiction film is to society what the horror film is to the person—a tale of catastrophe, a story of our worst nightmares. In the science fiction story, an ecological catastrophe *(The Naked Jungle)*, a technological accident *(2001: A Space Odyssey)*, or the not-welcomed meeting of two worlds *(The Day the Earth Stood Still)* serves to remind the audience that the inhabitants of Earth don't have enough respect for the environment, for science, or for each other; if this tendency persists, Earth will be destroyed or will destroy itself. In this context, the science fiction film is analogous to the biblical epic—both are morality plays celebrating past moral victories, while warning us to renew our moral fervor or there will be no future. These are the characteristics of the science fiction genre:

- The central character is an innocent bystander victimized by a technological accident or a phenomenon of another world.
- The central character may or may not overcome the challenge of the antagonist. *The Invasion of the Body Snatchers* is a good example of a science fiction film in which the main character begins and ends the story as a victim.
- The existence of relationships promises respite and perhaps an element of hope in the light of the daunting struggle.
- The antagonist may be a scientist or the product of science or nature. The scale of the antagonist is so great (the ants in the *Naked Jungle*), that the central character is reminded not only of her mortality, but also of how very human she is.
- The outcome in the science fiction film story is often more hopeful than the outcomes in either the *film noir* or the horror film.
- A certain nobility devolves to the central character based on her attempt to overcome her struggle with the supernatural *(Aliens)*.

- The environment can be urban or rural, earthbound or otherworldly. In any case, it is a benign, but necessary, host for the antagonist. The presence of Earth and how the environment (Earth or space) is presented reminds us of our place in the natural order.
- The story line of the science fiction film is often plot-intensive and presents a specific threat to the natural order. The plot outlines the central character's response to the threat.

The War Film

The war film genre is a national melodrama; these films are about transgression and power. How does the individual survive intact, physically and mentally? How are we, the audience, to feel about a particular war or about war in general? Many of the greatest films have concerned themselves with war—All *Quiet on the Western Front, The Big Parade, La Grande Illusion, Kanal, They Were Expendable, Paths of Glory, Dr. Strangelove or: How I Learned to Stop Worrying and Love the Bomb*—and those behind the lines who tried to cope with the war and its aftermath—*Open City, The Best Years of Our Lives, Forbidden Games, Who'll Stop the Rain?* More recent films such as *Europa, Europa* and *Schindler's List* focus on non-combatants as victims of war.

War, because it threatens all of us, is an important genre. Its characteristics are as follows:

- The central character has one primary goal—survival. This may mean personal survival, national survival, or the survival of the personal or political values he believes in.
- The character's values are tested.
- The polarities of human behavior—altruism and barbarism—coexist and are as much in combat as the combatants.
- By definition, violence plays a central role.
- Relationships, male–male and male–female, take on particular importance.
- Each film carries a particular political perspective of war. Many films are critical of it; others suggest war brings out the best and the worst in the characters.
- There is a primal quality and intensity to personal behavior.
- The antagonist is often never seen. *Paths of Glory* and *Full Metal Jacket* are good examples.

The point of view of the war genre ranges from romantic (*Sergeant York*) to cynical *(Too Late the Hero)*. Whatever the perspective, the individual character is the focal point. War isn't simply a test of character in these films; more often it is a plea for reflection about the issue of war. As Jean Renoir said about his great 1937 anti-war film, *La Grande Illusion,* two years later they fought again, but this time a bigger, more violent war. It appears the genre will continue to appeal to audiences.

The Adventure Film

What the situation comedy is to melodrama, the adventure film is to the war film. James Bond and Indiana Jones are positive cartoon heroes who not only survive war but seem to thrive on it. In their fantastic, aggressive adventures, there is a reassurance that men may start wars, but boys such as these can stave off the consequences. The characteristics of this genre are:

- The central character, most often a male, plays a messianic character whose role is to save either his nation or the world.
- He is thoroughly capable in his mastery of the tools and weapons of salvation, be they cerebral or physical.
- The main character exhibits a playfulness that can be childlike or childish.
- The challenges to the main character are considerable and numerous. This is a more plot-intensive genre than most genres.
- The antagonist is very often imbued with almost super-human intelligence, strength, or other powers. Whether it be the Joker or a shark, the more formidable the antagonist, the greater the success of the central character.
- Humor and self-depreciation are often a characteristic of the genre.
- Relationships are superficial. There is no time for intimate relationships in this genre.
- Sexuality and violence, although present, are neither sensual nor visceral. Again, there is no time to dwell.
- Ritual and mythology are more important than realism and complexity. Consequently, the genre readily embraces less realistic actions and modes; farce and technology coexist.
- Stereotypes abound in the adventure genre. Examples range from the mad scientist in *Dr. No* to the mindless Thuggees in *Indiana Jones and the Temple of Doom.* The racism implicit in that film and films such as *Rambo: First Blood Part 1* are by-products of the stereotyping rampant in the genre.

The adventure film has been a staple for the past decade. Indeed, many of the most successful films ever made were produced in the '80s and were adventure films—the Indiana Jones series, the Superman series, the Rambo series, Batman series—are the best examples. Adventure films have been so successful that characters from other genres *(Dirty Harry, Lethal Weapon)* have veered, in sequels, toward adventure and away from the genre of the original.

Adventure films have also been borrowing the dysfunctional family motif from the situation comedy, and *The Last Action Hero* borrows the alienated teenager from the melodrama. Although the mix does not work well in *The Last Action Hero*, the situation comedy element in *True Lies* does offset the soft plot of this particular adventure.

The Epic Film

The epic film is very often presented as a serious adventure film. The struggle of the main character is heroic but realistic. The main character may be a historical figure whose exploits have been memorialized in print (T.E. Lawrence's *The Seven Pillars of Wisdom)* or in literature (Joseph Conrad's *Lord Jim)*. The epic film may be biographical or historical but its main appeal is the moral or ethical dilemma (the personal issue) tested against a larger panorama—war *(Patton)* or colonialism *(Gandhi)*. Inevitably, the interweaving of personal and historical stories makes the epic film a film to experience.

Writers who excel in this form are Robert Bolt *(Lawrence of Arabia, A Man for All Seasons, The Bounty)* and Carl Foreman *(The Bridge on the River Kwai, The Guns of Navarone)*. Numerous contemporary writers are interested in this form. Robert Towne wrote *Greystoke: The Legend of Tarzan, Lord of the Apes;* Paul Schrader wrote *The Last Temptation of Christ;* and Bob Rafaelson wrote *Mountains of the Moon*. The characteristics of the genre are:

- A charismatic central character.
- An antagonist so powerful that the central character is elevated to a heroic position through his own efforts.
- A historical crisis, such as World War I and the Arab revolt in *Lawrence of Arabia*, or, in *A Man for All Seasons*, Henry VIII's desire to remarry, against Catholic canon, which led him to establish his own church.
- A moral struggle, by the protagonist, so overwhelming that success seems impossible. Colonial India and the nonviolent struggle for freedom by Mohand as Gandhi in *Gandhi* is an example.
- A depiction of the real world, rather than fantasy. Violence plays an important role in this genre, when it is displayed, it is all the more shocking because it signals the central character's willingness to sacrifice his life for a just cause.

- Poetic subtext. In the midst of all the violence of the story, the central character is sufficiently moral that his stand seems romantic, old-fashioned, and poetic. Consequently, the central character in an epic film is often immensely appealing.
- A complex central character. Paul Muni as Emile Zola in *The Life of Emile Zola* and Paul Scofield as Thomas More in *A Man For All Seasons* are good examples. The complexity also contributes to the appeal of this character.
- A sense of mission, such as is rarely exhibited by central characters. While Harrison Ford is an ambivalent Indiana Jones, Jeremy Irons is anything but ambivalent in *The Mission*.
- A complex story line that blends two stories—the personal story of the central character and the historical incident.
- A test of the central character. As a result of the test, he is challenged to pursue a course of action.
- A tragic fate for the central character. In this sense, the epic film story is closer to the melodrama than to the adventure film.

The Sports Film

The sports film is a particular sort of adventure film. It can be real *(Champion)*, cynical *(Raging Bull)*, or fantastic *(Field of Dreams)*. Unlike the adventure film, the focal point can be personal *(Bang the Drum Slowly)*, rather than apocalyptic. This doesn't mean that the sports genre is less exciting. *Rocky* is as exciting an experience as the best of the adventure films and is more emotionally satisfying than some. The characteristics of the sports film are these:

- The central character is a gifted athlete.
- He tests himself within the parameters of a particular sport.
- Only sports that have a broad appeal to society make a good background for this genre. Boxing, football, and baseball have been the sports of choice. The best films have been boxing films in which the character has much at stake, physically and spiritually. No one has made a good film about a tennis player! Only *Downhill Racer* has succeeded critically and financially aside from the main three sports (boxing, football, and baseball), although *Heart Like a Wheel, Chariots of Fire*, and *The Hustler* were successful.
- The apparent antagonist—the other team, the manager, or the owner—is not as important as the interior struggle of the central character. He is his own worst enemy, as in *The Hustler*.
- Relationships, whether they be male–female or male–male, are crucial to the emotional well-being of the central character.

- A mentor (a father, a coach or another professional) plays a key role.
- Family is an important component. Melodramas and gangster films are the only other genres in which family figures so prominently.
- The ritual—the big game or the big fight—plays a central role in the sports genre.

The Biographical Film

Biography, as in prose, is an important genre. What are our leaders, authority figures, great artists really like? We are fascinated with their greatness and talent. We want to know all about them. Underlying our fascination is our wish for immortality. In their own way, the subjects of biographical films (by their actions, achievements, character) have achieved immortality. Biographical films have these characteristics:

- The central character has a particular talent and a nonconformist personality.
- The central character's talent develops in conflict with the conventions of society.
- The drive for actualization is singular.
- The antagonist is not physical; it can be time *(The Life of Louis Pasteur)*, ignorance *(The Life of Emile Zola)*, or conventional thinking *(Patton)*.
- The seminal event is acted out publicly.
- The psychological makeup of the central character allows him to overcome the tragedy of life and succeed. Although Van Gogh dies at the end of *Lust For Life*, his success is evident in his life's work.
- There is a sense of mission that is religious in its overtone. Patton is as zealous, in his way, as Gandhi.
- Personal relationships often fail, but this only adds to the spiritual side of the central character.
- The critical moment, whether it is a discovery or a religious or political conversion, is the most important point in the story, far more important than the public acknowledgement of the character's achievement.
- The tragic aspect of the character's life is also important. Whether it be Patton's dishonor, Gandhi's assassination, or Zola's death, the reminder of mortality acts as ballast to the mythical subtext of these stories.

The Satire

Satire is a special form of genre. Although it is rare, its strength is such that you should know about the genre. Its characteristics are:

- The central conflict relates to a crucial social or political issue of the day. The environment, health care, the power of television, and nuclear war are all examples of recent satires.
- The film has a distinct point of view about the issue.
- Humor mixes freely with aggression.
- The central character is a vehicle to promote an issue.
- Fantasy and unreality are acceptable in this free-form genre.
- The level of aggression mounts rapidly, escalating to absurd levels before the film ends.
- Relationships can only be transient, given the urgency of the posed social or political threat.
- Random irrationality reminds us of the horror film. The genre succeeds when we see ourselves as victims of the danger and of the threat to society.
- This is a vigorous, energetic genre and is not at all tied to realism, like the melodrama or the *film noir*. High energy is rampant in these films.

Satire has experienced a resurgence in the '90s. Two themes stand out—the film industry and urban life in the city of dreams, Los Angeles. Both *The Player* and *Mistress* focus on the loss of humanity of the creative players in the film industry. The main character in *The Player*, a studio executive, brutally kills a writer and not only gets away with murder but advances in the corporate hierarchy of Hollywood. *Grand Canyon* and *Short Cuts* move from movie moguls to ordinary people living in Los Angeles who also seem to have lost their way and in *Short Cuts* also lose their humanity. The result is the need to escape—to the Grand Canyon in *Grand Canyon* or to have no means of escape in *Short Cuts*. The nastiness of each of the characters in *Short Cuts* suggests that malice and murder are not the province of the studio executive or of the ghetto—they're everywhere. Whether Robert Altman is criticizing all modern urban life or strictly Los Angeles in *The Player* is unclear, but what seems certain is that his interpretation of Raymond Carver assures that Los Angeles, so long the city of angels and dreams, is now the city of the nightmare, the modern equivalent of a Hieronymous Bosch painting.

Conclusion

Working with genre is the most topical and typical activity of today's screenwriters. Whatever story you choose to write, you're probably working with genre. Consequently, you must be familiar with the motifs of each. To involve the audience more rapidly in your story, use the expected signposts of the genre, which are a shorthand that audiences absorb from their earliest viewing.

References

1. Robert Warshow, "The Gangster as Tragic Hero" and "Movie Chronicle: The Westerner" in *The Immediate Experience* (New York: Doubleday, 1962), pp. 83–88 and 89–106.

6

. . . .

Working Against Genre

Because genre provides a writer with a shorthand that audiences readily understand, less time is needed to establish its characteristics. Just as character stereotypes are useful to the writer, so too are genres. However, stereotypes don't sustain our interest nor do they fascinate us enough to carry us, via curiosity or tension, through the balance of the story. In order to sustain an audience's attention, the writer must give us the unexpected and upset our expectations.

As mentioned earlier, genres are often influenced by current events. These historical, political, and social changes suggest new perspectives. For example, technological advances were a powerful feature of the post-war period. Dalton Trumbo, in his 1962 modern Western, *Lonely Are the Brave*, decided that in his conflict with primitivism and civilization, civilization would be represented by technology. Indeed, in the film, technology is the antagonist to Kirk Douglas's modern cowboy protagonist. Helicopters, jeeps, trucks, and advanced weaponry are the inanimate antagonists that challenge the Douglas character. Even a Social Security number poses a challenge to what he stands for—values of a former age, freedom, or, as he puts it, "A girl Paul and I grew up with . . . a wild-eyed mountain girl . . . her name is do-what-you-want-to-do-and-the-hell-with-everybody-else."[1]

How did the '60s influence other genres? Perhaps the most striking gangster film of the decade is *Bonnie and Clyde,* whose main characters are very different protagonists than Tony Camonte in *Scarface* or Rico in *Little Caesar* or Diggs in *The Asphalt Jungle.* The first difference is in their ages. The second difference is in their characterization. Bonnie and Clyde are depicted as innocents victimized by a society that offers no options to young people. This life-as-a-trap view was also present twenty-five years earlier in William Wyler's version of the Sidney Kingsley play *Dead End.*

The young age of the protagonists was a central feature of the films and plays of the 1960s. The society of the '60s was gripped by the young and the attendant foment in social values. The sublimated energy and idealism of the young is the central feature of *Hair,* and the subverted energy and consequent cynicism is the central focus of *The Manchurian Candidate.*

So far, the changes we have discussed are aligned with society's changing perceptions and issues. To explore the idea of working against genre, we now turn to more dramatic breakings away.

Changing a Motif

Genres, or story forms, characteristically have consistent motifs that recur in all film stories. Motifs usually relate to the main character, the antagonist, the environment, the nature of the conflict, and the tools for resolving the conflict. Underlying attitudes about the past, present, and future are also important qualities.

What happens when a writer challenges an important motif within a genre? By examining four particular genres, we will see how a writer can make a genre seem fresh, rather than simply giving it a contemporary sensibility.

The Western

Few significant writer–directors are as exclusively identified with the Western as Sam Peckinpah. While Peckinpah's film work parallels the period of decline of the Western, his films *Ride the High Country* and *The Wild Bunch* are among the most important in the genre. When we look at Peckinpah's work, we see a recurring effort to challenge the traditional presentation of the Western hero. In the classic Western, externalized action affords the hero the opportunity to be true to himself. Generally, he is not a character given to introspection, nor is he a character of psychological complexity. Only the Borden Chase and Phillip Yordan heroes portrayed by James Stewart in a series of films made by Anthony Mann in the 1950s, and the tormented Billy the Kid in Gore Vidal and Leslie Stevens's screenplay *The Left-Handed Gun,* suggest a psychological complexity that motivates the hero to externalized action. Peckinpah takes the psychological framework of the Western hero and tries to make him more complex, more realistic, and more difficult. The simple hero of the classic Western is replaced by one who is presented to us not only as that classic Western hero, but also as his alter ego.

In *Ride the High Country,* two old men, former famed gunfighters, are the composite heroes. Interestingly, the two men are played by Randolph Scott and Joel McCrea, each of whom portrayed classic Western heroes for the preceding twenty-five years. In addition to drawing upon our movie memories of these two actors, Peckinpah presents them as two men with diverging views about their present. One of them remains faithful to his past. The other wishes to improve his present by becoming a thief. The clash of values between them, represented by their past (the myth of the West) and their present (discarded but honorable), is really the clash between alter egos, the good and the evil present in all three-dimensional heroes. The casting adds a layer of movie mythology to the Western mythology.

Peckinpah carries on his exploration of composite heroes in *Major Dundee*. Both Dundee and Tyreen (Charlton Heston and Richard Harris) together portray the stubbornness (Dundee) and nobility (Tyreen) crucial to the hero's survival in the hostile environment of the West. The historical backdrop for this film is the Civil War, but the action of the film takes place in primitive Mexico, far from standing armies and urban centers.

Mexico is also the backdrop for the action of *The Wild Bunch*, set during the Mexican Revolution of 1913. Peckinpah again presents us with a composite hero in Bishop Pike (William Holden), the leader of the Bunch, together with his alter ego, Dutch (Ernest Borgnine), who portray the cruelty and the camaraderie that forms the moral code of the Wild Bunch. Even in its unusual depiction, this code remains recognizable as the code of the Western hero. By splitting the character, however, Peckinpah once again presents a more complex and realistic hero. The composite hero is more difficult to relate to, but he is the 1968 manifestation of those heroes who stand for the struggle of primitivism vs. civilization—a theme central to the Western.

This process of character splitting is not exclusive to Peckinpah and the writers with whom he worked. William Goldman does the same in *Butch Cassidy and the Sundance Kid*, as does Michael Cimino in *Heaven's Gate*. The gain in psychological complexity has made the Western hero in each of these films profoundly different and fresher than the classic one.

What if the central character in the Western is no longer a hero? What if he is as much a killer as Bishop Pike without the redeeming circumstance of being surrounded by characters who are even worse? This is the central feature of the protagonist in David Webb Peoples's *Unforgiven* (1992). Bill Mooney (Clint Eastwood) was a gunfighter who gave it up to appease his wife and after her death has children to care for and no money to support them. When a reward is posted by a group of prostitutes to bring to justice the two men who mutilated one of them, Mooney takes the job because he needs the money. Throughout the search he maintains his sobriety and his dead wife's values. But it does not last. Whether it is the cruelty of the town sheriff, the loss of his friend, or just the reassertion of the old demons, Mooney becomes what he was, a killer without remorse or glory.

This Western hero is not psychologically troubled like Lyn McAdam (Jimmy Stewart) in *Winchester '73*, nor is he relentlessly pursued as Bishop Pike (William Holden) is in *The Wild Bunch*. Mooney is the antithesis of the Western hero. Peoples has altered the nature and goal of the main character and made a pursuit Western seem to be a meditation on the values of the classic Western.

Maggie Greenwald has a similar goal when she makes the central character a woman who must dress and act like a man in order to make her way in the West. *The Ballad of Little Jo* (1993) alters the gender issue and the result is very effective. We will look at the Grunwald film in more detail later in this chapter.

Bad Girls (1994) by Ken Friedman and Yolanda Finch is another film that alters the gender of the protagonist and is a catalogue of what not to do if you want your screenplay to succeed. A momentary comparison between *The Ballad of Little Jo* and *Bad Girls* makes the point clear.

Although both films focus on a female Western protagonist, here the linkage to other Western motifs ends. In *The Ballad of Little Jo,* the main character takes on the characteristics of the male Western hero—she dresses like a man and acquires the skills men need to survive. She becomes capable with horses, guns, etc. In *Bad Girls*, the group of young women prostitutes does not acquire much in the way of skills. At least four times, one of them is captured and needs to be rescued by a man.

In *The Ballad of Little Jo*, the main character achieves a level of mastery that allows her to become part of the primitive rural values of the West (the opposite of the censorial civilized East she runs away from at the beginning of the film). There is no mastery or progression of the main character in *Bad Girls*. The plot simply does not afford the opportunities for growth.

Another motif that has been challenged by writers of the Western is the presentation of the town. In the classic Western, the town was viewed as a civilizing force, a place that represented the future. The church, the general store, and the marshal's office all represent the spirit of commerce, and law and order of the West. In the past three decades, writers have tried to challenge the presentation of the town. Dalton Trumbo, in *Lonely Are the Brave,* presents the town as one large holding center, a jail for the spirit. Ernest Tidyman, in *High Plains Drifter,* presents the town as some place much worse—it is the center of barbarism and, as Sodom in the Bible, a place to be destroyed.

Less malignant, but no less terminal, Miles Hood Swarthow and Scott Hale, in *The Shootist,* present the 20th-century Western town as a good place to die. In this film, John Bernard Books, grandly portrayed by an ailing John Wayne, is a gunfighter dying of cancer. He visits a town doctor (James Stewart) whom he had known in better times. Upon hearing the news that he will die, Books chooses to die in the town, but on his own terms—in a gunfight with three worthy town villains.

The recent *Tombstone* (1994) presents the town as a center of opportunity, a place where a man can make a living. The central character, Wyatt Earp has moved to Tombstone to improve his material well-being after having been the sheriff in Dodge City, Kansas. Here the town does not have the negative connotations it has in the classic Western. When trouble comes from the Clantons and the McCowerys, it is as if two sets of entrepreneurs were competing with each other, and after a time they revert to guns rather than opposing advertising campaigns.

In all of these films, the town is not viewed as it is in *High Noon* or in *3:10 to Yuma*. In each case, the town is a central, but different, feature in the film. In each case, an old story is renewed.

The Gangster Film

The gangster film continues to be presented in its classic form. Mario Puzo's *The Godfather*, Oliver Stone's *Scarface*, and David Mamet's *The Untouchables* attest to its continuing importance. However, as with the Western, variations and challenges to the motifs of the genre result in fresh and exciting films. As in the Western, the presentation of the hero is challenged. In the classic gangster film, the gangster hero is killed for transgressing the means to succeed in society.

Against a backdrop of an increasingly drugged, corrupt society, more and more gangster heroes are not killed. They survive and are, in their way, heroic, given the levels of corruption that surround them. The first of these heroes is Walker, played by Lee Marvin, in *Point Blank*. Walker's vengeful attempt to restore money stolen from him by his partner takes him on a journey through the organization of which his partner is now a part. As Walker eliminates level after level of the organization, his revenge has less meaning, as does the money he seeks to secure. Walker is a thief, but as portrayed in the Alexander Jacobs–David Newhouse–Rafe Newhouse script, he is an existential hero. He has the same energy and intuitive drive of the classic gangster hero, but he has modern self-doubt that makes him particularly empathetic, given that he is as much a killer as Tony Camonte in *Scarface*.

The same characteristics—energy and intuition—are joined by decency in the James Caan character in *Thief*. He, too, is an existential hero and he, too, lives to walk away from those who are dishonest with the thief.

Perhaps the most interesting gangster hero is Lou, the petty criminal portrayed by Burt Lancaster in *Atlantic City*. Lou is an aging bodyguard to a once-famous criminal's moll (Kate Reid). With the good old days behind him, Lou finds a new lease on his reputation with Sally (Susan Sarandon). She is young and in trouble because of her criminal brother-in-law and former husband (Robert Joy). Lou rescues Sally and in his moment of decision he must kill. Yet, he walks away happier than before, and alive. In a world of criminality and corruption, Lou is an empathetic hero and he lives on.

Police and detectives as heroes have also been presented in a different light. The messianic *Serpico* is not dissimilar from Dan Banion in *The Big Heat.* Both have a moral fervor we associate with the energy needed to turn back the forces of criminality that challenge the social order, but there are variations. In *Bullitt* and *Madigan,* the main characters, played by Steve McQueen and Richard Widmark, respectively, have upper-class tastes. In *Tightrope,* the main character, portrayed by Clint Eastwood, suffers from a guilt complex arising from his domestic life. He is a single parent as well as a busy detective with a major murder case on his hands. Is he protagonist or antagonist? This blurring of the distinction takes on new levels in a film such as Barry Keefe's *The Long Good Friday.* The gangster is the protagonist and an active political movement, the IRA, is the antagonist.

Not only are the gangster and the cop presented differently, but so is the traditional environment of the gangster film—the big city. This environment is presented as the seat of power, particularly material power. In two recent films, buildings became cities unto themselves. In *Die Hard,* a post-modern tower is the center of power where a policeman (Bruce Willis) must stop a robbery. In this milieu, the gangsters are robbers posing as international terrorists.

In *Someone to Watch Over Me,* the center of power is the building in which a murder witness lives. The detective assigned to guard the witness falls in love with her. This cross-class entanglement suggests another path to material success—climbing the social ladder—which moves beyond the gangster's approach of theft and murder.

A cross-cultural perspective on the center of power is explored in *Witness.* In this film, the main character, John Book, escapes from his corrupt colleagues who threaten to kill him and the murder witness he is protecting. Book and his witness escape to rural Pennsylvania, the home of the Amish, where the murder witness will be among his own people and harder to find. This shifting of the environment for the gangster film is the second challenge to a genre motif.

A third challenge is the alteration of the expected narrative shape of the gangster film. Characteristic of this genre is the strong plot, foreground over background action. Also characteristic is the drive of the main character to succeed in rising to the top in the gangster world, to solve the crime for the police.

In *Carlito's Way,* David Koepp explores a gangster trying for a different kind of personal success—he wants to leave the life of crime and live a normal life. Unfortunately, Carlito (Al Pacino) is loyal to his family and friends, with the result that he is inextricably drawn back into the life of crime and must suffer the classic fate of the gangster hero, death.

This shift in the character's goal alters the balance of the foreground and background stories in the film. The result is a less exciting but more deeply felt sense of the character, his fate and the impression that in certain ethnic communities, the fate of the members is predetermined and tragic.

Another example of the shift between plot and the interior concerns of the character is David Mamet's *Homicide.* Here the central character is a Jewish policeman named Gold. The plot has Gold and his colleagues trying to apprehend a young Black drug dealer. The background story concerns Gold as a Jew, how he feels about it and how he is pushed to try to be loyal to other Jews. An old Jewish woman has been murdered and Gold's growing interest in the case involves him with a Jewish terrorist organization. Should he help them? Should he break the law, go against his own code of behavior to validate himself as a Jew?

The meditation that proceeds in the background story eventually supercedes the hunt for the drug dealer. Although the plot does resolve itself, the background story leaves Gold as confused as he was early in the film. Nevertheless, the shape of this police story with its shift away from plot toward the interior life of the main character provides a striking example of working against genre expectations.

Film Noir

Film noir, the genre of deception and betrayal, provides writers with a narrow band of options to reorder. The protagonist, unlike the Western or gangster protagonist, is a victim and doesn't lend himself to redefinition (at least not yet). The antagonist, on the other hand, provides writers with considerable scope. Generally, the antagonist is the spider woman *(Black Widow)* that destroys its mate, or the alcohol *(The Lost Weekend)* or drugs *(The Man with the Golden Arm)* that destroy the main character. However, writers have been increasingly adventurous in their antagonists; politics and history have helped.

A number of the key *film noir* works of the past twenty years have made antagonists representatives of the government. Beginning with the Angela Lansbury character in George Axelrod's *The Manchurian Candidate,* the government and those in power or closest to the power have manipulated the main character for political ends. In *The Manchurian Candidate* Lansbury has her own son trained as a killer for the purpose of political assassination. This satire–tragedy puts political goals above personal affiliation. Here a mother sacrifices her own son to the cause.

No such personal sacrifice is at stake in William Goldman's *All the President's Men*, but the belief that the government functions by the people and for the people is challenged. This sobering tale, based on the Bernstein–Woodward book on Watergate, has terrifying overtones. This view of the antagonist is also present in Alvin Sergeant's *The Parallax View*, in Robert Stone's *Who'll Stop the Rain?*, and in Robert Garland's *No Way Out*.

Another variation in *film noir* is the addition of pimps, promoters, and sociopaths as frightening antagonists. In Paul Schrader's *Hardcore*, the principal antagonists are the purveyors of pornography; in Elmore Leonard's *52 Pick-Up*, the antagonist is a sadistic purveyor of pornography; and in *Klute*, the antagonist is the pathological client of hooker Brie Daniels.

Since sexuality and aggression are motifs of *film noir*, the blending of two motifs, aggressive sexuality and the antagonist, brings a less personal, but no less menacing, position to the role of the antagonist. It is as if the workplace in *film noir* has become as dangerous as the home.

Film noir has also invaded the terrain of other genres. The pastoral small town is the setting for *Blue Velvet*, but in this story of voyeurism and violence, a small town is no haven for its characters. Instead, it is the scene for nightmarish aggression and a level of sadistic sexuality rare in *film noir*. The small town no longer projects the good-neighborliness of *It's a Wonderful Life*. Nor does the Pentagon prove to be a safe haven in *No Way Out*. It is as fraught with danger as the city in a classic *film noir*.

Film noir tends to play itself out through the actions of a desperate main character at a critical moment in his or her life. A good example is *Sunset Boulevard*. We meet Joe Gillis when he is a down-and-out writer in Hollywood, at the point where his car is about to be repossessed. Without a car in Los Angeles, his career will be over, he might as well give up his dream of being a Hollywood scriptwriter. It is at this point when the main character enters a relationship with a woman who he hopes will rescue him from what appears to be his fate. In *Sunset Boulevard*, the woman is Norma Desmond, whose driveway he has entered to evade the repo men pursuing him. In *film noir*, the fate he meets at the hands of Norma Desmond is far worse than anything the repo men could have done.

This is the narrative shape of classic *film noir*. The relationship and the consequent betrayal embrace the degradation the main character must accept if he is to strengthen this false, final relationship. He erroneously believes that the sexual-aggressive nature of the relationship will strengthen him.

What happens when the writer tries to alter this classic narrative shape? Paul Schrader, who is responsible for a number of excellent *film noir* stories, including *Hardcore*, *American Gigolo*, *Taxi Driver* and *Raging Bull* has written *Light Sleeper* (1994), a film that alters the narrative shape of *film noir* by including a relatively happy ending.

Light Sleeper tells the story of John LeTour (Willem Dafoe), a former drug addict and current drug dealer. He works for Ann (Susan Sarandon). In the course of the story, he meets Mary Ann (Dana Delaney), his former wife, who left him because of the drugs. He genuinely wants to rekindle their relationship and tells her he is clean, drug free, but she does not believe him. He persists and visits her dying mother. His kindness touches Mary Ann and she agrees to go with him. They make love but she tells him it won't happen again. He carries on his passion for her. When he drops off drugs to a classy client (Victor Garber), he sees her in the apartment in a drug-induced state. We are surprised that she is on drugs. He waits outside for her, but she jumps from the balcony of the apartment to her death. Angry, hounded by police to turn informer, he tells the police where he last saw her alive. The furious client arranges to have him killed, but LeTour turns the tables and kills the man and his bodyguards. Although LeTour goes to jail, Ann has decided to wait for him. They decide that their relationship, first presented as mother-son, is genuine and can last. There in jail, hands together, the new lovers patiently vow to stay together after he is released.

This optimistic ending of *Light Sleeper* is but one alteration to the classic narrative shape of *film noir*. There are many others. Since the main character is a desperate man, we expect him to relapse into drug use and eventually to die, but he doesn't. He does enter a desperate final relationship with his former wife, but his fate and hers are the opposite of what the genre leads us to expect. Nor is he killed in the attempt to kill the client who provided his wife with the drugs that killed her. The fact that in the end he is alive, happy, and in love again leaves us with some hope, a state utterly foreign to *film noir*.

The narrative shape of *Light Sleeper* resembles the dreamy sequel to a *film noir* story. It's as if LeTour has hit bottom just prior to the beginning of the film and that the film is about his resurrection. In this sense, *Light Sleeper* begins where classic *film noir* ends. Whether this more hopeful vision of the urban nightmare is Schrader's redefinition of *film noir* for the '90s or whether he simply wanted to create a Christ parable with a changed ending, *Light Sleeper* changes our experience of the *film noir* genre.

The War Film

Rather than choosing the combatant as the protagonist, as is usual, two recent films chose as the protagonist, a young noncombatant whose life is very much influenced by war. In both *Empire of the Sun* and *Hope and Glory*, the protagonist is a 12-year-old boy. In one case, the boy has to cope with the Japanese occupation of Shanghai during World War II and subsequent imprisonment in a concentration camp; in the other case, the boy has to cope with the London Blitz and its consequences. The boys identify with the romance of war and discover its reality as well. The challenge to the motif is that the protagonists are not totally absorbed with survival, as their youth allows for a much broader engagement with the war and its meaning. They are as involved with growing up as they are with the war.

Forbidden Games and *The Tin Drum* also use young protagonists. Each film is placed in the native country of the protagonist, and *Forbidden Games* takes place during World War II. Because these protagonists are not combatants, they have very different perspectives on war and the issue of survival.

Another war film that treats the protagonist differently is *Full Metal Jacket*. In the story, Matthew Modine is an observer. The passive nature of this character is discussed in a later chapter. For now, it is useful to point out that this protagonist functions as much as a witness as an active participant. He watches and photographs the brutality of war in Vietnam as it occurs around him. The more classic protagonist is Charlie Sheen's character in *Platoon*, who wants to survive and does, albeit with less idealism. The two characters couldn't be more different.

Mixing Genres

For the writer, challenging a motif within a genre offers an opportunity to present a story in a fresher way, while mixing two distinct genres in one story offers a different, more radical opportunity. Genres often have such different meanings to an audience that mixing two can have a dissonant, troubling impact. With other genres, the mix may be more complimentary and can make the film seem more energetic, fresh, and renewed. In both cases, the impact can be surprising. Mixing genres has resulted in some of the most startling and important films of the last decade; such as *Raging Bull*, *Blade Runner*, *Diva*, *Something Wild*, *Raising Arizona*, and *Blue Velvet*.

■ ■ ■   ### A Case Study of Opposites I: *The Stalking Moon*

No two genres could be more different than the Western and the horror film. Yet, in Alvin Sergeant's *The Stalking Moon*, we have both. As a Western, the film is the story of an army scout (Gregory Peck) who is about to retire. On his last assignment, to capture a group of Indians who have escaped from the reservation, he finds a white woman and her Indian son. The woman (Eva Marie Saint) is to return to her family in the East. To hurry her leave-taking, she goes with the scout, who eventually takes her to his home in the mountains. There they await the arrival of her vengeful husband, the chief of the band, who will do anything to return his son to his side. So far, this is a Western with a surrogate family in the making—scout, white woman, and Indian boy. However, the horror genre intercedes when the Indian chief, who we never see until the last five minutes of the film, inflicts horrible death on all who stand in his way. The sudden violence and the scope of the killing suggest an inhuman power. The chief, Salvahee, takes on a primitive and supernatural destructive power as he wreaks insurmountable horror on those with whom he comes in contact and brings violence to the surrogate family.

The mixing of these two genres, one that focuses on the world of dreams and the other on the world of nightmares, is effective because those two worlds are flip sides of each other. They coexist in your subconscious and it's not hard to imagine one quickly turning into the other.

The fact that they are opposites helps the two genres coexist. The result is a dramatically effective gripping story that is certainly unexpected.

▪ ▪ ▪   A Case Study of Opposites II: *Wolf*

The horror film embraces the non-realistic manifestations of the nightmare; the melodrama tends to be about realistic people in realistic situations. The blend of non-realistic horror story and realistic melodrama is the mix of opposites we find in Jim Harrison and Wesley Strick's 1994 film, *Wolf*.

Wolf tells the story of Will Randall (Jack Nicholson), an editor with a large publishing house. Mature and middle-aged, he is about to be moved out of his job to be replaced by his young, aggressive protege (James Spader). Driving in Vermont late at night, he accidentally hits a wolf, then tries to move the body off the road. The wolf, which is not dead, bites him and runs off. And as expected, Will becomes a werewolf.

In the classic werewolf tale, the wolf victimizes and destroys those he loves and eventually is destroyed. In *Wolf*, Will is not destroyed but renewed, made young, by becoming a werewolf. The tired, middle-aged man becomes sexually vigorous and vocationally effective. His new-found aggressiveness applied in the corporate world makes him succeed over his rival.

The horror dimension follows the story line of the main character—how he deals with becoming a werewolf when the moon is full, his fears that he murders people (including his estranged wife). He ends up biting both his rival and his lover (Michelle Pfeiffer).

In the horror genre, the main character needs to be destroyed because the surfeit of aggression and sexuality makes him a danger to himself and society. Implicit is the idea that the character is evil and thus must be destroyed.

In *Wolf*, the writers carefully separate good from evil. A good man who becomes a wolf may be sexually active and aggressive in business but essentially he will be a good wolf-man. An evil man (Spader) who becomes a wolf will become a killer and deserves to be destroyed. Simply becoming a wolf is no longer a reason for the main character's destruction, a deviation from the fate of the typical protagonist in the horror genre. In *Wolf* the main character transcends victimization, a point we shall return to later.

In the melodrama, the main character challenges the power structure but in the end becomes its tragic victim despite a heroic effort. The melodrama *Wolf* centers on Will's age. Although highly thought of by his writers, Will is middle-aged and his publisher (Christopher Plummer) wants someone with a more aggressive, marketing-oriented approach. It is the classic case of the broom that follows the corporate takeover; the main character is swept aside. The concern with his age reflects the current fascination with the young in the media; studio executives in Hollywood and reporters on newspapers are younger than ever. Even the character's wife is having an affair with his young successor. Will challenges the publisher and the age issue by devising a strategy to keep the writers with him in a new company and by taking up with the young, troubled daughter of the publisher.

The Nicholson character offers some compatibility between the two story forms of the horror film, where the main character is a victim and the melodrama where he struggles valiantly but in the end fails, a victim of the power structure. The same is true of the antagonist. In both genres, Spader's character, the young, evil, ambitious male, is the antagonist.

Wolf uses the elements of the horror film—sexuality and aggression—to overcome the weakness and powerlessness typical of the melodrama protagonist. The main character uses these qualities to awaken, to overcome the byproducts of aging, fatigue, and depression in order to become renewed and successful. Because he is essentially good, he can use the sexuality and aggression for positive purposes. Although this alters the narrative shape of both genres, it seems to make the transition work. The result is a touching, adult sense of the fate of the monster. By altering the narrative shape, these opposite genres work well together.

■ ■ ■   A Case Study of Similar Genres: *Blade Runner*

The science fiction genre is similar to the horror film. Often it focuses on apprehensions about the future or on technology and its negative trade-off with humanist values. The protagonist may be like Captain Kirk, struggling with the issue of aging *(Star Trek: The Wrath of Khan)*, while the antagonist is a mad man, Khan, who may bring about Armageddon.

The protagonist in the science fiction film always has hope, while the protagonist in *film noir* displays a desperation that precludes hope. In *film noir*, the protagonist views life experiences more as a last chance and the antagonist is much more personable than Khan. Indeed, the protagonist–antagonist relationship in *film noir* is often characterized as a dance of death, with the dancers as two lovers rather than foes.

Science fiction and *film noir,* although both proximate the world of the nightmare, are not a natural mix. Indeed, at the levels of protagonist, antagonist, and setting, they conflict with one another. In *Blade Runner,* we can explore where the mixing of the two genres works and where the contradictions are so great that they undermine the drama's credibility.

This science fiction story is the story of an ex-cop, Deckard (Harrison Ford), who is now a blade runner. A blade runner tracks down and destroys replicants, which are technical duplications of human beings used as slave labor on the Offworld space colonies. The manufacturer of these combinations of commerce and technology, the Tyrrel Corporation, works with the motto, "More human than human." Six replicants have escaped and returned to the polluted, polyglot metropolis of Los Angeles, and the blade runner must track them down and destroy them. Machines that become more human than human are a genuine danger.

The *film noir* story is that of Deckard, the desperate ex-cop who falls in love with the replicant Rachel (Sean Young). Does he destroy her or does he become more human than human, too? The *film noir* is framed by the futuristic metropolis of Los Angeles—a jungle of technology, overpopulation, and constant rain.

The *Blade Runner* script is both inventive and disappointing. The struggle between humanity and technology, the basis of the science fiction story, introduces elements of pathos and hope into the *film noir* story, which in turn provides a believable context for the science fiction. We can imagine the Los Angeles of 2019 as something like the city we discover in *Blade Runner.* However, in dealing with the protagonist and the antagonist, the two genres contradict each other and eventually defeat a fascinating narrative effort.

In *film noir,* the protagonist is a victim. In the science fiction film, he is an idealist who struggles with the abyss toward which technology pushes him (and us). It is hard to imagine a cynical victim and a romantic idealist in the same person, yet this is precisely what *Blade Runner* proposes in Deckard.

In terms of the antagonist, the science fiction story suggests that Tyrrel, who invented the replicants, is the antagonist. In a sense, he is the antagonist in the *film noir* story as well. He did ask the police to destroy the runaway replicant, Rachel, with whom Deckard falls in love. More important, however, he is the man who incorporated a finite life span in Rachel and thus put a very short term on the duration of Deckard's and her love. Rachel is destined to die sooner than one would expect in a love match with a human; Deckard is destined to be alone.

As an antagonist, Tyrrel is an eminent but not gripping presence in both stories. Although he is rarely present, there is considerable ambivalence about Tyrrel, about commerce, and about technology. But there is nothing visceral in this antagonist; he is little more than a symbol because the story demands of the two genres have pushed the antagonist far into the background.

The mixture of the two genres, when presenting the protagonist and the antagonist, works to undermine the effectiveness of both genres. The film script remains a fascinating failure.

A similar mix was attempted in Edward Neumeier and Michael Miner's *Robocop,* with more success. The protagonist, Murphy (Peter Weller), is believable as a victim. He is a policeman killed in the line of duty and is restructured as a robot–policeman, a Robocop. His personal struggle is that he was once human and is now the product of technology. By the end in the film, he finds some humanity among his technology. The part of the antagonist is split between Murphy's murderer and the corporate head of security, in whose department Robocop's construction was requisitioned (a surrogate inventor). Particularly with regard to the protagonist, this mixed genre film works.

■ ■ ■   A Case Study of the Police Story as Nightmare: *The Fugitive*

Writers Jeb Stuart and David Twohy mix two story forms; the police story and *film noir*, in *The Fugitive* (1993), which was based on the famous television series. Although the police story uses its central character to solve a crime, Richard Kimble (Harrison Ford) in two-thirds of the film appears as a man found guilty of his wife's murder. After Act I, he spends as much time searching for the true murderer as he does evading Lieutenant Girard (Tommy Lee Jones), the man who is relentlessly pursuing him. In *film noir* the main character is a victim, so the pursuit maintains Kimble as a victim on one level, for most of the film, giving it the principal duality that prevents *The Fugitive* from being strictly a police story. The victim quality increases our sympathy for him.

The screen story opens with the murder of Richard Kimble's wife. Kimble, a well-known surgeon in Chicago, returns home to find a one-armed man in his home; he struggles with him, but the man escapes. Kimble is accused of the murder, found guilty, and sent to prison to await execution. En route to prison, another prisoner shoots the bus driver and in the resulting accident Kimble escapes. The balance of the police story deals with Lieutenant Girard's hunt for Kimble, who eventually returns to Chicago to try to find the one-armed man. By looking for an amputee with a prosthetic similar to the one Kimble detached from the killer the night his wife was killed, Kimble does find the one-armed man and he leads Girard to him. The investigation, however, brings Kimble face-to-face with the true antagonist, his friend Charles, also a heart surgeon. Charles, in the employ of a drug company, had hired the one-armed man to assassinate Kimble, not his wife. The plot ends with the real killer, Charles, apprehended and Kimble, now in the protective custody of Girard, soon to be a free man.

These two genres of police story and *film noir* tend to have complementary shapes, with the police story being plot-driven and *film noir* being driven by the background story about the relationship that will bring destruction to the victimized main character. In *The Fugitive*, the differing shapes do not undermine one another because in the police story both Girard and Kimble are working to solve the crime despite Girard's pursuit of Kimble. In the *film noir* dimension of the story, Kimble is the classic victim protagonist, and the destructive antagonist, usually a woman, is a policeman. The parallels between Girard and Javert in *Les Miserables* are obvious. Although Kimble and Girard are rarely together in the conventional sense, the strongest relationship in the film is between these two men and until the conclusive scene in the hotel it is clear that Girard means to bring Kimble to justice and to death. Because of the common characters, the two story forms do not undermine one another. If anything, the emotionally powerful *film noir* dimension, helps the viewer overcome the disappointing foreground resolution of the plot. The Girard-Kimble relationship is simply far more interesting than Kimble's relationship with the one-armed man or Charles.

The result is a film that seems to have the best of both genres—an exciting plot in the police story and a powerful emotional relationship in the *film noir* tradition. The sum is greater than the parts.

▪ ▪ ▪ A Case Study of Screwball Comedy: *Something Wild*

The screwball comedy is the flip side of *film noir*. In both genres, the (usually male) protagonist is viewed as a victim, and the antagonist is often the woman he chooses (or is chosen by) and with whom he gets involved. The prime difference between the genres is that the outcome of the screwball comedy is happy, while the outcome of *film noir* tends to be tragic. The action line in both genres is the story of their relationship.

Max Frye's screwball comedy *Something Wild* is the story of Charlie Diggs (Jeff Daniels), a corporate executive with a rebellious side to his nature. He is picked up by Lulu (Melanie Griffith), who virtually kidnaps him for a weekend, one that becomes wild beyond all expectation when they meet Lulu's ex-husband. The relationship between Charlie and Lulu is prone to much role reversal and sexual aggression. She is unpredictable, seductive, and dangerous, but she appeals to the rebel in him and he falls in love.

The *film noir* story in *Something Wild* has much to do with deception. Lulu deceives Charlie and Charlie deceives Lulu. When they meet her ex-husband, played by Ray Liotta, the deception becomes lethal. Lulu's ex-husband wants to kill Charlie and almost succeeds. The principle of deception is pervasive. It goes on in the city as well as in rural settings; it takes place within relationships as well as within families. Lulu and her mother have an elaborate code of interaction, all based on a series of lies and delusions. This is the perfect milieu for the tragic outcome of *film noir*.

The upshot of mixing these genres, however, steers us away from the logical tragic conclusion toward a happier outcome. The film provides considerable tension between the two genres. The goals differ and, consequently, the treatment of protagonist and antagonist differs. The screwball comedy aspect of the film softens our sense of him the protagonist as a victim. Indeed, he has to overcome his victimization if he is to transcend the classic *film noir* protagonist. There is some loss of credibility in this leap.

A similar fate is cast for the antagonist. Lulu moves from being a leopard woman to being a pussycat, and the transition gives her little to do in the second half of the story. To keep the story going, the ex-husband becomes the antagonist.

The result is a dramatically mixed experience, but also a rich one in terms of the alternation of comic and tragic goals. The energy that results from the clash of two genres heightens our fascination with the story and with what might happen next. However, the shifting natures of protagonist and antagonist result in a less emotionally involving experience than if the film focused on one of the genres. This particular experiment in mixing genres is designed to appeal to us as voyeurs, rather than as participants.

■ ■ ■ A Case Study of Genders and Genres I: *The Ballad of Little Joe*

Many Westerns have introduced a dimension of melodrama into their stories. *The Gunfighter, The Left-Handed Gun,* and *High Noon* all include an overlay of melodrama, but few Westerns have used it as a major element. *The Ballad of Little Jo*, however, relies on melodrama as much as on the typical Western form.

Maggie Greenwald has written the story of a young eastern woman who must leave home. She has had a child out of wedlock and now, shunned by her family, is traveling west to try to make a life for herself. What she quickly discovers is that as a woman she will be viewed as a chattel suitable for sexual pleasure. To avoid this fate, she takes on the appearance of a man—the clothing, the hair, and the affectation. At first unsure and shy, she begins to live and work in a mining town. Fearful that she will be discovered, she takes work as a winter sheep herder. In isolation she can avoid the detection of her true identity.

She enjoys the solitude and her growing competence is clear. She begins to acquire the survival skills that men have mastered. And eventually she earns enough to start her own farm. One day in town, she takes on a Chinese railworker as her cook to prevent him from being hanged. Suddenly she has companionship and quickly he discovers her true identity. They become lovers.

As time passes, her happiness is threatened by the local cattle company, which through intimidation and murder has been buying adjacent land. In the end, she decides to defend her land and stays. Both she and her lover die on the land, and it is only at her death that the town discovers her true identity.

As a Western, *The Ballad of Little Jo* has many of the classic elements. The main character is heroic. The story is shaped around the struggle between primitiveness and civilization, although uncharacteristically, the central character here opts for primitivism with its tolerance of her individuality—her relationship with a "Chinaman" and her deception. *The Ballad of Little Jo* presents a violent milieu, but there is little ritualized killing on screen. Most of the killing takes place off-screen, and there is no gunfight at the end of the film. Its resolution certainly differs from the conventional Western. There is no fierce antagonist to make Little Jo's actions stand out more heroically. The land, however, does play the classic Western role. Beautiful but dangerous, it offers opportunity to the character, but in the end the harshness of life on that land ends her life.

As a melodrama, *The Ballad of Little Jo* is the story of a woman challenging the male power structure. By pretending to be a male, she demonstrates her desire to benefit in the society in the same manner available to men. At one point her Chinese lover warns her that if the men of the town find out she is a woman, their humiliation will be such that they will kill her. This film deviates from melodrama by adopting the Western convention of the victorious main character.

Although the melodrama tends towards realism and the Western less so, Maggie Greenwald has not presented an elegiac West. The Western dimension of this screenplay is realistic rather than heroic and ritualized, which reduces the conflict between the two genres. If there is a genuine difference between this Western and most others, it is in the absence of an antagonist. Here the melodrama form helps out. By providing the entire male population as a power structure opposed to women, every male encountered prior to the Chinese man becomes at one point or another a threat to Little Jo. In this sense men in general become Little Jo's antagonists. And her struggle to avoid discovery, even in both instances when her true identity is revealed, does become heroic, given the level of threat.

Although the two genres do not share many elements, their combination in the movie strengthens and makes the 19th-century story into a modern struggle between male and female. *The Ballad of Little Jo* is an excellent example of mixing genres to good effect.

■ ■ ■ A Case Study of Mixing Genders and Genres II: *The Crying Game*

The Crying Game, which is on one level a political thriller about IRA terrorists, is also a melodrama about gender and sexual preference.

The film opens with the IRA kidnapping of a black British soldier, Jody. If the British do not release IRA prisoners, the soldier will be killed. Fergus (Stephen Rea), who is assigned to guard the soldier, becomes his friend. Before his death, Jody asks Fergus to take care of Dee, his lover back in London. Fergus agrees.

The next phase of the film, in London, focuses on Fergus's efforts to get to know Dee and his falling in love with Dee. All is well until he discovers that Dee is male. This apparently ends the budding love affair, but it is soon re-kindled as Fergus simply cannot get Dee out of his mind.

Fergus's IRA cohorts resurface in London and demand his participation in the assassination of a government official. He has no choice, but Dee prevents him from fulfilling the obligation, believing that Fergus wants to leave to take up with the other woman, Jude. Betrayed, Jude returns to kill Fergus, but Dee kills her instead. Fergus sends Dee away and stands in as the murderer. In jail, Fergus is visited by Dee, who is impressed with his commitment to him/her. The film ends with the fantasy of their possible future love together.

In the political side of the story, Fergus is the main character. He is in the IRA for life. If he does not kill, the IRA will kill him. And the British might kill him anyway. The main character is presented as a potential victim attempting to avoid a particular fate. When a plot provides enough surprises, the sense of excitement and emotion around the fate of the main character can be considerable. (*The Day of the Jackal* is a good example of a plot-centered thriller.) Neil Jordan is not very interested in plot and there is a minimal investment in surprise here. It falls to the melodrama to engage and move us.

The melodrama in *The Crying Game* focuses on a heterosexual white male who, against his previous disposition, begins to fall in love with a black male transvestite. His tragedy is in the end an altruistic sacrifice, but he is alive and eventually he will be able to return to Dee. As he did in *The Miracle,* where incest was the taboo, Jordan flirts with the possibility that love can overcome taboos of race and gender.

The success of *The Crying Game* stems from Jordan's interest in the melodrama, which helps compensate for the plot flaws in the thriller. Indeed, the melodrama is so provocative that it all but makes the audience forget that *The Crying Game* began as a political thriller. The script is also aided by the fact that both genres rely on realism. Compatibility in the role of the main character in both the thriller and the melodrama, essentially realistic, also strengthen the film. The absence of a strong antagonist in the melodrama leaves the role to poor Jude, from the thriller. Her death, on one level, kills off the female rival to Dee, but on another level makes no emotional sense in the way the fate of a true antagonist should.

■ ■ ■   ## A Case Study of Adventure Film as Satire: *Raising Arizona*

The Coen brothers's *Raising Arizona* is both an adventure film and a satire. Since both genres move away from naturalism or realism, this particular mix of genres is both stimulating and fresh. The adventure film genre is narrative-intensive and pits a romantic protagonist against a mythic antagonist. The levels of conflict between protagonist and antagonist are increasingly intensified and fantastic as we move through the story. In the end, the goal of the adventure genre is to claim goodness over evil and to have a good time doing it. The genre is very much adolescent wish-fulfillment.

In the case of satire, the goals are much more serious. The satire genre tackles serious issues of social concern with a sense of aggressive comedy. The genre is critical, pointed, funny, and fast. Energy is essential. The antagonist is the issue—television, nuclear war, medical incompetence, government bureaucracy. The protagonist—well, we are all thrust into the position of the protagonist.

Raising Arizona is about a couple's (Nicholas Cage and Holly Hunter) desire to have a child. They can't, so they decide to kidnap one from a rich businessman whose wife has given birth to quintuplets. The kidnapping and the subsequent efforts to prevent others from taking the child is the heart of the story. In the end, the desperate couple decides to return the baby to its family. The adventure story relates to the kidnapping and to the efforts of two convicts and a bounty hunter who try to steal the child from the kidnappers.

The satire on contemporary North American values revolves around children. This most precious resource, the story suggests, is nothing more than a valuable commodity, like them, and, like bonds or gold, the baby is no more than a possession. The story satirizes this view of children by making the thieves childless and desperate for a child to complete their empty lives. The Coen treatment is energetic and filled with action. Car chases, robberies, and explosions occur with startling frequency around the baby, while pointing us toward the question of the value of children in today's society.

The mixing of these two genres works in *Raising Arizona,* because of the freedom inherent in both genres. Anything goes. There are few restrictions on protagonist–antagonist interaction, except that in both genres, it tends to be intense, active, and frequent. Pace, energy, and comic aggression are key to mixing these two genres. The Coens fulfill that requirement and the result is a fresh, funny, and touching film story about family values in the 1980s.

We have suggested that writers can work against genre expectations by challenging the motifs of particular genres or by mixing two genres to tell their story. In both cases, the result is an unexpected and often more energized view of what could otherwise have been a formulaic story.

■ ■ ■ A Case Study of Failed Mixed Genres: *Basic Instinct*

Mixing the police story and *film noir* can work effectively as in *The Fugitive,* but the mixture fails in *Basic Instinct.* The reasons for this failure provide important lessons for aspiring screen writers.

Joe Eszterhas's *Basic Instinct* tells the story of Nick Curran (Michael Douglas), a San Francisco detective with a troubled past. He has been drug- and alcohol-dependent and he has killed bystanders in the line of duty.

A woman has killed a rock star with an ice pick during intercourse. The woman suspected of the murder, Catherine Trammell, is a novelist whose last book included a scene about killing a rock star with an ice pick. She also seems to know a lot about Nick; he is the research for her next book.

The police story proceeds along the lines of an investigation to solve the crime. For half the story, Catherine Trammell (Sharon Stone) is the primary suspect. But at one point in the investigation, suspicion shifts to someone trying to frame her. That person increasingly seems to be Beth, the police psychologist (Jeanne Tripplehorn), who knew Catherine when both were psychology students at Berkeley. Catherine's bisexuality alludes to an affair between them, an affair which led to the death of Catherine's faculty advisor. The instrument of death was an ice pick. Beth is apprehended and then shot after having killed Gus, Nick's partner. The original crime seems solved and possibly an old crime as well, as Beth's actions imply she is the killer.

The *film noir* dimension of *Basic Instinct* unfolds via Nick's fascination with Catherine. She knows a great deal about him, and he is provoked by her taunting him about his past—his wife's suicide, his drug and alcohol abuse, and his penchant for punishing or masochistic sex. The fact that Catherine seems more interested in him as research is compounded by her narcissistic excitement and her desire for women, specifically her feminist lover, Roxy (and earlier, Beth). His is a true *"noir"* love in that he is driven by passion and excluded from a permanent relationship by implication. Catherine is absolved of the opening murder, and the story ends with her and Nick in bed. She prepares him for sado-masochistic sex and the film ends as she reaches for an ice pick.

Beyond the lack of credibility in the plot (it is hard to believe that Beth is the killer), it is difficult to believe that an investigation by the police Internal Affairs Department could be conducted with such a dearth of intelligence. Finally, the police story fails because the red herring of Catherine Trammell as the false antagonist of the police story is at odds with her role in the *film noir* story, her role as the true antagonist. Which brings us to Nick Curran.

We have a contradiction in our expectations of Nick in the police story and the *film noir*. In the police story, he is the hero who solves the crime. In *film noir* we expect him to be the victim of the antagonist. We are faced then with a character who has to be both hero and victim, two roles that are at best difficult to reconcile. Coupled with the complication of an antagonist who is the antagonist in the *film noir* but a false antagonist in the police story, we have a situation of dramatic incongruity. Joe Eszterhas is a clever screen writer but he is not a magician. The result is the use of irreconcilable deployments of the protagonist and the antagonist in each of the two genres. The resulting loss of credibility is understandable, and the result is a failed screenplay.

■ ■ ■   A Case Study of Changing Motifs and Mixing
Genres: *Crimes and Misdemeanors*

Woody Allen's *Crimes and Misdemeanors* is a remarkable example of
audacious storytelling. Allen tells two independent stories linked by a single
character, a rabbi, and an ephemeral idea that morality is both relative and
relatively elusive in our modern urban world. It is a complex enough challenge
to combine two stories in one film. It becomes even more complex when the
two stories are presented in different narrative forms—a straight melodrama
and a situation comedy. Allen then goes one step further and decides that
within each story, the melodrama and the situation comedy, he will challenge
the most important motif—the fate of the protagonist.

The melodrama is the story of opthamologist Judah Rosenthal (played by
Martin Landau), a man whose mistress threatens him with personal and
financial disclosure. She threatens to ruin him unless he leaves his wife and
takes up with her full time. Judah relies on two people with whom he shares
this pending disaster. One person is a patient, a rabbi who, in spite of going
blind, is optimistic and encouraging to Judah—tell your wife; it will all work
out. The other is his brother, a small time hoodlum who suggests that the only
way to deal with this situation is for Judah to get his mistress out of his life
permanently. How Judah deals with this personal crisis is the story line of the
melodrama. Judah's sense of immorality and his anxiety are central to the
decision he makes and the range of feelings he experiences once the decision is
made.

The situation comedy follows the efforts of Cliff, played by Woody Allen, to
sustain his integrity in the face of a career during which he has experienced
limited success and a marriage that has been a total disaster. Cliff makes
documentary films. He is currently working on a film about Professor Levi (a
character based on Primo Levi, the writer and Auschwitz survivor), a
concentration camp survivor who postulates on the meaning of love and
morality in modern life. Enter his brother-in-law (Alan Alda), a successful
television producer. To appease his sister, Alan Alda's character offers Cliff a job
making a documentary about himself. Cliff fools himself into thinking that he's
taking the job for the money. He hates everything his brother-in-law stands
for—success. In Cliff's mind, you can't have wealth and integrity. Naturally the
story line displays his ambivalence.

The documentary on his brother-in-law brings about a crisis—professional
and personal. While making the film about his brother-in-law, Cliff meets an
associate producer, Hallie, played by Mia Farrow, with whom he falls hopelessly
in love. He also botches the film. In the end, Cliff loses both the film and the
relationship with Hallie. Not even Professor Levi can help Cliff overcome the
cesspool of materialism that swirls about him. The professor inexplicably kills

himself, thus ending the film project that would have at least provided Cliff with some integrity.

Cliff's moral position is very vulnerable on every level, and he is left perplexed and saddened by the various outcomes—all of which are bad.

In rereading this description it doesn't sound very funny, but the story line of all situation comedies might be tragic from a different point of view. As Alan Alda's character says, his definition of comedy is tragedy plus time. So, too, is the situation comedy about Cliff tragic.

The melodrama in *Crimes and Misdemeanors* is about recognizable people in a power struggle. Jonah's melodrama story, on the other hand, reflects the most important power struggle of the 1980s, the battle of the sexes.

In *Crimes and Misdemeanors,* the two genres work to complement each other. There are points where the differences add a level of tension, a dissonant chord, that surprises us and helps us move the story beyond our genre expectations.

In terms of character, the central character in each story is recognizable— the ambitious Judah Rosenthal and the idealistic Cliff. Each character is ambivalent and has an interior conflict about his value system. Each wants to be perceived as a success, but each carries a family history. Judah has a religious background. His father's words continually resonate, "The eyes of God are on us always." To find his way through his father's warning, Judah becomes an opthamologist, but he is always losing his way (according to his father). Cliff has a history of failed relationships. Both he and his sister share this penchant and its implications. They fail in life.

The two stories are also similar in the types of conflict that prompt their respective crises. In both cases, the source of the conflict is a woman—Jonah's mistress or, in Cliff's case, a wished-for mistress. Both characters desperately proceed to deal with these two women. In each case, the character convinces others to aid him in his struggle. Judah uses his brother; Cliff uses Professor Levi. In each case, the struggle unleashes an intense, almost desperate attempt to cope with the resulting events.

The two stories differ primarily in their resolutions. Woody Allen twists each tale away from the genre convention. Melodrama usually ends in the tragedy of the thwarted ambition of the central character—the execution of Montgomery Clift's character in *A Place in the Sun,* the absence of the mother from her daughter's wedding at the end of *Stella Dallas.* This is not the case with Judah Rosenthal. Although a party to murder, he is not arrested, nor will he be absent from his daughter's wedding. Judah is scotfree and has freed himself from his anxiety and guilt as well.

In the situation comedy, the film generally results in success for the main character: Jack Lemmon gets the girl, but loses the job at the end of *The Apartment,* and James Garner gets the girl (or boy, depending on your

interpretation) at the end of *Victor, Victoria*. No such luck for Cliff. This
resolution is closer to that found in melodrama. Cliff loses everything—his wife,
the girl of his dreams, the film he didn't want to make (about his brother-in-
law), and the film he wanted to make (about Professor Levi). Cliff, the man who
is interested in ideals, ends up powerless, and Judah, the man who is interested
in power, ends up with even greater power.

The mix works in this case because of the proximity of the two genres, a
distinct advantage. Situation comedy is the flip side of melodrama. *Film noir* and
the screwball comedy are also mirror images of each other. Consequently, a film
like *Something Wild* has a greater likelihood of working than a film that uses
wildly different genres—the horror-comedy *An American Werewolf* in London,
for example. It is easier to succeed with genres that share basic qualities.

In *Crimes and Misdemeanors*, Allen poses numerous narrative challenges
for himself and for his audience. By telling two different stories, by using two
different genres, and by twisting genre characteristics within each story, he
creates a modern parable. What is the nature and role of love and morality in
our lives? His meditation is structured, formal, rather than alluded to as an
afterthought or aside. He doesn't use the classic qualities of an empathetic main
character or a monstrous antagonist. He confidently proceeds to tell two stories,
using two genres, and allows us to ponder the questions in our lives.

Conclusion

It is critical for the writer to understand genres in order to write
mixed-genre screenplays. Clearly, writing against genre has become the cross-
word puzzle of the screenwriter—difficult, but addictive. Know your genres
and you will be able to work against them; then you'll be able to move beyond formula into the interesting and energetic options that can generate.

The option of mixing genres offers the writer much in the way of narrative opportunities—surprise and novelty at the very least. But there is also
the option of layering the story in new and interesting ways. Just as challenging a genre motif alters our experience of the screen story, the mixing
of genres can undermine our expectations and provide new dimensions to
old stories to entice the fickle film audience.

One recent example illustrates the point. *Diva* is a dark story, but its
mixture of wish-fulfillment (the musical) and *film noir* (the dangerous side
of male–female urban relationships) makes the story seem more real and more
satisfying. In this case, the mixing of two genres sidesteps the optimistic fantasy of the musical and the pessimistic, nightmarish dimension of *film noir*.
The result is more than interesting and provides a more genuine, deeply felt
experience than the film would have presented in only genre.

The examples mentioned in this chapter only scratch the surface of mixed-genre screenplays. So many of the big films released in the early 1990s were mixed-genre films—*Dick Tracy, Die Hard II, Total Recall, The Fugitive, Schindler's List*—that it seems mixed-genre stories are beginning to be the standard and genre stories are becoming the exception. This is a total reversal of the screen story situation of only a few years ago.

References

1. Dalton Trumbo, *Lonely are the Brave* (Universal Pictures, 1962).

7

■ ■ ■ ■ ■ ■ ■ ■

Reframing the Active/Passive Character Distinction

On the most superficial level, film is a medium founded on the illusion of believability—what we see looks real (most of the time). As a result, the focus of the producer and, consequently, the writer, turns to making what we see as engaging as possible. Otherwise, attention and audience are lost. Whether one calls the connection between screen and audience engaging or electric, game or gripping, it is the elusive characteristic that all producers look for as intensely as Francisco Pizarro looked for gold and Vasco da Gama looked for spices. In our business it's what everyone wants.

What are the implications for the character? More particularly, does every main character have to be active, energetic, and attractive, as well as find herself in an abundance of conflicting situations? There is little question that this option offers to us characters who are appealing and easy to identify with, but it also offers us characters we rarely know and who are rarely in our own lives.

In this chapter, we challenge the notion that the central character must be active and energetic to ensure sufficient conflict and drive to carry us through a 90-plus-minute narrative story. We would like to suggest that there is a much broader set of options available to you.

We acknowledge that in particular genres it is more useful to have active, energetic main characters. It is hard to imagine how the plot of *Die Hard* would unfold if John McClane (Bruce Willis) were a reflective or passive character! But ambivalence and confession are very interesting in the Phillip Marlowe that Elliot Gould portrays in Robert Altman's *The Long Goodbye.* Indeed, this main character is a perfect reflection of Los Angeles in the 1970s; more than one form of pollution influences Marlowe's behavior. The notion, here, is that a wide range of options is available when you begin to move away from the active main character. To chart this path, we begin by studying the conventions that surround our main character.

Conventional Notions of Character

The troubled teenager, the ambitious lawyer, the poor prizefighter, the belligerent policeman—all are characters we know. We see them in film after film, although they may enter their stories via a variety of options that suggest a new or fresh story. Key to our discussion is that all of these characters conform to our notion of the character. By profession and by nature, they are prone to act against barriers to their goals; each, in his own way, is keen to overcome his current situation or station in life. In a sense, these characters are not willing to wait, to think, to discuss, or to feel paralyzed. They are characters who act.

The Active Character

Central to the conventions of characterization is the character who, in the superficial sense, will act. Not only does this type of character fit more easily into the story line filled with events, but in all likelihood his actions will help shape that story line. In this sense, the active character helps you do your job—to tell the story as effectively as possible.

The active character is, by nature, a character who gets involved in relationships and in events. Active characters are less predictable in their responses to people and events, and this involvement and potential for surprise are useful and helpful qualities for the screenwriter. It isn't surprising, then, that the active character has become a convention for screenwriters.

The Energetic Character

Second only to the active character is the energetic one. Clearly, a character who is energetic will respond quickly to a situation of conflict or a barrier to her goals. This response may be anxious or aggressive. In either case, the response is dramatically useful because it highlights the conflict. Generally, the more difficult the barrier, the more intense the character's response. The question in the audience's mind is whether the character can overcome the oppositional force.

Audiences relate quickly to energy. Energy is attractive. It needn't be negative or positive, but it does enhance the feeling that your character has power. This power is open-ended in a way that powerlessness is not. Consequently, the energetic character is a very inviting character for the audience.

The Intentional Character

Although the active character and the energetic character are the most common conventions used to create a main character, they are incomplete unless your character has a goal. Intentional characters are those characters who have goals that motivate them. Most often, secondary characters have more clarified, singular functions in the screen story and, as a result, appear to be more intentional. Main characters are generally in conflict about their goals, and through the actions and events of people they work through the conflicts and move toward their goals.

The audience must understand the conflict as well as the character's goal. Only then can the energetic efforts of the main character engage us in his struggle.

The active, energetic, goal-directed character is the conventional screen character. Charm, wit, and sexiness are all add-ons that deepen our engagement with the main character. Each invites us, in a different way, to get involved with the main character.

Real Life and Dramatic Life

In real life, we find the full gamut of characters—from active to passive, energetic to depressed, happy to angry, frustrated to fulfilled. These characters exist, whatever their state, in the ebb and flow of everyday life, with both its ordinariness and its excitement. Elemental tasks mix with significant events and, as with many of us, these characters' lives are surrounded by the confusion that so often engulfs people and events. Dramatic life is considerably more shaped. Conflict, critical events, and intentional characters are codependent variables that make up the screen story.

One of our goals in this chapter is to suggest that how you interpret dramatic life in film can help you draw real-life characters into your stories. Before you can do this, however, you have to understand the limits and opportunities of real life and dramatic life.

Real-Life Characters

The primary problem for the screenwriter is that if the real-life character is not active, not particularly energetic, and does not have a goal, she is difficult to place in a screen story. Characters such as this are potentially unappealing and disinterested in their fate. Consequently, they don't lend themselves to involving audiences with their story.

We have purposely overstated the traits of real-life characters. Often, active, energetic, and goal-directed people pass through our lives, they are people to whom we feel drawn. But what of all those other people who are in the middle, who are the opposite of the conventional main character? Must we discard all of them as potential main characters? The answer is no.

Movie Characters

The opposite of the real-life character is the movie character—the character to whom we have grown accustomed through our exposure to movies and television. Because we have had so much media exposure, writers are as likely to draw on a movie character for characterization as they are to draw on a character known to them in their everyday lives.

Movie characters are an exaggeration of dramatic characters. They are as shaped as characters in real life are not. Movie characters tend to be goal-directed, energetic, and active, but they go even further. They are often charismatic, at least in the case of main characters, in spite of their proximity to a stereotype. Movie characters seek out resolutions to the conflicts they encounter, but they do so in an exaggerated way. They apply their energy with a vigor virtually unknown in real life. The complexities of everyday life are alien to these characters. Movie characters represent the opposite of the more complex characters we examine shortly, characters who represent a shift away from the active character, characters who are more recognizable in real life.

Dramatic Characters

Dramatic characters lie between movie characters and real-life characters; they are not as resolution-oriented as a movie character, but because of the conflicts in which they find themselves, they must find a resolution. Such characters may feel ambivalent; they may choose not to act or they may not exhibit the kind of energy we associate with the conventional main character. Dramatic characters may act as observers, may be catalysts, and very often are in the middle of the action of the story most reluctantly. They may not understand the forces at work in the situation and they may not function well even if they do understand the situation.

We get involved with these characters because they find themselves in the midst of crises that take over their lives. This dramatic situation allows us to engage with a character whether that character be active or passive.

The further the character is from the movie character, the more likely we will recognize him in our lives. As a result of this identification, our response to this character is likely to be more complex than it would be toward a movie character. The dramatic character provides a wide range of options from which the writer can choose to engage the audience.

Real Life as Drama

One of the most powerful films of the early '70s was a small domestic drama by Ken Loach entitled *Family Life*. The movie followed the life of a young woman who was falling into a schizophrenic state. Needless to say, she wasn't a very active character. Indeed, after two hours she barely spoke. Yet, her story breaks the heart. Her conflict is multileveled. She is the youngest of two daughters and is controlled, rather than parented. Her stronger sister has broken out of the stranglehold of this family and has made a life for herself. The doctors who treat the young woman disagree on her psychological state. A psychiatrist experimenting with treatments has luck with her and she improves. However, when he loses his position to a more conventional doctor, the young woman moves from group therapy to shock treatment and she is lost. The story has dramatic values at the level of family and institution (hospital). The character has a goal—to get better—but she is not strong enough to overcome the goal of her family (to keep her under control) and the goal of the institution (to keep people like her under control).

In real life, this young woman is quite recognizable, but she is a stranger and an exception to the screen story. The story works because of the nature of the dramatic situation. The story has narrative drive.

Narrative Drive

Stories such as *Family Life* have a crisis that is sufficiently acute, and, if there is no quick resolution, the character will be lost forever. This sense of urgency is compelling and gives the story narrative drive.

A sense of urgency for the fate of a character can be replaced by a sense of urgency for the fate of a community (*Matewan*), of a society (*The China Syndrome*), or of the world (*Wargames*). In all cases, the sense of urgency creates the story parameters. Will the world be saved? Will the characters survive and hopefully thrive?

However, a sense of urgency is not enough to grab the audience. There has to be an interesting story to tell. For example, the training of an assassin to kill on command and the execution of that command at the highest levels of government is the narrative drive of *The Manchurian Candidate*.

The more reflective or passive the character, the greater the writer's reliance on a sense of urgency and a strong story. *Psycho* is populated by characters of varying psychological states. The main character, portrayed by Janet Leigh, steals money and runs away. For 40 minutes of screen time we are with her as she plots and ponders, decides, and finally changes her mind. Guilt is her most prevalent characteristic. After 40 minutes, Hitchcock kills her off and we are left without a main character. Yet the film remains etched in our memories. Why?—aside from Hitchcock's brilliant craftsmanship. Urgency and lots of narrative drive. The story doesn't end with the death of Marion Crane.

Narrative Energy

Often, a character's energy is the same as the story's energy. This is the case in *The Lady Eve* in which Barbara Stanwyck's Eve is certain that she will wrap Henry Fonda's Adam around her pinky. The narrative energy is the way in which she goes about it. There is a lot of story to *The Lady Eve*. There are many examples of this type of story—*Papillon, The Great Escape, Champion, Stella Dallas.*

Energy and drive, however important to the screen story, needn't reside in the main characters. The story and the secondary characters can compensate for the ambivalence or conflict of the central character. More often we are presented with stories that have considerable narrative drive and with characters who are ambivalent, conflicting, or reflective—the writer in Sunset Boulevard, the decent insurance clerk in *The Apartment*, or the reluctant book promoter in *Crossing Delancy*. In each of these stories the drive or energy comes from the story. In each case, there is a secondary character who is driven and whose actions are critical to the evolution of the story. The most memorable of this trio of screen stories is *Sunset Boulevard*. Gloria Swanson's portrayal of the aging silent screen star is one of the greatest moments in cinema's short history.

The Problem of Passivity

Avoid passive central characters: This is good advice for beginning screenwriters who face multiple problems of structure, language, and character, but it is too restrictive for writers who are comfortable with structure and storytelling. Clearly, the character who is totally passive leaves little room for opportunity to interact with the world. However, film stories have been made about such characters—*Oblomov* and, more recently, a Polish film called *A Short Film About Loving*. But, as described earlier, other characters and the story have to compensate for passivity in the major character.

What is not possible, except in an Andy Warhol movie, is a screen story in which all the characters and the level of action and narrative remain quiescent. That would not leave much room to deal with stories in which characters are relatively passive, reflective, ambivalent, and nonexpressive. In this type of story, the writer runs into real trouble. A passive cast covers a lot of states of behavior and the full range of professions as potential subject matter for the writer. In the remainder of this chapter we discuss examples of screen stories in which the active—-passive balance clearly tilts toward passive characters.

▪ ▪ ▪ A Case Study of a Passive Main Character I: *sex, lies, and videotape*

The main character in Steven Soderbergh's *sex, lies, and videotape* is aware that she is unfulfilled, but totally unaware as to why. She is a passive main character. The young married woman is having sexual problems. She has a concerned therapist, a promiscuous sister, and a wandering husband. She is unaware and frightened by much of her behavior, particularly about her lack of sexual feelings.

An old friend arrives to stay with them and in his straightforward way alienates the husband, shares his sexual sublimation with the wife (he videotapes women talking about their sex lives), and stimulates her sister to new heights of arousal. His presence also destabilizes the young wife's slender hold on what passes for a married life. Her marriage collapses, she has a sexual experience with the voyeur, and becomes better friends with her sister.

This simple story parallels the Sleeping Beauty story, except, here, Sleeping Beauty is awake—at least consciously—but she doesn't understand a thing about her life, about her failures, or about her potential. Total lack of awareness is not an active, reflective, or even reticent position for a major character. Indeed, it is a position that promises a character scorn or rejection. Only the despicable behavior of her husband and sister put her in a least-sympathetic position. This is not the position for involvement and identification with the main character.

The old friend is hardly the typical Prince Charming. He is a voyeur with no clear means of support, and his position with the other characters is too ambiguous to make him appealing. He is, however, mysterious, which makes us curious about him and about his fate. But he doesn't replicate the powerful position that Georgia had in *Four Friends* or Ray had in *Who'll Stop the Rain?*

The young wife is probably similar to young wives we know in real life—confused, a submerged personality—but she is not a character we often meet in movie life.

▪ ▪ ▪ A Case Study of a Passive Main Character II: *My Own Private Idaho*

The main character in Gus Van Sant's *My Own Private Idaho* is a narcoleptic (River Phoenix). When there's a troubled situation, he goes to sleep. He is the antithesis of the type of goal-directed character whose goal and energy drive the story.

Mike is a street hustler in Portland, Oregon. His is an unpredictable life of the moment. He dreams of home—Idaho—and of a mother who will nurture him. When he meets Scott, a rich, rebellious street kid, Mike is attracted to him and helps him search for Mike's mother. They find Mike's brother, who tries unsuccessfully to disabuse Mike of his illusions of their mother. The search takes them to Italy, where Scott falls in love with a young woman. The two men part, Mike returning to his former way of life and Scott becoming what he always was—a person of privilege, a person who belongs. The film ends with Mike asleep on a road in Idaho. His search in its way continues. But the road for Mike goes nowhere.

Mike is passive in a different sense than the character in *sex, lies, and videotape*. She is passive in her marriage and in her sexual modesty until she is transformed by a man who uses the camera as a tool or wand to awaken her. There is no awakening for the main character in *My Own Private Idaho*. He not only remains on the margins of society; he seems to have little impact even on those with whom he has a relationship. Scott tolerates, even accepts his neediness. Not so Mike's brother. He is infuriated by Mike's unwillingness to face the truth of his life. Although there is one moment in the script when Mike attempts to be with another (Scott), he is for the most part withdrawn, acting out a psychodrama or actually sleeping in response to the pain of the moment. In the sense of realizable goals, Mike has none; he has only the desire to find his mother. Mike is a passive character in the most complex sense. It is far more difficult to relate to a passive character like Mike's than to a character who is eventually transformed. For the audience, therefore, he represents an emotional enigma who resists rescue because his mental state is his failed attempt to rescue himself.

■ ■ ■ A Case Study of Main Character as Catalyst I: *Who'll Stop the Rain?*

In *Who'll Stop the Rain?*, Michael Moriarty portrays John, a left-wing journalist for an independent newspaper. His columns from Vietnam haven't stopped the war and he sees himself as an impotent idealist. As the story begins, John decides to smuggle heroin into the United States. Everyone else is making their own way with this war, why not him? He depends on Ray, a friend from the Marines, now in the Merchant Marine, to smuggle in the heroin, but John has been set up. He is the perfect dupe, an innocent willing to take desperate action and in doing so endangering himself, his family, and his friend.

Who'll Stop the Rain? is a tale of the rite of passage from idealist to survivor. John's ideals don't shelter him from a corrupt F.B.I. agent and his criminal colleagues. John, who is not a conventional main character, starts the action that sets off the narrative. The balance of the story—the effects on his family, the threat to his life, the further disillusionment he experiences—are all consequences of that original action. In every case, he is victimized by those consequences. He is acted upon and is passive for the most part.

John doesn't even re-enter the story until the middle of Act Two, during which he becomes no more than a device for the criminals to try to regain the heroin from Ray (Nick Nolte). Throughout Act Two, Ray is the character who acts; he runs away with the heroin and John's wife (Tuesday Weld) in order to protect both for John. Only in Act Three does John face a choice. He is willing to die to save his wife. In his mind he is already dead. While he doesn't die, his idealism does. At the end of the film, he is a survivor, but not much more. His future, in spite of the last image on the screen, does not have an endless horizon.

Since the main character is not prominent in the narrative, the story has strong secondary characters. Ray is the man whose sense of friendship is generous, and he's worldwise in ways that John is not. The film also has a powerful narrative and a corrosive sense of language that is both literary and scatological.

■ ■ ■ A Case Study of Main Character as Catalyst II: *Silent Tongue*

The main character of Sam Shepherd's *Silent Tongue* is an Indian woman named Silent Tongue. Although her history and her actions drive the story, she appears very briefly in the story. In this sense, she is a main character who is a catalyst to the story rather than a character whose actions are central to many scenes in the screen story.

Silent Tongue is an Indian woman who is abducted by an itinerant Scot. He rapes her and takes her as his woman. Over the years she bears him two daughters. He also has an older white son. When the screen story begins, the man, now twenty years older, runs a traveling show full of freaks, magic shows, bluster, and a medicine he sells to cure all ills. He is a man who will sell anything and has. The story opens with the return of a stranger, elderly but fit. He too comes from another land, Ireland, and he is desperate for the well-being of his son. A year earlier he had purchased the Scot's eldest Indian daughter for his son. She died in childbirth and the son is destroyed with grief. He will not even bury the body; he sits and guards it. The Irishman has come to buy the younger daughter to replace the daughter who is dead. The Scot is indignant but he has his price. Frustrated, the Irishman kidnaps the younger daughter. The Scot and his son pursue hotheadedly.

In his efforts to rescue his son, the Irishman makes a bargain with the younger daughter. This is where the story takes a startling and spiritual turn. The spirit of the dead sister begins to torment them all. She wants only to be burned so that her soul can be freed, and she pursues a course that will assure the liberation of her spirit. Her sister respects her wishes.

Because of the dead woman's desire, the Irishman must take his son back from the despair he had dwelled upon and later the Scot must be taken and tortured by the Indian as he deserves.

In the end, Silent Tongue and her two daughters get what they needed and wanted—freedom and respect. Her spiritual strength and determination drives this story in spite of the fact that she appears only briefly in the narrative.

■ ■ ■ A Case Study of Main Character as Observer I: *Inside Moves*

Rory (John Savage) introduces himself to us by jumping out of a 10th-floor window and failing to kill himself. Disabled, he faces a limited life. This is a depressing beginning to one of the more uplifting films of the decade!

Rory is befriended by a group of disabled persons who hang out in an Oakland bar. One of them, Jerry, invites him to a basketball game where Rory is impressed by the expressiveness of his new friend. In fact, Jerry is a loudmouth who acts as if he can play the game better than the pros. He tells the star player how he blew the game and challenges the star, Alvin, to a one-on-one playoff. Alvin accepts and almost loses to Jerry. Rory watches and it begins to dawn on him that if Jerry (with a gimpy leg) can almost beat a pro, there are possibilities to his life.

Rory slowly begins to engage with life; he takes an ownership stake in the bar. As Jerry's career ascends, Rory begins to grow. He becomes interested in a woman; the future is beginning to have options. But his ascent is tied to Jerry. Only after he has observed or responded to Jerry's achievements, does he try to broaden his life.

Rory is always passive, observing. It is Jerry and the other disabled people who catalyze his final choice—to live fully, rather than in a limited way that is akin to suicide. The secondary characters are very active and energetic, in spite of being confined to a wheelchair, or blind, or without arms. The narrative is elaborate and filled with events and people. There is a lot of story for Rory to observe and with which eventually to engage.

We never know Rory very well, but we can see his tentativeness and we can relate to his emergence. He is never more than an observer. His condition doesn't permit him to play basketball like Jerry or to be a romantic activist with the waitress he loves. All of Rory's efforts are tentative. In the end, his efforts secure our respect for his decency and for his insight into himself and into Jerry, but it is late in the story for his character to win us over. Consequently, Rory is very far from the conventional main character in film, but he is never very far from characters we know in real life.

■ ■ ■ A Case Study of Main Character as Observer II: *Black Robe*

Brian Moore's *Black Robe* (1991), set in early 17th-century Quebec, has as its main character Father Laforgue, a Catholic priest (Lothaire Bluteau). The priest is being taken inland to Huronia, and his guide is an Indian named

Chomina (August Schellenberg). Accompanying him is a young fur trader, the family of Chomina, and a number of his men.

The priest is an ascetic in a physical land, traveling with physical people. But beyond that, they believe in a higher order, a spiritual being that differs from the priest. The Catholic priest believes in Jesus and organized Catholic religion; the Indians believe in the spirit of animals and the land.

The journey to Huronia is a dangerous one where the priest is totally dependent on his Indian guides. He also chooses not to experience the Indian values/interpretation of life. Not so his fur trader companion, who becomes quickly involved with Chomina's daughter. The priest watches, desires, and flagellates himself so that he can transcend or avoid his earthly feelings.

The priest remains on the periphery of the action, always observing, never entering it. Although he is present and is clearly the main character, his position remains as an observer. He does not change in the course of the story, which is unusual, because he maintains the observer position. He represents one corner of the spiritual struggle in the story; it seems the less fulsome interpretation of spirituality. Although the priest lives at the end, while Chomina dies, it is the spiritual life of the Indian that seems complex and appropriate to the primitiveness of the land. The priest's position in comparison seems outside the land, not transcendent, but residual. In this sense his observer status as main character consolidates the narrative view that, relatively, the coming of the white man and his religion to North America was not so much a progressive step as a new step, a different step, a misstep.

■ ■ ■ A Case Study of Main Character as Outsider: *Four Friends*

Steven Tesich wrote *Four Friends,* an autobiographical story that spans the 1950s to the 1970s. The story opens with young Danilo and his mother joining their Yugoslavian father in East Chicago, Indiana, and takes us through the sexual revolution of the '60s, to when Danilo takes his parents to the boat on which they return to Yugoslavia, while he remains to make his life in America.

Danilo's is an immigrant story. He stays quietly on the sidelines and allows his friends to speak for his rebelliousness and sexual expressiveness. He is alienated from his parents; against his father's wishes, he goes to college where he befriends a rich American. He becomes engaged to his friend's sister, again against the wishes of his father. *Four Friends* ends with Danilo reconciled to his adolescent girlfriend, Georgia, and resigned to the idea that his father will never understand him.

Most of the action of the story occurs around Danilo and there is a lot of story to tell. The tale of the '60s, from JFK to Vietnam, is interwoven with

Danilo's story. Many of the characters are more vivid than Danilo (Craig Wasson). Georgia is the catalytic figure in the story. She is expressive, exploratory, and spontaneous—all the qualities absent from Danilo.

The story maintains Danilo as an outsider looking in on a society from an idealistic perspective. For him, America is the land of his dreams. What he sees rarely conforms to his dream, but that is because he remains on the outside. Danilo is passionate and energetic, but he simply cannot express those feelings; he is constrained by his posture as outsider. Consequently, he is a man on the margin, a position that poses a variety of difficulties for a main character, not the least of which is identification.

One benefit of presenting the main character as outsider is the opportunity to reflect on the action of the story as well as to participate in it. Although this isn't taken up in Tesich's character, Danilo's inexpressiveness provides pauses when we can reflect about how he feels. Consequently, there is a constant tension (not knowing how the character will react) that is useful in maintaining our involvement. However, it is not a tension that leads to concern for Danilo, but to curiosity about him and the story. This seems to be the fate of placing the main character in the position of outsider.

▪ ▪ ▪ A Case Study of Main Character as Medium: *Field of Dreams*

Bill Kinsella (Kevin Costner) in *Field of Dreams* is a main character who has a vision—he must build a baseball field in the middle of his Iowa cornfield. Kinsella is a three-dimensional character. He's a nice guy; he's a dreamer; he isn't materialistic—but that's about it to his character. A series of subsequent voices and visions populate his team with Shoeless Joe Jackson and the other scandalized White Sox from the 1919 team accused of throwing the World Series. Kinsella gathers a black writer and an old doctor, and they join the ghost players in the idealized diamond in the sky. Kinsella finally gets to see his dead father and reconcile himself to the former baseball player whose memory he had long scorned.

Perhaps we all long to say something to parents we have lost. Kinsella's wish doesn't get fulfilled until the end of the film, and until then, there isn't much to him. Unlike some of the other passive, reticent, or ambivalent main characters we have discussed, Kinsella's flatness is not compensated for by a rushing flow of narrative or by another major character who drives the story. The writer (James Earl Jones) is interesting but too ambivalent to compensate for the shortcomings of the main character.

Yet, the story has a powerful emotional resonance in Act Three, in spite of the use of larger-than-life characters and a main character whose primary function is to act as a medium for this 1980s fantasy. Perhaps Kinsella, too, is recognizable as one of us.

■ ■ ■   A Case Study of Splitting the Main Character: *Mystic Pizza*

Another approach to the active/passive split in the main character is to challenge our involvement in a manner that fractures our identification with one character, whether that person is active or passive. In *Mystic Pizza,* there are three main characters, two sisters and a friend, all in their late teens and all preparing for their adult lives. Each character is different: One sister is loud and sexy; the other is quiet and cerebral; the friend is ambivalent. Character splitting offers us choices in terms of identification and involvement. On a continuum, the characters are active to passive around their sexuality, just as they are active to passive about a career, a husband, and their futures. The element that ties these three characters together is their need to work to secure a future. All come from working-class families and each of them works in the restaurant named Mystic Pizza.

The story has none of the narrative drive or the overdeveloped secondary characters present in other films discussed in this chapter. What does propel us through the story is, in part, a choice of characters to identify with, the honesty of the characters, and the parallels of the stories of each character.

In each case, the story unfolds through a relationship. The difference is the background of each character. Although there are significant differences among the three, their personal bond suggests that we concern ourselves with the fate of all three young women. These main characters are recognizable to us; they live among us and, in some cases, could be us.

■ ■ ■   A Case Study of Antagonist Compensating for Main Character: *The Little Foxes*

Alexandra (Teresa Wright), the young protagonist of Lillian Hellman's *The Little Foxes* is an innocent. Her mother, Regina (Bette Davis), is an antagonist and the opposite. Regina is so worldwise, manipulative, and evil, we can't believe she has given birth to someone quite so angelic. This polarity is so extreme that it compensates for the slightness of the protagonist.

Set in the deep South in 1900, *The Little Foxes* tells the story of a wealthy Southern family. Their goal of growing richer is stymied by their reliance on the banker in the family, Alexandra's father (Herbert Marshall). The ailing man is urged to return from a convalescence in Baltimore. Business dealings, particularly with his wife and her brothers, threaten his wealth, health, and cost him his life. Alexandra is witness to all of this. The issue for her is whether she wants to remain an innocent or face up to the fact that her mother is willing to do anything and sacrifice anyone to fulfill her own ambition.

This particular strategy has been frequently used to restructure the active/passive nature of a protagonist. The most recent example is the Luke Skywalker—-Darth Vader relationship in *Star Wars.*

Conclusion

In all the case studies discussed in this chapter, the main characters were not active or energized. Danilo *(Four Friends)* is a reactive character, and Rory *(Inside Moves)* and John *(Who'll Stop the Rain!)* are characters who act out of desperation. These actions bring each of them to the brink of disaster. They are reticent, passive, ambivalent main characters, and all are recognizable to us. They are tentative and all too human. They are flawed and, in each case, they have been considered failures for much of their lives. Their commonality lies in their recognizability. They remind us of people we know, rather than of movie characters.

In order to make these characters succeed dramatically, however, the writers had to modify their narrative approaches. These characters need dramatic situations and stories that are particularly energetic. The stories also needed memorable secondary characters, such as Ray Hicks in *Who'll Stop the Rain!* or Jerry in *Inside Moves.* They are certainly more memorable than the main character.

Finally, these stories require a very special antagonist, an antagonist who in her nature can compensate for the shortcomings of the main character. Regina, in *The Little Foxes,* is but one of a long line of great antagonists.

The benefit, should you choose to use active/passive characters, is a move away from movie main characters and a move toward real-life characters. This shift, as we have seen, can take you toward other options for your character. In the next chapter, we discuss one of these options—identification with the main character.

8
∎ ∎ ∎ ∎ ∎ ∎ ∎ ∎

Stretching the Limits of Character Identification

Audiences identify with characters in difficult situations and with characters they like or wish to be like. This identification is useful in a variety of ways; it quickly simplifies the relationship between the audience and the story. The audience enters the story through the character with whom they identify.

Identification also provides an umbrella of tolerance. Once involved with a character, viewers tend to overlook the more subtle issues of story credibility and are forgiving of the occasional use of coincidence. Writers don't want their viewers to become too aware of the various manipulations that are the mechanics of the screen story. This awareness is always a danger when identification with the main character is moderate or absent.

But what happens in a screen story when the main character is less than admirable? What is the balance between character exploration and audience empathy? Is there an underside to viewer identification? When does identification turn to voyeurism? These character-related issues are explored in this chapter.

Sympathy, Empathy, and Antipathy

Viewers relate to characters for different reasons. They relate to Sophie (Meryl Streep) in *Sophie's Choice* out of sympathy. She is a concentration camp survivor and her situation invites our sympathy. But do we empathize with her? Do we identify with her? No. The same can be said about Sol Nazerman (Rod Steiger) in *The Pawnbroker* and Lena (Isabelle Huppert) in *Entre Nous*.

The factors that prevent us from becoming more deeply involved with these characters are different in each case. We don't empathize with Sophie because she is never very forthcoming. Whether one considers this with-holding or lying is semantic. In the case of Sol Nazerman, he is too enraged, too angry at the whole world, to invite us to know him beyond his anger and his pain. In the case of Lena, she is a woman who makes a choice to marry in order to save her life. Later, she wants to escape from the man who provided her with her married life. We feel sorry for Lena, but we also feel sorry for her husband. There is little room to move to empathy.

In each case, the characters are trapped by past events and their con-temporary life is hell. They escaped from hell (the Holocaust) only to find a new hell. The level of tragedy in each of their lives precludes an empa-thetic identification and keeps our involvement with them at the level of sympathy.

Empathy implies a restrained identification with a character. Not only do we feel *with* them, often we feel *like* them. Wes Block (Clint Eastwood), a troubled detective in *Tightrope,* is a concerned single father as well as a professional with personal doubts. His flaws make him all too human, and, as a result, we empathize with him. The same can be said for Isabelle (Amy Irving) in *Crossing Delancey.* She is a professional person with no personal life. When an unorthodox opportunity arises to become involved with a man who cares about her, she doesn't know how to respond. Her vulnerability in this circumstance makes her appealing and empathetic. We care about her, just as we care about Wes Block.

In the majority of cases, the writer will use an empathetic or at least sympathetic main character. Occasionally, the writer will develop a char-acter for whom our dislike outweighs our like. Antipathy for a main char-acter is not as rare as we might think. We might feel ambivalent about Harry Mitchell (Roy Scheider) in *52 Pick-Up* or hostile toward the manip-ulative Richard Boyle (James Woods) in *Salvador* or loathing toward the cowardice of the conformist (Jean-Louis Trintignant) in *The Conformist,* but in each case, there is something about the character that involves us. The actors are portraying characters we like to hate—philanderers, manip-ulators, and cowards. Yet, we do get involved with them in a fashion. Harry Mitchell, in *52 Pick-Up,* is being blackmailed about an affair. The twist is that his girlfriend is part of the blackmail scheme. At risk is his marriage to a high-profile local politician. His wife's career is also placed at risk. His behavior is not admirable, but at least we can understand his desire to save his wife's reputation. Here lies the key to this type of character—there must be one redeeming quality that humanizes him. We can relate to that ele-ment.

When we look at Richard Boyle, in *Salvador,* we see the same quality. He will do anything for a story, but his love for a Salvadoran woman (he has a wife in the U.S.) is so intense, so genuine, and so different from the rest of his behavior that we can relate to this relationship and begin to see a more positive side to Boyle.

In the case of *The Conformist,* the title character's strong relationship with a woman other than his wife is the quality to which we relate. The other woman is the wife of a political dissident in Paris, who the conformist must set up for assassination. His desire to save the wife is so strong that we see a commitment for another not reflected elsewhere in the film. The fact that he allows her to be killed, in spite of her pleas to him, re-establishes his cowardice and is the most troubling moment in the film. Until then, however, this relationship is an attempt to reach us.

Identification Vs. Voyeurism

Our relationship with main characters isn't always straightforward. Perhaps the person who understood that best was Alfred Hitchcock. He wanted us to be involved, to identify with his characters, but he also wanted us to see them, physically and emotionally, from a detached view— as if we were voyeurs. If we can sympathize with their plight, empathize with their positive goals, and watch their obsessions, we become implicated with the characters; we share their guilt.

Marion Crane (Janet Leigh) in *Psycho* and John Ferguson (James Stewart) in *Vertigo* are obsessed characters who steal or manipulate and yet we are, in a complex and not always comforting way, involved with them. These two characters have a great deal in common with the most voyeuristic of Hitchcock's characters, L. B. Jeffries (James Stewart) in *Rear Window.* All three characters are straightforward, outwardly normal people who are trapped. In the case of Marion Crane, she is trapped in an extramarital affair that will only move ahead with enough money. So she steals the money and is then plagued by guilt over her actions. This guilt suddenly turns into expiation when she decides to return the money. Finally at peace with herself, she is killed by Norman Bates and we are left in the voyeuristic position of her killer.

John Ferguson, in *Vertigo,* falls in love with a woman he has been hired to follow. As a policeman and now as a private detective, his acrophobia (fear of heights) is exploited when his subject, Madeline (Kim Novak), falls from a window, an apparent suicide. Riddled with guilt, he finds a woman who looks like Madeline, and in reality is Madeline, and makes her over to look like the woman he lost. When he discovers she has duped him, he returns to the scene of the first "death," but this time she does slip and fall. His guilt is rekindled and he is left suspended, as are we.

In both cases, each character has positive and negative characteristics. Through their negative actions we are distanced from the characters and assume the position of voyeurs. As we distance ourselves, we begin to feel guilty, as if we were abandoning people to whom we had started to relate. Our guilt becomes particularly acute as their situations deteriorate (death for Crane, death of a loved one for Ferguson). Hitchcock has succeeded in implicating us with their guilt.

This type of balance is not exclusive to Hitchcock, but is most often found in this genre. *Bedroom Window, Blue Velvet,* and *Dead Ringers* are recent examples.

Self-Revelation

Another approach to overcoming the negative qualities of a character is to provide him with an opportunity to reveal the real self. As with people, we generally see the social or public self. If the character is a rogue, writers usually give him some charm, and we come to think of him as something of a rascal, not as an evil or totally negative person. If he is not charming, the moment of revelation is a very useful device to gain our understanding, complicity, or tolerance for the character. If this moment is particularly unexpected, the writer can even generate empathy for the character.

A good example of this type of character is Midge Kelly (Kirk Douglas) in *Champion.* This Carl Foreman screenplay chronicles the rise and fall of a world champion boxer. Until a point halfway through the film, we sense that Kelly is a restless, ambitious man who wants to rise above his childhood poverty. He is opportunistic at every turn. Halfway through the film, Douglas has a scene in which he talks about what it was like to be a poor boy. The humiliation he suffered remains a vivid scar, and at that moment we begin to forgive or at least tolerate his cruelty to those closest to him.

In *Blame it on Rio,* Matthew Hollis (Michael Caine) takes a vacation with a divorced friend and their teenage daughters. Matthew's marriage is foundering and he takes solace from his friend's daughter. The affair that follows is kept from his friend, but not from his own daughter. Matthew is not an admirable man in this Charlie Peters-Larry Gelbart script, but the writers give Matthew many moments of revelation. From the beginning of the film, Matthew begins to confess directly to us and this continues periodically throughout the film. The result is that we tolerate the character.

Another approach to the moment of revelation is taken in *True Believer.* Edward Dodd (James Woods), a famous civil rights lawyer of the 1960s, is now a lawyer primarily for drug dealers. His moment comes when a new assistant, Roger Barron, chastises him for not taking on a controversial murder case. He is no longer the man for whom Barron traveled to New York. This is a humiliating moment for Dodd, who is hungry for the glory and publicity of those early days and now has to settle for less idealistic clients. We learn about Dodd's past and we sense who he was. Can he be that person again? Until this point in the story, Dodd is presented as a mesmerizing speaker in court and as a lawyer who has fallen from grace. He has talent, but conviction without idealism seems ignoble. Can Dodd once again be noble? Although he is energetic, it is not possible to sympathize or empathize with him. Only when we learn who he was, do we feel sorry for him and hope that he can recapture his idealism.

A moment of revelation is important for a less-than-sympathetic main character and is a device often used by writers to involve us with character. When a screenwriter is more painstaking about the story, we find these moments apply to more than just the main character. Virtually all of the characters in John Patrick Stanley's *Moonstruck* have their moments of revelation, and the three key characters in David Mamet's *Things Change* have their moments as well. It is important to remember that the moment of revelation is very often associated with a story point in which the characters have undergone a humiliating experience. When they are vulnerable, they reveal their private sides. Then, whether saint or sinner, we are hooked by the character.

Heroism

A moment of revelation, particularly when a character is feeling vulnerable, requires courage. We don't mean Arnold Schwarzenegger's commando-type heroism, but courage on a more human scale. Main characters, whether we identify with them to a greater or lesser degree, require a good measure of heroism in order to overcome the dramatic hurdles that stand in their way. Heroism can be defined, for our purposes, as a main character's attitude plus action in surmounting challenges that prevent the character from achieving a goal. The use of heroism provides a means of viewing the character in a more sympathetic light and offsets our lack of empathy for the main character.

One route to heroism is the quality of the challenge. The challenge can take the form of a remarkable antagonist, like the Joker in *Batman*; it can be the setting, as in *The Emigrants* (the land) and *Lawrence of Arabia* (the desert); or it can be class rigidity, as in *Pelle the Conqueror*. In each case, the level and quality of the challenge make the main character heroic.

However, not every character is as tenacious as T.E. Lawrence or as rich and talented as Batman. When we look at the rigid Colonel (Alec Guiness) in *The Bridge on the River Kwai* or the selfish captain in the same film (William Holden), we find their behavior in the second half of the film no less heroic. The angry father (George C. Scott) in *Hardcore is* faced with the heroic search to find a teenage daughter who has run away from their religious home, only to become an actress in hardcore pornographic films. He has to overcome many qualities in his own background in order to proceed with his search.

The character we recognize most often as neither sympathetic nor empathic is Lyn McAdam (James Stewart) in *Winchester 73*. We don't know much about Lyn, other than that he is angry and is an excellent rifleman. Only as the story unfolds does the character have a number of moments of revelation. Each time he tells us a little more, until Act Three, during which we learn what has embittered him—the death of his father at the hands of his own brother. In his attempt to confront and kill his brother, he has to overcome many challenges. During the course of his successes, he makes the transition from angry protagonist to vengeful hero. His challenges—outlaws, Indians, and more outlaws—seem increasingly daunting, but the success of his challenges measures his determination.

Charisma

Whether a main character is empathetic or antagonistic, a quality that can be as useful as heroism is the elusive charisma that makes everyday people attractive. Although charisma is more often thought of in connection with politicians and movie stars, it can also be used in the development of characters. It is particularly important in the character, who, on first meeting, presents in an unappealing manner. Good examples of this quality range from the eccentric T.E. Lawrence in *Lawrence of Arabia* to Travis Bickle in *Taxi Driver*. Both are men with a mission seemingly beyond their own means. Screen stories naturally gravitate toward characters who have power *(Patton)* or who want power *(The Candidate)*, the famous *(All the President's Men)*, and the infamous *(The Last Ten Days of Adolph Hitler)*.

What is charisma and how can it be developed in a character? Irvine Schiffer, in his book *Charisma*,[1] suggests certain characteristics that create charisma. They are:

- An element of foreignness
- A subtle imperfection
- A calling or sense of mission
- Polarized aggression or intensity
- A sexual dimension
- The ability to convince others.

The charismatic character, then, is somewhat different from other characters; he arouses our curiosity and attracts us by his intensity and sense of mission. These characters have a powerful sexual dimension and they are not perfect. They might have a bad back, wear glasses, or be exceedingly short. The key element is that we quickly notice that they are different and are not put off by them, but instead are curious about them. Charisma is helpful in balancing negative and positive characteristics and helps us get involved with that character.

The Tragic Flaw

Very often when a central character is a negative one, our acceptance of him hinges on a tragic flaw in his character. Not dissimilar from Macbeth's sense of invincibility (some might call it susceptibility to delusion) or the lean and hungry look of Cassius in *Julius Caesar*, there is often an extreme quality that is both the source of strength as well as the source of duplicity in these main characters. Lonesome Rhodes's (Andy Griffith) earnestness in Budd Schulberg's *A Face in the Crowd* is the basis for his wide appeal in small groups and then large groups (on television), but is also the source of his duplicity. Steven Gold's (Tom Hanks) immaturity in David Seltzer's *Punchline* is the source of his rage with people on stage and off, but it is also the source of his strength as a comic. The audience is attracted to the power, but repelled by the nature of the tragic flaw.

In order to understand better how tragic flaw plays itself out in screen stories, it is useful for us to acknowledge that this quality is played out in a literary manner. Tragic flaw adds subtext and is the link between the character and the society that has produced this character.

For example, Sidney Falco (Tony Curtis) is a New York press agent in Clifford Odets and Ernest Lehman's *Sweet Smell of Success*. He lives in a tough city in which he must depend on the kindness of gossip columnists to make a living. Unfortunately, there are no kind gossip columnists in New York. Sidney Falco's tragic flaw is his ambition. He will do anything and sacrifice anyone in order to succeed.

On the other coast, Joe Gillis (William Holden), in Billy Wilder's *Sunset Boulevard*, wants the good life of Hollywood. He takes advantage of Norma Desmond's self-myopia and tries to rewrite her script for Mr. DeMille. Here, too, ambition leads Joe to desperation, opportunity, and finally to his own death.

The world views of Falco and Gillis and implicitly the world view of their entertainment industry, which trades on celebrity, are no more kindly treated than are the characters. In both cases, the viewer has a fascinating insight into character pathology and the strength of desire needed to succeed in the industry. And in both cases the language and the dialogue are brittle, hard, and brilliant. The dialogue alone creates for us the excitement, the dynamism, of being inside the industry.

Falco and Gillis are men of their time and place. Other places and other times yield other memorable characters. King (George Segal), in Bryan Forbes's *King Rat*, lives in the world of the Japanese prisoner-of-war camp. While others die, he thrives, thanks to opportunism. Charles Tatum (Kirk Douglas), in Billy Wilder, Lesser Samuels, and Walter Newman's *Ace in the Hole*,(later retitled, *The Big Carnival*) is even more blinded by ambition than Sidney Falco. He is a New York newspaperman exiled because of his alcoholism to work in New Mexico. While there, he encounters a story that may take him back to New York. A man is trapped deep in a cave. The man could easily be rescued, but Tatum convinces the sheriff and others to delay in order to get some publicity for the town. While the man slowly dies in the cave, a wave of pity carries the story to the national airwaves. People drive to the site; large equipment is set up to start the digging; admission is charged to gain entry to the site. Charlie finally makes it to the national airwaves and back to New York—until the man dies in the cave. Then, his story begins to unravel and Charlie, brilliant reporter, is turned into a murderer—all because of his immoral sense of ambition.

There are numerous other wonderful examples of tragic flaw, the self-absorbed Blume (George Segal) in Paul Mazursky's *Blume in Love* and the mad Rupert Popkin (Robert De Niro) in Paul Zimmerman's *King of Comedy*, among them. The use of the tragic flaw attracts and repels the viewer, all the while making a negative main character tolerable.

■ ■ ■   A Case Study of Charisma: *White Hunter, Black Heart*

White Hunter, Black Heart (1990) is the story of John Huston (as played by Clint Eastwood) in the making of *The African Queen*. Peter Viertel's novel is adapted by Viertel, James Bridges, and Burt Kennedy, and the fixation of the screenplay is Huston's indifference to making a difficult location film in Africa and his total devotion at that time to shooting elephants. This leads to the death of a devoted black guide and only then does Huston turn back to the purpose of his being in Africa, to make the film.

The screenplay does not dwell on the famous participants in the film— Bogart, Hepburn, Spiegel, Harry Cohn—rather it stays with the character of Huston and his obsessions. What is fascinating about the screenplay is Huston's vigorous narcissism. He loves to talk, to challenge, to bully, to decide, to contradict, all just to hear the tonal rhythms of his own speech. It's as if he's making up dialogue, rather than behaving out of an ethos, a humanity. His speech on London and Nazi sympathizers during the Blitz, a tale told to a British expatriate anti-Semite during an elegant African evening, is a classic of liberal ideology and cynical manipulation. His is a character who loves to watch and so do we.

Whether it is his love of language or outrageous behavior, Huston is energetic, deterministic, and flawed, the perfect charismatic character.

The question here is whether these qualities are enough to draw us into the story. They certainly fascinate us, but the tragedy that befalls Huston (the loss of the guide) does not strike us as tragic for him but rather tragic because of him. In consequence, we remain outside his character, impressed by his energy but never identifying with him. The result is a bold experiment where we see the character rather than feel as the character does.

■ ■ ■   A Case Study of Charisma and Tragic Flaw: *Raging Bull*

Jake LaMotta (Robert De Niro), in Paul Schrader and Mardik Martin's *Raging Bull,* is a charismatic, but flawed, character. He is an intense Italian-American who play acts and is not perfect. Physically and emotionally he is always attacking. He has a primitive animalistic aggression that is both the source of his power as a boxer and the source of the poison to all his personal relationships.

As LaMotta moves toward the championship, he loses two wives and a brother—the people closest to him. Consequently, this champion loses everything. His impulsive aggressiveness results in the loss of his material goods as well as his imprisonment. The film ends with LaMotta rehearsing his nightclub routine. He is the warm-up act for strippers—a far cry from being the champion boxer of the world.This character attracts and repels us at the same time. We are attracted to his restless energy, but we are repelled when it is used to beat up his wife. We are attracted by his ability to remain standing in the ring, no matter how badly beaten, but we are appalled by the savagery of the two men in the ring. LaMotta is charismatic, but he is also terribly flawed. His flaw destroys him, leaving no more than a pathetic, second-rate comedian living off the remains of his reputation.

■ ■ ■   A Case Study of Self-Revelation and Heroism: *The Manchurian Candidate*

Raymond Shaw (Lawrence Harvey), in George Axelrod's *The Manchurian Candidate,* is not a likable central character. He is arrogant, rude, and angry. He is also a man who has been brainwashed in Korea to be a Communist assassin. He is particularly dangerous because of his skill as a marksman, because of his unawareness of his chosen role, and because he is beyond suspicion. He is the stepson of a United States Senator, chosen to be the vice presidential candidate of his party, and he is a Congressional Medal of Honor war hero.

Raymond's character, however, is of greatest interest to us. He is a negative character, and yet, by the end of the story, we empathize with a man who has killed at least five innocent people, including his own wife. This comes about in one key scene. Raymond, drunk, is confessing about his character to his friend and commanding officer, Ben Marco (Frank Sinatra). He tells Ben that he knows he is not a lovable person and repeats it throughout the scene. He then describes that time in his life when he was lovable. He describes his meeting with the woman, Josie Jordan, with whom he falls in love. Since her father is the Senator that Raymond's mother once slandered as a Communist, there is no love lost between the two families. With Josie, Raymond laughs and becomes lovable. However, his mother finally breaks up the relationship and Raymond returns to his unlovable self. In this scene, Raymond also expresses his hatred for his mother and his inability to go against her.

Both his break-up with Josie and his relationship with his mother become critical in the second half of the film. Josie re-enters his life and Raymond enjoys a brief happiness when they marry. Then, his mother re-establishes her special hold over Raymond and we learn that she is the Communist agent who will control Raymond, the assassin, in the United States.

The fact that Raymond reveals his inner self to us, the fact that his self is so totally different from the Raymond we have seen so far in the story, both shocks and moves us. He evolves from assassin to pawn and we empathize with a character who was, up until that point, negative in every sense. As a pawn, we see Raymond in his Act Three struggle with and against his mother, a heroic struggle of a weak son attempting to overcome an overpowering mother. At the end, in his struggle against his mother, Raymond becomes a real war hero that the Communists created.

■ ■ ■ A Case Study of Identification and the Negative Main Character: *Paper Mask*

The negative main character has a great deal in common with the classic main character. Each has energy, appeal, charm, and a goal, but the negative main character differs in the nature of that goal. Through an identification process, we understand and can share the positive goal of the classic main character. But through the same process we can identify with the negative main character in spite of the nature of his goal.

Matthew Harris (Paul McGann) is a hospital orderly in John Collee's *Paper Mask* (1992). He really admires the doctors: They own the hospital and have the respect of the women who work there. One night he witnesses an automobile accident in which a young doctor is killed. He moves the body into the mortuary and there steals the doctor's identity papers. The rest of the story is Harris's attempt to create a career as a doctor in two hospitals. At first he is awkward but, helped by a veteran nurse, he almost succeeds, until an old acquaintance, a fellow orderly, moves to his new hospital. At this stage, so close to success, Matthew refuses to give up. He kills his friend and the pretense goes on.

As one might imagine, Harris can be undone at any point—faulty medical practice being the primary problem. Equally possible is that he might slip up and reveal that his identity is a false one. Or there is the recognition factor: How long can one hide from the past?

Clearly Harris's goal is to lie about himself and his profession. Without proper training, he hopes to put himself in a position where people will trust him with their lives. Because of his lack of training, they are at far higher risk than they realize. His goal makes Matthew Harris a negative main character.

Nevertheless, the vigor, the charm, and the relentlessness with which he pursues his goal create a certain amount of empathy for him, but not enough for us to identify with him. How then does writer John Collee create an identification with Matthew Harris? He uses the plot structure to create the necessary identification. Collee constantly puts Matthew Harris in danger of being caught—by a nurse, by a hospital administrator, by a friend from the past; Harris is a man in constant danger. By using this plot device, we have no choice but to identify with Harris—we identify with the negative main character, who is a person in constant danger.

▪ ▪ ▪   A Case of the Negative Main Character: *The Conformist*

The Conformist (1971), Alberto Moravia's story of the making of a Fascist in Mussolini's pre-war Italy of the 1930s, is the classic portrait of a negative main character. Marcello Clerici is an upper-class gentleman from an unorthodox family—his mother is a drug addict and his mad father is confined to a mental institution. They were people of standing, but Marcello does not identify with them, he wants order in his life. So he becomes engaged to a flighty, nouveau-riche young woman, and he wants to become a member of the Fascist party. Marrying the young woman only requires that he go to confession, a temporary return to the Catholic Church. Joining the Fascist party is more complex—he must trap his former professor, a radical voice of dissent, now in Paris. He agrees.

On his honeymoon in Paris, he goes to see Professor Quadri, tries to befriend the professor and his wife, Anna, and then betrays them. Quadri and Anna are assassinated en route to their rural home. At the end of the war, Marcello decides he no longer wants to be a Fascist, so he betrays the blind friend who first introduced him to the party.

There is nothing admirable about Marcello. He is a coward and morally a cynic. He joins the Fascists to be empowered in the new society. He marries a woman for whom he has only contempt. And when he does fall in love, with Anna Quadri, he does nothing to prevent her death.

How then do the writers create empathy for Marcello? First, they show a scarred past—he is raped by the chauffeur, whom he believes he has killed in anger. In his contemporary life, it is clear that neither his mother nor father can be a role model for him. Finally, the writers show us that Marcello knows what he is doing but his self-contempt is so great his negative actions fit in with his self-image. The writers show a level of consciousness, choice, rather than desperation in the why of what Marcello does and in this way create empathy for a character who has no admirable qualities, who is not charismatic, and whose goals are reprehensible.

■ ■ ■ A Case of an Ambivalent Main Character: *Chilly Scenes of Winter*

Although the classic main character and the negative main character share many qualities, except the goal, this is not the case with the ambivalent main character. He has no clear goal, a distinct problem for the dramatic elements of the story in which such a character is placed.

In Joan Micklin Silver's adaptation of Ann Beattie's novel *Chilly Scenes of Winter* (1979), which was originally released as *Head Over Heels*, Charles (John Heard) is the ambivalent main character.

Charles is a government bureaucrat bored by his work and beset by a family that needs rescuing (mother and sister). He is a man weighed down by emotional responsibility and intellectual lack of opportunity. Then he meets a young, recently separated woman at work (Mary Beth Hurt), falls in love with her, and pursues her. Unfortunately, she too is an ambivalent character, unsure of her next move. In the end, she returns to her husband, leaving the main character with his memories and his fantasies.

The main character in *Chilly Scenes of Winter* has some charm; he is intelligent, but he is troubled, unfocused. Most of the people around him share that state. Although all are eccentric, there is very little plot, it rests on the dialogue to energize this story. It tries valiantly to do so but cannot compensate for the limitations of Charles as a character. The ambivalent character can engender a degree of empathy but in the end his lack of definition limits the degree of empathy and identification the audience has with such a character.

■ ■ ■ A Case Study of Identification and Voyeurism: *Blue Velvet*

Jeffrey Beaumont (Kyle MacLachlan), in David Lynch's *Blue Velvet*, seems to be a nice, middle-class young man in a small town. He is intelligent and curious. When he finds a severed ear in a field in Lumberton, he wants to find out to whom it belongs. His search leads him to a beautiful nightclub singer. Aided by the local police detective's daughter, he infiltrates the singer's home and begins to watch her. But he watches her, not as a man with a mission, but as a man in lust. He is aroused by her and when she discovers he's broken into her apartment and has watched her undress, she turns the tables on him and rapes him.

This description of the action of Act One of *Blue Velvet* begs a number of questions, not least of which is: Where is this story going? Of direct interest to us is that Jeffrey is a character with whom we can certainly identify; he has all the qualities we admire. But then he begins to behave like a voyeur. The events that Jeffrey watches are so violent, so unusual on the screen, that we are repelled and yet drawn to them.

As the story progresses and we return to the mystery (the missing ear), behavior returns to a more predictable mode. Jeffrey is again a protagonist we can admire, even if we don't fully understand why he is so driven (curiosity is not enough of an explanation). In this film, the role of the antagonist, Frank (Dennis Hopper), is important. He is cruel misogyny and criminality personified; he is unpredictable and vengeful. When Frank beats Jeffrey for his interest in the singer (as a jealous suitor would), we sympathize with Jeffrey's Boy-Scout behavior. Jeffrey is earnest again, just the opposite of Frank. The antagonist takes over the voyeuristic dimensions (we become fascinated and repelled by him), and we identify with Jeffrey .

Lynch plays with identification and voyeurism throughout the film. Since he is robbing us of our illusions of the sanctity of small town life, there is little, if any, solace here for the viewer. The best we can do is identify with Jeffrey, who has raised our suspicions of his goals and motivations.

■ ■ ■   A Case Study Beyond Voyeurism—the Discovery of Empathy: *The Boys of St. Vincent (Parts I & II)*

The Boys of St. Vincent (1993), written by Des Walsh, John N. Smith, and Sam Grana, provides an excellent example of the discovery of empathy in an absolutely vile character.

The film is set in a Catholic orphanage in Newfoundland. In the first part of the two-part film, the focus is on the boys, and particularly on Kevin and his abuse at the hands of the head of the orphanage, Father Lavin. The first film concentrates on the investigation of a suspicion of sexual abuse, how it is discovered and then covered up. The second part of the film, set fifteen years later, focuses on the trial of Father Lavin. The main character in Part II is Father Lavin (Henry Czerney), who has now left the church and made a life in Montreal. He has two children, a wife, and a job—in sum, a new life. The charges and the trial pose questions of responsibility for both victim and victimizer. By focusing on Father Lavin, the film humanizes the perpetrator as it carries us beyond a voyeuristic position into a relationship with a character whose actions are despicable beyond description.

Although the writers do stay with Kevin and his struggle over whether to testify, they also create another main character in Father Lavin. His struggle is over whether to hide his past or to own up to it, particularly with his family (his wife). In terms of a negative main character, we have seen Lavin's goal, his sexual satisfaction, and his sadism played out in terms of his love object, Kevin, in Part I.

The Father Lavin we meet in Part II has a temper, but he seems to have tempered his desire for young boys, has married and created a new life. But what creates empathy for Father Lavin are his meetings with a psychiatrist who has to assess him for the purposes of the trial. Those sessions create a good deal of empathy because Father Lavin provides us with a private moment, a confession, where we learn that he, too, was adopted and sexually abused as a young child. He did raise himself up in terms of class, education, and status, but the neglected child in Lavin is filled with the pain that fuels the adult Lavin's rage. That moment takes us past viewing him strictly as a repellent perpetrator, and into a relationship with him. That empathetic relationship is shocking because of how negative our sense of the man, his abuse of power and privilege vis-à-vis young helpless boys, has been. Although he returns to his angry state when his wife at the end tells him she's leaving him, we remain acutely aware that this man is no longer a conventional negative character. He is complex, vulnerable, and sadistic. We have a relationship with him, empathy having replaced the distance of voyeurism.

Conclusion

The use of empathetic and energetic main characters is more widespread than it first seems. To establish the viewer's identification with the main character, the writer can either create sympathy for the main character or present the vulnerable side of that character to invite empathy. The writer can use a main character who challenges the audience's positive relationship with him and stretches the limits of identification. In order to do so, certain conditions must exist that allow us to become involved with such a character.

First, the main character should be charismatic. Jake LaMotta and George Patton are good examples. Second, the sense of mission the character exhibits implies an aura of heroism that is particularly appealing to audiences. These characters also generally exhibit a tragic flaw that prevents them from being successful human beings. Generally, these characters exhibit an aloneness that implies a sense of tragedy. Finally, these characters tend to exhibit their flaw through self-revelation. This moment creates a vulnerable main character who may be unlikable, but who briefly becomes a fuller human being. Although they revert to their former selves soon thereafter, our feelings toward them are never the same after the moment of self-revelation.

It is possible to use main characters who stretch the limits of identification. Certain conditions should prevail, however, to allow for our engagement with the main character. If those conditions don't prevail, the writer will ensure that we are voyeurs rather than participants.

Stories can function and remain interesting when the viewer is a voyeur. Particular filmmakers—Hitchcock, Lynch, and Godard—prefer that the viewer occupy both positions, voyeur and participant. The balance of the two positions depends on the narrative structure of the story as well as the nature of the main character. If the writer wants us to occupy the voyeuristic position, a more distant and unappealing main character will ensure that outcome. On the other hand, if the writer wants to place us as participants, our identification with the main character must be challenged. The result is that your audience will create relationships with a wide range of main characters.

References

1. Irvine Schiffer, *Charisma* (Toronto: University of Toronto Press, 1973).

9

. . . .

Main and Secondary Characters

Traditionally, the main character is played against secondary ones in order to demonstrate that only the main character can surmount the obstacles posed by the story. But this promotes the notion of a singular hero set against the world. By altering this relationship, a scriptwriter can suggest that no one character is privileged, that the main character has to deal with the same limitations as all the other characters.

To explore this relationship, we look first at the classic example of the main character vs. secondary characters. In Budd Schulberg's *On the Waterfront*, the main character, Terry Malloy (Marlon Brando), faces a dilemma. He can be a criminal like his brother and a member of the union mob organization of which his brother is a part, or he can follow his more ethical instincts and try to lead a responsible (read moral or anti-mob) life. As with every good main character, Terry has it in him to go either way— criminal or good guy. He also has the energetic self-reflection to be troubled by his situation, and is empathetic and charismatic. In short, he is the type of main character who focuses the story and helps the storytelling.

The secondary characters line up on both sides of Terry's moral dilemma; they are either saints or sinners. The principal sinners are the head of the union, Johnny Friendly (Lee J. Cobb), and Charlie-the-Gent (Rod Steiger). Charlie, as Terry's brother, and Johnny, his principal benefactor, are in positions to put particularly strong suasion on Terry. Indeed, the quality of Terry's livelihood depends on the quality of his relationship with Charlie and Johnny. The story begins with Terry luring his friend Joey to the roof, where the two raise pigeons. Up there, Johnny's henchmen throw Joey from the roof, because he was ready to testify against union corruption and was therefore a threat to Johnny. Terry helped Johnny to get rid of the threat, and Terry is immediately implicated. Although his conscience is troubled ("Joey wasn't a bad kid"),[1] Terry accepts a cozy job on the waterfront.

On the side of the saints are two important secondary characters— Joey's sister Edie (Eva Marie Saint) and Father Barry (Karl Malden). Through his involvement with Edie and the priest's belligerent call for moral warfare on the waterfront, Terry's conscience and consciousness are stirred. But it is only when Johnny Friendly forces Charlie-the-Gent to prevent Terry from speaking to the Crime Commission that the two brothers confront the nature of their relationship in the famous I-could-have-been-somebody speech. Now it is Charlie who suffers pangs of conscience. He releases Terry, an action that results in his own death. If there is one action that makes Terry's decision personal as well as moral, it is the death of his brother. Terry has made his choice to destroy the sinner, Johnny Friendly. It almost costs him his life, but, in the end, Terry has heroically acted on his choice.

All four of the secondary characters mentioned are strong characterizations, differentiated from Terry in their clear stance in the drama, either as saint or sinner. Only Charlie veers in certainty. In this sense, Terry's choice becomes heroic, because he has to overcome his own uncertainty.

Each of the secondary characters acts as a catalyst to provoke action by Terry. They are foils that reveal different aspects of Terry's character, serve to illuminate Terry's conflict (saint or sinner), and help him resolve his problem.

On the Waterfront represents the classic notion of main character and secondary characters. In no way does this notion suggest that secondary characters have to be uninteresting and maim the stature of the main character. Eve (Anne Baxter), in Joseph L. Mankiewicz's *All About Eve,* and Norma Desmond (Gloria Swanson), in Billy Wilder and Charles Brackett's *Sunset Boulevard,* are among the most memorable screen characters, yet both are secondary characters in classic dramas in which the main characters, Margo Channing (Bette Davis) and Joe Gillis (William Holden), are challenged to surmount the obstacles posed by the story.

Secondary characters can be interesting; they can have their own goals (as Eve does in *All About Eve*). Often, their goals are so important and so oppositional to the main character that they become the antagonists. Johnny Friendly, in *On the Waterfront,* and Eve, in *All About Eve,* both present themselves in the role of antagonist. As antagonist, the secondary character often takes on as complex a personality and passion as the main character. Indeed, the more powerful the antagonist, the more heroic the struggle of the main character and the more likely we are to confirm the main character's primacy in the world the film story creates.

At what point does dramatic democracy set in to promote a more complex view of the main character, one of the many struggling to work out his position during a particular film story? The answer is writer-dependent. Many stories have explored this concept. The result can be interesting or confusing to the audience. It is in this type of drama that the skill and originality of the writer is tested, and we begin to move away from the classic balance between main characters and secondary characters.

■ ■ ■   A Case Study of Dramatic Democracy: *Love with the Proper Stranger*

Arnold Schulman's *Love with the Proper Stranger* is a story in which there are two characters who are equivalent in their attempts to resolve their dilemmas—to live life as their parents did (to marry) or to live a more independent life filled with sexual gratification (to be single).

Angela (Natalie Wood) and Rocky (Steve McQueen) are Italian-Americans. Both come from immigrant parents who have instilled old values in the lives of their children. Both children are in full rebellion. But how serious is the rebellion? Will they ever be free? Do they want to be free?

The story has a very creative opening. In a busy musician's hiring hall, Rocky is looking for work. He wants to be paged to appear busy, and he is paged. But it's not a scam; someone really is looking for him—Angela. He doesn't recognize her. She tells him she's expecting his baby and he still doesn't recognize her. All she wants from him is the name of a doctor so she can get an abortion. This is not an auspicious beginning to a relationship that is the subject of the balance of the screen story. But, surprisingly, the film starts the relationship at a point where many other screen stories end.

We find out a great deal more about Angela's family life during the course of the film—her guilt-rendering mother, her over-protective smothering brother—but we can't conclude that she is the main character. We also meet Rocky's parents and his latest girlfriend (Edie Adams). These characters present their unappealing version of domesticity. Both Angela and Rocky are on the run from domesticity, a view they associate with marriage .

Ironically, Angela and Rocky move through this story headed toward marriage, but when one proposes, the other opposes on the grounds of familiarity. Rocky offers to marry Angela because it is the right thing to do; Angela doesn't like the reason behind his offer.

These two people, so intimate before the story began, learn to like one another and eventually fall in love with each other. Whether they transcend the domesticity from which they ran is avoided in the romantic, open-ended ending—they kiss in front of a big crowd outside of Macy's.

What is most significant is that neither Rocky's nor Angela's struggle is made more heroic than the struggle of the other. These two characters find a solution, but we are not certain (as we would be if the ending were more heroic) that this is the end of their relationship problems. This is just the end of this film. We hope they will find happiness, but we have an uneasy feeling that their struggles will continue. This paradoxical conclusion is an inevitable result of viewing as equivalent plights of both characters. This dramatic democracy is more credible, but it undermines the degree of resolution and catharsis one associates with the classic main character–secondary character balance.

■ ■ ■ A Case Study of Plot Over Character: *Groundhog Day*

It is unusual when plot supersedes character in our involvement in a story but this is the case in Danny Rubin and Harold Ramis's *Groundhog Day* (1993). As with the vigor of plotting in Dale Launer's work (*Blind Date, Ruthless People*), *Groundhog Day* works with a powerful plot conceit to overcome the deficit of character in the screenplay.

Phil Conners (Bill Murray), a TV weatherman has an oversized view of himself. When he is assigned once again to the annual live report from Punxsutawney, Pennsylvania, on Groundhog Day, it's too much. Accompanied by a producer (Andie McDowell) and a cameraman, Phil is obnoxious, uncooperative, and dying to get back to Pittsburgh. But a storm prevents his return and when he wakes up the next morning, he finds himself living through a nightmare—it's Groundhog Day again. A few more repeats of the day and Phil realizes he's trapped in the worst day of his life. The rest of the screenplay relates to how he responds, uses, and changes in response to being trapped.

Phil's character is clearly unappealing and, although they differ, the producer and cameraman are not fascinating. She is ingenuous; the cameraman is sarcastic. Their characters do not compensate in the story for Phil's flatness. What does compensate is the adventuresome quality of the plot. Phil is by turns cynical, opportunistic, criminal. Once he discovers that he can't be punished for what he does, he becomes quite inventive about what he can get away with each day. This polar swing in behavior liberates the plot just as Phil himself is being trapped. Only when he experiences something he deeply wants, the love of his producer as a mate, does Phil regret being trapped in Groundhog Day. At that point his behavior becomes saintly, too good to be stuck anywhere, and the day finally changes, just as Phil has.

The interesting element in the film is how plot development compensates for a main character who does not engage us empathetically. Since the secondary characters are also stereotypes, they don't compensate for the main character's shortcomings. In *Groundhog Day*, only the plot and its inventiveness of characterization and character compensate.

■ ■ ■ A Case Study of Multiple Main Characters: *Mystic Pizza*

Some films opt for three rather than one protagonist. An early example is Robert Sherwood's *The Best Years of Our Lives*. Post-war adjustments were thematically appropriate to that time. The more recent *Mystic Pizza* is appropriate to the 1980s. Feminism, upward mobility, acquisitiveness, and education all play parts in the film.

Kat (Annabeth Gish), Daisy (Julia Roberts), and Jo (Lili Taylor) are three young women who work at Mystic Pizza, in Mystic, Connecticut. Daisy and Kat are sisters. All three women wonder about the future and, through their male–female relationships, learn that there are no easy answers about their futures. All they have is an enduring caring for one another, hopefully, this will help them through their lives.

Having three main characters divides character identification as well as the capacity to make anyone's struggles heroic. Indeed, the fact that each meets her travails in a different fashion–Kat with a naive romanticism, Daisy with a street-smart aggressiveness, and Jo with an adolescent propensity for avoidance—suggests that sister knows best. For example, if Kat had Daisy's street-smarts, she wouldn't have fallen in love with a married man. The differences in character and approach to problem resolution threaten to destabilize the unity of the story, but they don't.

Because the time frame is short and because each character's story chronicles a relationship, there is a sense of unity. These stories are all slices of the same pizza, to use the metaphor the screen story uses. These are winning characters; their intentions and actions are understandable, not alienating. Their mutual friendship creates a net under the individual stories and the result is an emotional unity that is as strong as a single protagonist screen story.

The men in each relationship are the antagonists of this story. When the three women salute one another at the marriage that ends (and begins) the story, we admire them and resent those who come between them—their men. Writers Amy Jones, Perry Howze, Randy Howze, and Alfred Uhry have fashioned a sisterhood story that transcends the downside of using more than one main character and alleviates the consequences of the main character–secondary character balance. This screen story is very much in balance.

■ ■ ■ A Case Study of Main Character as Antagonist: *Reversal of Fortune*

Does the negative main character need to be surrounded by one group of characters even more negative and another that group is positive? This is the central question posed from a narrative perspective by Nicolas Kazan in his screenplay for *Reversal of Fortune* (1990).

The central character, Claus von Bulow (Jeremy Irons) is accused of attempting to murder his wife, Sunny (Glenn Close). His stepchildren, together with the maid, are certain that von Bulow gave his wife an injection causing shock and irreversible, permanent coma. von Bulow is convicted. He retains lawyer Alan Dershowitz (Ron Silver) to appeal his conviction. This is the heart of the story. Throughout we learn about von Bulow's relationship with Sunny and his womanizing, including his mistress at the time of Sunny's falling into a coma. Whatever the motive, von Bulow is as Dershowitz characterizes him, a character everyone hates.

As a character, von Bulow is in the middle of the drama—is he guilty or is he innocent? Only he stands to lose all. Surrounding him is Sunny, her children, and his mistress. As scions of wealth, all are characterized as vapid, vain, and vulnerable people. Their weakness as people seems to have led to a fate where they can be used by people such as von Bulow—hard, cynical, driven by the goal of desperately needing money to maintain the lifestyle they believe they deserve. Neither Sunny or Claus von Bulow elicits empathy from the viewer.

On the other side, there is Dershowitz, his team, the maid. Dershowitz and the others are hot, emotional, vulnerable, affectionate, as warm-blooded as von Bulow and the rich are cold. They are the positive energy in the story and their goal, the search for justice, falls on the dubious mantle of von Bulow. Clearly this group of secondary characters provides a positive polarity that the audiences can relate to. And Dershowitz's goal, to win, always to win, is easily identified whether it be with sports or jury trials. The audience relates to his goal rather than to the goal of the main character, von Bulow (whose goal is to survive). He becomes the surrogate for von Bulow. If Dershowitz wins, so too the protagonist. But if he wins, this negative main character, a man who attempted to kill his wife, will be set free. The remarkable quality of Kazan's script is that we understand that and consequently when the main character does win, there is none of the satisfaction that is, for example, experienced when Richard Kimble is free at the end of *The Fugitive*. Instead, we are left with an appreciation that the laws of the land and the laws of living don't always coincide in their results. Particularly for the rich like von Bulow, the results can be striking.

■ ■ ■   ## A Case Study of Balance: *Who'll Stop the Rain?*

Who'll Stop the Rain?, by writers Judith Rascoe and Robert Stone (on whose novel the film is based), reverses the classic case of balance. John Converse (Michael Moriarty) is the main character, a man trying to decide if he is an idealist or a cynic. The Vietnam War and the '60s are making him increasingly cynical. He decides to sell heroin acquired in Vietnam and engages Ray Hicks (Nick Nolte), now in the merchant marines and a former Marine with John, to help.

Ray is a loyal friend to John and helps transport the heroin to the United States. Unfortunately, John has naively joined a smuggling operation that doesn't tolerate amateurs. Ray protects the heroin and John's wife (Tuesday Weld), and rescues John from the American connection, an F.B.I. agent (Anthony Zerbe) who employs two of the most venal co-agents (Richard Masur and Ray Sharkey) imaginable. They are ruthless, cruel, and hideously funny. All of these characters are more energetic and heroic than John. Indeed, John seems inept and indifferent to his fate; he is a depressed main character.

Ray, on the other hand, is energetic, charismatic, and inventive. He is heroic in terms of overcoming the obstacles that endanger John, his wife, and himself. Ray is selfless and, in the end, sacrifices himself in the name of friendship.

Who'll Stop the Rain? positions the main character–secondary character balance directly opposite the position of the classic model. The strategy is to undermine the sense that the main character is privileged. The consequent antiheroics of John may alienate those in the audience who want a hero with whom to identify. But John's position provides a more reflective and realistic self-exploration of the Vietnam–U.S. relationship. Just as John Converse reflects on his feelings about himself, the war, and his future, so too do we. The primacy of the secondary characters in *Who'll Stop the Rain?* prompts the desired conclusion.

■ ■ ■   A Case Study of Main Character as a Witness: *Full Metal Jacket*

Private Joker (Matthew Modine) in *Full Metal Jacket*, written by Stanley Kubrick, Michael Herr, and Gustav Hasford, is as much a witness as he is a main character. The story breaks down into two sections (another innovation of this screen story). The first part is the story of basic training; the second story is about combat in Vietnam, particularly of one patrol in Hue, during the Tet offensive.

In the first story, the Sergeant and Private Lawrence are more important than Private Joker. Joker is the witness to a psychodrama played out between the Sergeant and Private Lawrence. The answer to how far the Sergeant will go to turn his men into killing machines is very clear. He'll go to any lengths— humiliation and destruction. The Sergeant succeeds in his mission as evidenced by the fact that at the end of the movie, Lawrence kills the Sergeant, then kills himself. Private Lawrence and the Sergeant are protagonists and antagonists depending on your point of view. These two secondary characters take over the drama and Private Joker survives as a witness and goes on to combat.

In combat, Joker is a photographer, a visual witness to a battle in which the antagonist is unclear. We never see the enemy, but see the killing. The patrol is whittled down one by one. The men are frustrated, angry, and afraid. Finally, they capture the sniper. She is dying and she is alone. So many have died at the hands of one sniper! Here, again, the members of the patrol, whether animalistic or rational, brave or cowardly, frightened or filled with bravado, are more complex and compelling than Joker.

Joker does survive, as is appropriate for a witness, but the majority of secondary characters, who have faced life and death and found mainly death, have struggled more expressively to surmount the obstacles placed before them.

In *Full Metal Jacket,* it is clear that no one character is privileged. All characters are trying to survive and all are limited by the same parameter—the war. Joker survives, but this outcome is neither heroic nor cathartic.

■ ■ ■ ## A Case Study of Interior Main Character and Exterior Secondary Characters: *Paris, Texas*

Travis (Harry Dean Stanton) is a 1980s poor version of Orson Welles's *Citizen Kane.* A relic from his past provides a key to his current behavior and character. Or does it? Sam Shepard and Wim Wender's *Paris, Texas* is the story of a man who has lost his memory and must reconstruct his life. His brother Walt (Dean Stockwell) and his son, Hunter (Hunter Carson), help. It is not until Travis takes his son on a journey to find the boy's mother, Jane (Natassia Kinski), that we get a true sense of Travis as a man who is incapable of coping with his own shortcomings. His possessiveness has cost him his wife. His self-absorption has robbed him of raising his son. Like Kane, Travis is fixated by the relationship of his parents and the circumstances surrounding his early life in Paris, Texas— where modern cosmopolitanism meets primitive ruralism. His life cannot sustain the clash and he has been among the walking wounded ever since.

In terms of character, Travis is lost, a position that is not conducive to mastery or primacy over other characters. If anything, it is the reverse. The secondary characters seem more rooted (brother and sister-in-law) and more exposed (wife). They are all more vital and engaged than Travis. But in the absence of primacy, Travis does occupy a dramatically more democratic position vis-à-vis the secondary characters. The secondary characters try to help Travis, but his is an interior problem and he has to help himself. For all their externalized actions, the secondary characters do not seem paralyzed by their deeper fears. Each is fearful and alludes to interior lives, but each, including the most poignant, Travis's wife, is able to act in ways unavailable to him. As a result, Travis leaves his son with his mother at the story's end. Travis is alone and seems to realize the rightness of that stance. He has used his son to find his wife, and Travis realizes that though he may need a reconstituted family, his passive character prohibits him from being part of a nuclear family. And so he leaves, alone.

■ ■ ■ ## A Case Study of Role Reversion: *Something Wild*

Charles Driggs (Jeff Daniels), the main character of Max Frye's *Something Wild,* is a closet rebel who happens to be a stockbroker. He is a conventional middle-class main character, and he allows himself to be accosted and then kidnapped by Lulu (Melanie Griffith). The consequent adventure is filled with sadomasochistic dimensions. Lulu ties him up, rapes him (he doesn't object), and eventually calls his boss, while Charles, naked and tied up, has to make excuses for being away from the office for the afternoon. Later, Charles accompanies Lulu to her high school reunion and meets her ex-husband. He almost loses his life in trying to take Lulu away from her husband, a violent, unpredictable psychopath.

Charles is overwhelmed by Lulu, a dynamic, unpredictable woman whose sense of danger stimulates him. In a stereotypical sense, Lulu takes on male behavioral characteristics in Act One while Charles assumes female behavioral characteristics. Because of this blurring, it's difficult to identify Charles with the classic main character (hero). Not until Lulu's ex-husband appears do we have a secondary character who is an antagonist—another requisite for prompting heroic action on the part of the main character.

The degree of role reversion intensifies when Lulu saves Charles from harm at the hands of her ex-husband. It is Lulu who decides whether she will have a relationship with Charles.

To the degree that he has lied to Lulu about himself, Charles is as much a sociopath as she. They are misanthropic and belong together in a relationship based on mutual deception and role reversion.

Charles, Lulu, and her ex-husband are all outsiders. In Charles's case, he has been more repressed about it. While these three are opposed to one another, their characters are quite similar. In this sense, they are different from the classic presentation of secondary characters who represent different sides of the issue faced by the main character. These secondary characters, Lulu and her ex-husband, have a dark side, as does the main character, Charles. The lack of a clear-cut choice—to be an upright citizen, broker, or to be a criminal, saint or sinner—makes the resolution, the death of Lulu's ex-husband, less a climax than a relief from an untenable situation. His death does not resolve the issue of the relationship between Charles and Lulu.

The central question about the balance of main to secondary characters in *Something Wild* is: Has the role reversion subverted the separateness of the main character and is Charles defined enough to be further segregated (for heroic ends) by the active antagonist to qualify him as a classic protagonist? The answer is no. The role reversion has subverted Charles as a classic main character. His shared deception with Lulu has dramatically democratized Charles and Lulu. An argument could be made to consider Lulu the main character; although she isn't the main character, she is too much like Charles to be considered a conventional secondary character either. Only the ex-husband's posture as antagonist works to save Charles's status as a classic protagonist, but it isn't enough. The balance between main and secondary character has been successfully subverted.

Conclusion

In the classic screen structure, there is a particular balance between the main character and the secondary characters. The main character is in the midst of the drama, surrounded by secondary characters who articulate options for him. They may act as catalysts to promote a choice or they may provide examples of the options for the main character. In either case, the main character is implicitly big enough and complex enough to make a choice and because he is implicitly larger than the secondary characters, his actions seem heroic.

What happens to this balance when the secondary characters are more important than the main character? Or when they are equivalent? The result of both cases is a form of dramatic democracy where neither main nor secondary characters appear to be more privileged. The trade-off, between classic main character and the main character who shares the same quandaries and questions as the secondary character, is the loss of the hero. If one character is no more privileged than any other character, heroic action becomes, simply action, and the dramatic struggle of the main character becomes, in one fashion or another, the struggle of each character.

When the main character is no greater an influence than any other character, a variety of options ensue. Clearly, the writer has more freedom in the main character—secondary character balance. Because the classic such mix is formulaic, the democratization of the characters offers more freedom of choice in the relationship of main to secondary characters. The secondary character who is the antagonist is pulled closer to the protagonist. The struggle between them flattens. Perhaps the similarities between protagonist and antagonist are more memorable than the differences. There is a gap in the story that can move the writer to look to the interior struggles of all the characters, rather than to look to the externalized actions that confirm the primacy of the main character. The options are numerous and interesting.

Dramatic democracy allows for identification with the main character, but it robs the viewer of the satisfying catharsis of the classic screen story balance of main to secondary characters. In fact, the viewer may be left uneasy, as at the end of *Full Metal Jacket* or *Something Wild*, or emotionally exhausted, as at the end of *Paris, Texas* or *Who'll Stop the Rain?* This state has clear consequences for the marketability of a screen story as more important writer-directors such as Woody Allen *(Crimes and Misdemeanors)* and Spike Lee *(Do the Right Thing)* opt for this balance between the characters of their stories. The option (different stories, different outcomes, surprise) is a more encouraging one for those writers whose status is less secure. Dramatic democracy yields options that are not available in the classic balance between screen characters.

References

1. Budd Schulberg, *On the Waterfront*, 1954.

10

· · · · · · · ·

Subtext, Action, and Character

Subtext, often associated with the interior dilemma of the character, is more reminiscent of theater than film. However, subtext is an important dimension of good screen stories, and it always relates to character. In order to present a model of screenplay subtext, it is necessary to look at the structure of the screen story.

The structured screen story presents characters at a particular point in their lives, facing a particular problem. This problem is given dimension by the secondary characters, who articulate two options for the main character. The dilemma and character are supported by a story line that provides opportunity for the main character not only to interact with secondary characters, but also to be confronted by events that will help her to make a choice. If the story is properly structured, not only will there be a mounting sense of urgency about making that choice, but there will be major plot points that chart the way for the central character.

So far, the story appears to be all action line. Where does the subtext develop and does it interact with the action line?

Foreground and Background

To explain the subtext-action-character relationship, it is better to revert to other terminology. We will call the action line the foreground story. The foreground story is the plot that embraces people and action outside the character. The background story, which yields the subtext, relates to the main character's interior problem or issue. The central character works out this interior issue through relationships with the secondary characters. A specific example of this foreground-background relationship is found in Jack Soward's *Star Trek: The Wrath of Khan.*

The foreground story is the struggle between Khan and Kirk. Khan, an aberrant genius long exiled on a distant planet, is accidentally discovered by the starship Reliant, which has been on a scouting mission for the Genesis

Project Scientific Station. Khan is only interested in revenge on his nemesis, Kirk. The *Reliant*, now commandeered by Khan, orders Carol Marcus, chief scientist of the Genesis Project, to give up all scientific data. This is a highly irregular procedure, so Carol sends a distress signal to Admiral Kirk, who is on a training mission with Captain Spock of the *Enterprise*. Kirk responds and he and his inexperienced crew take off to the Genesis Station.

A struggle for control of the Genesis Project follows as well as a space duel between Kirk and Khan. To complicate matters, Kirk and Carol were lovers and their child, David, now grown, works with his mother. David is not fond of the father he never knew. Spock, however, is totally unambivalent about Kirk and the fate of the *Reliant*. He sacrifices his life in order to save the crew members of the *Enterprise*. Spock's crypt is sent to its final resting place on the planet created by the Genesis Effect. This action line is the foreground story.

The background story is the interior issue of Admiral Kirk's aging. He no longer has a command but an administrative position; he needs glasses. And he seems to have a fondness for antiques—Dickens, Shakespeare. During the course of the story, Kirk echoes that he feels old. Taking command of the *Enterprise*, the challenge of an old adversary (Khan), and the discovery of his family (Carol and their son David) challenge him. At the end of the film, after the memorial ceremony honoring Spock, Carol asks him how he feels and Kirk answers, "Young. I feel young."

Clearly, the events in the action line can help or subvert this interior issue. In *Star Trek: The Wrath of Khan*, with so many young people playing an important role and with the Genesis Project providing the birth of a planet, the young-old dilemma is given dimension.

The balance of foreground and background is usually this: In Act One both foreground and background stories are introduced; in Act Two the background story is fleshed out; in Act Three the foreground story is prominent and the background story is resolved. The foreground story is action-oriented; let's call it motion-oriented. The background story, on the other hand, is emotion-oriented; it is what the main character feels most deeply about.

In order to highlight the subtext or background story's relationship to character, it is useful to examine, in detail, Billy Wilder and I. A. L. Diamond's *The Apartment*. The foreground story is a tale of corporate advancement in a New York insurance company. C. C. Baxter (Jack Lemmon) is a low-level clerk. He is ambitious and his colleagues give him the means for advancement. Baxter allows first one person, then later four people, to use his apartment for trysts, casual and less casual. Each promises recommendation to the head of personnel, J. J. Sheldrake (Fred MacMurray). When Sheldrake wants to use Baxter's apartment, Baxter's future is secured. At the beginning of Act Two, Baxter is promoted. How far he advances in the company is now totally dependent on Sheldrake.

When Baxter takes care of a little problem for Sheldrake (Sheldrake's girlfriend attempts suicide in Baxter's apartment), the reward is further advancement. When a former girlfriend tells all to Sheldrake's wife, his feigned divorce becomes real and he asks Baxter for the apartment. But Baxter refuses, because by now, he too is involved with Sheldrake's girlfriend. Baxter loses his job and his advancement within the company is over.

The background story is the story of Baxter's interior dilemma—he wants a personal life, but his personal life is always negated by his will to advance. The focus for this personal dilemma is Fran (Shirley MacLaine), an elevator operator Baxter likes. When Baxter gets his first promotion, he asks her out. She agrees, telling him she has to see another man to say goodbye and will then join him in front of the theater. Fran never makes it to the theater. Instead, she gives into the charms of J. J. Sheldrake and goes to Baxter's apartment, leaving a sick C. C. Baxter in front of the theater. She has stood him up and he's hurt, but not discouraged. The opening of Act Two follows Baxter's interest in Fran as well as Fran's relationship with Sheldrake.

In the first half of Act Two, Fran and Sheldrake have a relationship and Baxter's on the outside. Only during his second foray of interest in Fran (at the Christmas party) does Baxter realize she is Sheldrake's girlfriend when she uses a cracked make-up case he had returned to Sheldrake earlier in the story. Sheldrake jokes that women take these flings so seriously. Baxter, realizing the truth about Fran, leaves and gets drunk on Christmas Eve. Meanwhile, Sheldrake and Fran are arguing in Baxter's apartment. She presents him with a Christmas gift; he didn't remember to buy one for her, so he offers her $100 to buy herself a gift. Sheldrake then dashes off for an evening with the family and Fran attempts suicide by taking Baxter's sleeping pills. When Baxter returns, a lovely woman on his arm, he finds Fran and is frightened by her state. With the help of the doctor next door, he revives Fran.

The suicide attempt is the midpoint of Act Two. The balance of the act focuses on Fran's recovery in Baxter's apartment and their developing relationship. She isn't aware of it, but Baxter is. His happiness is brief.

In Act Three, Baxter rehearses his speech for Sheldrake. He will take Fran off his boss's hands, because he loves her. However, when he sees Sheldrake, Sheldrake makes the speech. He tells Baxter that his wife threw him out, so he's planning on getting a divorce and taking up more legitimately with Fran. At this point Baxter faces his moment of truth. He chooses to give up his advancement and walks out on Sheldrake. He'll not be an accomplice to Sheldrake's plan, especially since he loves Fran. He is no longer willing to sacrifice his personal life for advancement.

Baxter's character is critical to the successful interplay of foreground and background. We have to believe that he can be an opportunist or a sensitive idealist. The story has to be structured so it provides scope for both sides of his character. Next, the quality of the secondary characters must allow for the two options—opportunist and idealist—to resonate. Sheldrake and the other insurance company executives are singularly opportunistic; each wears his insensitivity like an oversized badge. Fran and Baxter's doctor-neighbor, however, are idealistic; they are friendly and straightforward. They never manipulate, nor are they cruel. These two characters analyze the world—Fran categorizes people as "takers and those who get took" and the doctor sees those who are a "mensch" (human beings) and those who are not.

The subtext arises from the interplay between the emotion-laden background story and the motion-laden foreground story. The result is layered. How far is C. C. Baxter willing to go to succeed? Besides defining that limit, the subtext also suggests the degree of dehumanization the individual will tolerate to improve his material wellbeing. But is it worth his spiritual wellbeing? In the end, Baxter opts to be a human being and Fran decides to join him. They question their material wellbeing at this moment ("I don't have a job. I don't know where we'll go"), but the issue of spiritual sovereignty is, for these two characters, indisputable. They are whole and they are happy; this is the implication of the background story and the source of satisfaction for the viewer.

In a sense, deeper satisfaction for the viewer devolves from the subtext of the story, rather than from resolution of the plot. The subtext issue is the interior one and thus more deeply associated with the main character. The plot, on the other hand, presents a line of action that is the surface of the story. The foreground story may be quite distant from the interior life of the main character. There are intersecting points of background and foreground, but the foreground story doesn't necessarily offer the viewer the level of involvement available from the subtext.

It is, however, not enough to believe that the character can go in one direction or the other. For subtext to be deeply meaningful to the main character, character and subtext must be integral and interwoven. An example will illustrate how this relationship works.

John Fusco's *Thunderheart* (1992) is the story of an FBI investigation of murder on an Indian reserve in the Dakota Badlands. Roy Levoi (Val Kilmer) is the main character, an FBI agent assigned to look into the struggle between radical and conservative elements on the reserve, a struggle that has led to murder. The foreground story in *Thunderheart* is the investigation and solution of the murder. The background story is the struggle between traditional Indian values and commercial white values. Fusco fuses the main character to this background story by making him half-white, half-Indian.

Those characters who relate to the white values in the story—the older FBI agent (Sam Shepard), who becomes the antagonist, and the conservative Indian elements he works with—definitely appeal to that side of Roy Levoi that wants to be accepted as a white man.

The other group of secondary characters, the Indian side, includes an Indian sheriff, a female Indian teacher, and the Indians' religious leader, all representing older values involved with magic, nature, and history. They represent the past for Roy Levoi and each in turn prods him to admit to his Indianness.

When the crime is solved and Roy learns that his FBI partner pushed another Indian to commit the murder, he is outraged. When the Indian teacher is killed, there is no turning back. He will go against his white partner, risk his life, and demand justice. By the end of the story, Roy Levoi has accepted his Indian side and implicitly devalued his white half.

The subtext or background story—to accept Indian values or white values with their implications for the future, the environment, and the community—is at the center of *Thunderheart*. And because Roy Levoi is half-white, half-Indian that struggle is all the more personal and meaningful.

Screen stories work best when subtext and character fuse as strongly as is the case in *Thunderheart*.

The Balance Between Foreground and Background

Some screen stories, which are plot-intensive, are all foreground. In these stories, the character facilitates the plot and her inner life is ignored. *Ruthless People* and *Fatal Attraction* are two examples of foreground scripts. In *Ruthless People*, the premise that money can't buy love attaches most easily to Bette Midler's character, but she experiences no deeper inner conflict, nor does Danny DeVito's character, who instigates the idea of murdering his wife for her money. What is interesting about *Ruthless People* is the difficulty in determining the identity of the main character and, once that determination is made, how little the main character matters. Contrary to classic screen narrative, the main character's role in *Ruthless People* is incidental.

In *Fatal Attraction*, the premise that one-night stands can be fatal falls best on the shoulders of Michael Douglas's character. But again, there is no interior conflict. Both mistress (Glenn Close) and wife (Anne Archer) are important to the plot, but less critical to the interior life of the Douglas character. His conflict is totally externalized. Noteworthy is the success of both these films. Both are well-structured, compelling screenplays, but they do not have that additional layer, the background story, that involves us in a complex relationship with the main character. Other examples of screen stories that are all foreground include *Blind Date, Risky Business, Ferris Bueller's Day Off,* and *Back to the Future.*

Screen stories that allude to the main character's interior life, but for all intents and purposes are foreground treatments, include *Black Rain, The Accused, Presumed Innocent, Some Kind of Wonderful, Valmont,* and *Ghost.* In these screen stories, the effort at creating an interior conflict for the main character can confuse the viewer. In the cases of *Black Rain, Presumed Innocent,* and *Valmont,* the unfulfilled promise of greater complexity from the character eventually undermines the effectiveness of the foreground story. In *The Accused, Some Kind of Wonderful,* and *Ghost,* the main characters aren't complex; they are young innocents. We don't expect complex inner lives and, consequently, these characterizations don't undermine the foreground stories.

A number of films do, however, try to introduce a modest background story that adds a layer to the story but does not derail the foreground story. These stories are primarily genre stories that are heavily plot-dependent; consequently the effort at a background story is surprising, yet in each case the script is strengthened for the effort.

John Bishop's *The Package* (1989) is the story of a U.S.–Soviet military plot to assassinate Gorbachev and/or the U.S. president and to promote a continuation of the Cold War. The cold warriors hire an assassin, a former covert military man (Tommy Lee Jones). The plot, headed by an army colonel (John Heard), is organized with the help of high military officials on both sides. An army sergeant (Gene Hackman) is used as a dupe for the plot. He is angry and effective and in the end prevents the assassination. He doesn't want to be a victim of a plot he doesn't comprehend but what he knows endangers him and all those close to him.

The Package has an elaborate intelligent plot, but it is the background story that strengthens the film. Quietly, the sergeant's story is about the old-fashioned virtues of military life— camaraderie, loyalty, effectiveness. The alternative represented by the colonel and the assassin represents a military that has become political. The sergeant doesn't want to be political; he simply wants to be a good soldier and in the end he is. But it requires disobedience, unlawful behavior, and individual initiative. His background story struggle affirms the virtues of military life and individual initiative, devoid of politics.

The Package is a thriller, whereas *Striking Distance* (1994) is a police story. In the police story, there is a crime and the plot chronicles the difficulties of the investigation but eventually, the crime is solved and the criminal apprehended. The background story in *Striking Distance* is about family values. Rowdy Herrington and Martin Kaplan have written about a Pittsburgh detective, Thomas Hardy (Bruce Willis), whose testimony indicts his partner and cousin for brutality. The result is that he is shunned by his colleagues on the police force. The consequent suicide of his partner and the death of his father (also a policeman) in a high-speed chase with Hardy at the wheel lead Hardy to leave the force for the River Police, a demotion.

The foreground story concerns the hunt for a sadistic killer of women who were associated with Hardy. Through both phases of his career, in homicide and the River Police, Hardy contends that the killer is a former policeman.

The interesting background story about duty and family is played out effectively, since one of the accused is Hardy's cousin. His father and his uncle are career policemen and clearly Hardy hopes to be a career policeman as well. The problems that divide the family and provide the background story are the roles of his partner and his cousin Joey. Will Joey's father cover up the fact that his son is a criminal? And how should Tom respond to the criminality of his partner and cousin? Duty and family become the subtext and the background story.

Finally we turn to a situation comedy, a genre that is also plot-driven. Gary Ross's *Dave* (1992) is the story of Dave (Kevin Kline), who looks identical to the President of the United States. When the president, a self-serving political ne'er-do-well, has a stroke, Dave is drafted to be his stand-in. Dave himself is decent and generous; even the president's wife notices how different the "president" has become. What will the fate of the nation be at the hands of Dave, a stand-in president? Clearly it's going to be better. Can Dave get away with this positive deception? This is the plot of the film.

The background story of *Dave* relates to the values the presidency should stand for. Should they be the idealistic, positive Capraesque values, or should they be modern, cynical, and self-serving? The background story provides a layer to the mistaken-identity plot of *Dave* and makes it more meaningful to the audience, which is precisely the benefit of a background story. *The Package, Striking Distance,* and *Dave* are foreground-intensive stories strengthened by the modest addition of an effective background story.

■ ■ ■   A Case Study of the Primacy of the Foreground Story: *Music Box*

Joe Eszterhas's *Music Box* is the story of a Hungarian-American accused of war crimes during World War II. If convicted, he will be stripped of his American citizenship. The majority of the story takes place in Chicago and pivots around the hearing during which Michael Lazlo (Armin Mueller-Stahl) is accused of lying on his American immigration application. He is specifically accused of being a Hungarian policeman who cruelly aided and abetted the deportations of Jews from Budapest in 1944. To the end of the film, he denies his complicity.

We enter the story through the eyes of his daughter, Ann Talbot, an attorney played by Jessica Lange. Lazlo asks her to defend him in the hearing. Reluctantly, Ann complies and, in her efforts to defend her father, learns more than she ever wanted to know. Whether she is prepared to deal with his past is her personal dilemma (the background story).

The presentation of the story is very straightforward. In the foreground, father and daughter are introduced. We see that Ann Talbot is a successful, aggressive lawyer and a good daughter. Then her father is accused of war crimes. He invites his daughter to join him when he goes to see the immigration people. She agrees, already defensive about her father (the background story is introduced), and he asks her to defend him. Other characters are introduced—her son, her ex-husband, her ex-father-in-law, the prosecuting lawyer, and her female assistant. The investigation begins, followed by the hearing that includes a number of witnesses, survivors of the Holocaust, principally women. The hearing concludes in Budapest.

Throughout the story, Ann learns more facts that challenge her view of her father (the background story). Ann continues to function as a good lawyer, in spite of the credibility of the eyewitnesses. However, when her assistant turns up information about her father's finances, she begins to learn about his past associates. Finally, she pieces together the truth. Having gotten her father acquitted (the resolution of the foreground story), she is faced with a personal dilemma—to allow the acquittal to stand or to reveal what she has learned about her father. This is the moment of truth and the moment of resolution of the background story. Family solidarity or moral justice, which should she choose? As his daughter, her choice is that much more difficult to make, but in the end she turns against her father.

The foreground story in *Music Box* is elaborate and well-plotted. The impact of the foreground story resolution is strengthened by the background story. The daughter's inner life—her view of herself as a daughter, and the solidarity and strength that come from being a member of this immigrant family—is challenged by the choice she has to make.

In *Music Box*, the foreground story is dominant, but the existence of the background story strengthens the screen story and results in a greater emotional resonance of foreground and background.

■ ■ ■   A Case Study of Subversion of the Foreground Story: *Homicide*

Homicide (1992), written by David Mamet, is on one level a classic police story. Police stories tend to be plot-intensive—crime, investigation, apprehension. The story ends when the policeman or detective finds, takes into custody, or kills the bank robber or serial killer who has been the center of the investigation.

David Mamet, as mentioned earlier, is very taken up with the confused identity of his main character, Detective Gold. Can one be a policeman and a Jew? This is at the heart of the background story. Mamet builds up the background story as if it is another plot—the murder of an elderly Jewish storekeeper and the subsequent investigation. Nevertheless, its resolution is not at all clear in the way the foreground story resolves. Indeed, the background story with its overlay of Jewish terrorists and a neo-Nazi organization and the effort to get Gold (Joe Montegna) involved, all but makes us forget about the foreground story. Gold suffers losses (his partner, his own well-being) in expediting the foreground plot (the apprehension of a drug dealer-killer). Nevertheless, his confusion about his own Jewishness seems to supersede all other elements of the story. At the end, Gold is lost because he doesn't know who he is. The background story has posed a problem for him and his failure to find an answer subverts resolution of the background story and makes us all but dismiss the plot, its resolution, and its importance in the narrative.

■ ■ ■ A Case Study of Moving Toward a Greater Background Story: *Q & A*

In certain genres the viewer expects a strong plot in which foreground has primacy background. This is particularly true in gangster films; *Scarface* is a good example and *The Godfather* is exceptional in its attempt to balance the foreground and background stories. However, *Q & A*, written by Sidney Lumet, turns our expectations of the genre upside down. In *Q & A*, the background story is more prominent and important than the foreground story.

The foreground story of *Q & A* is the investigation by the District Attorney's office of a killing. Policeman Mike Brennan (Nick Nolte) has shot and killed a Puerto Rican drug dealer in what he claims is self-defense. The investigation is commissioned by Quinn (Patrick O'Neal), head of the DA's office, who assigns O'Reilly, a recent law school graduate, to the case. O'Reilly (Timothy Hutton), who has just joined the office, was a policeman and is the son of a policeman. This will be his first case.

The foreground story follows O'Reilly's investigation. He is assigned two police detectives to assist in what appears to be a straightforward investigation. But the investigation doesn't prove to be so straightforward.

The dead man's boss, Bobby (Armand Assante), suggests that Brennan killed not in self-defense but in cold blood. The story is further complicated by the fact that Bobby's wife is a woman O'Reilly used to live with and who suddenly left him. Other complications are the loyalties that develop along lines of race, color, and culture. The case becomes even more complicated when the Mafia becomes involved. Finally, Brennan starts killing witnesses, and the Q & A develops into an effort to stop the killings and to understand why they are occurring. In the end, Brennan and Quinn are implicated in the killings. The simple case of defensible homicide has become more complex; indeed, the extent of the killing defies rational explanation.

This foreground story provides the action line for a story that is more interior than it first appears. The background story that gradually unfolds is a story of prejudice and the hatred born of that prejudice. *Q & A* is populated by five groups—Puerto Ricans, Irish, Blacks, Jews, and Italians. Each group is very loyal to its own members. Positioning O'Reilly, the main character, against Brennan, one of his own, immediately forces the main character to make a choice—be true to his own at all costs or go against his own. This is how his options are put to him by Brennan and Quinn.

However, this particular conflict isn't as strong as the reason why Bobby's wife Nancy left O'Reilly the night she first introduced him to her father. She had never told him, nor could he have guessed from her appearance, that her father was black. She saw his prejudice at that moment and she left him. Seeing her again, O'Reilly is faced with his own prejudice.

The central conflict for the main character is whether he can look beyond race and color to the person and situation, or whether he will remain prejudiced. The background story is rife with prejudice. Every group expresses hatred toward the other four groups and their hatred is evidenced in language and action. Simultaneously, the pressure within each group is to support the other members of the group, even if one member of that group is a criminal and another is a cop.

Other cultures are present as well—the police culture, the criminal culture, and the transsexual culture. In each case, group solidarity and opposition to other groups is not just registered, it is demanded by members of the group.

Because of the dilemma faced by the main character, the story becomes not so much the story of a criminal investigation (foreground), as it is a study of a system choking on prejudice and hate (background). Can the individual maintain his nationality, his humanity, and his morality in such a system? There are no easy answers from Lumet and, as a result, the screen story ends by posing more questions than it answers. But it does stir many emotions, principally because the background story is so powerful. In contrast, the outcome of the foreground story, the death of Brennan, is neither satisfying nor cathartic because the background story has displaced it in relative importance.

■ ■ ■   Case Studies of the Writer Elevating the Background Story: *The Fabulous Baker Boys* and *Flesh and Bone*

Steve Kloves has written two films, *The Fabulous Baker Boys* (1989) and *Flesh and Bone* (1994), where the interior life of the main character dominates the narrative. In the first film, a musician (Jeff Bridges) is a passive relative to his brother and partner. Their musical career is flagging. When the business-minded brother decides to hire a female singer, their career improves. Two problems arise: The passive brother is an inveterate womanizer who falls for the woman (Michelle Pfeiffer), and his career is a creative dead end. He does not have the self-confidence to pursue the jazz career he desires. When the story ends, he has broken off with his brother, the singer leaves him, and he may or may not pursue jazz.

In *Flesh and Bone*, a son (Dennis Quaid) has a murky past. As a boy he helped his father (James Caan) burglarize farms in Texas. The story opens with a burglary gone wrong. The result is the killing of three of the farm occupants; only a baby girl lives.

Twenty years later the boy, now a man, is a small businessman in Texas. He keeps to himself. A woman enters his life (Meg Ryan) and later we discover she is the young baby who survived the killing. His father comes back, too, and when he finds out about the girl's past, he wants to kill her. In spite of his love for the girl, the son struggles with what he should do. In the end, he rescues her and kills his father. Whether he will take up with her and be happy is left unsaid.

Steve Kloves has chosen two main characters who are extremely interior— one might almost call them wounded—and placed them in stories with very little narrative. Each background story has to do with individual vs. family obligation. How much should the individual give up on behalf of family— creative aspiration, ethical consideration, happiness? It's as if neither main character can be truly happy, and the background stories in each film provide one last chance at happiness. The attitude of these films is *film noir* but the form is melodrama with the parent/brother standing in as the power and the son/brother standing in as the transgressor.

In both *The Fabulous Baker Boys* and *Flesh and Bone*, Kloves elevates the background story over the foreground, and the result is a unique choice for character over plot at a time when plot over character dominates commercial screenwriting.

■ ■ ■   ## A Case Study of the Background Story: *Moonstruck*

John Patrick Shanley's *Moonstruck* is a good example of a background screen story. In the foreground, Loretta (Cher) is a mid-30s Italian-American who is about to marry for the second time. She agrees to marriage in spite of her lack of passion for her husband-to-be (Danny Aiello). He asks her to invite his estranged brother (Nicholas Cage) to the wedding, as he is flying to Sicily to tend to his dying mother. Loretta falls in love with the brother and passion reawakens. While everyone around her is looking for passion, Loretta finds it and keeps it.

The background story focuses on the pivotal search for passion by Loretta. Her father, her mother, her aunt and uncle, an unknown New York University professor, all seek the same state—to be moonstruck. Loretta achieves this stage by moving from a passionless relationship with one brother (Aiello) to a totally passionate relationship with the other (Cage). It is Cage, with his focus on opera (intense passion) and extreme emotions (love for Loretta and hate for his brother), who is her primary catalyst.

Shanley is much more interested in exploring the state of being moonstruck (the background issue), than he is in weaving an elaborate plot. Consequently, we have a very simple foreground story and a consistent meditation among each of the characters on the moonstruck issue of the background story.

What is surprising about the story is the amount of feeling it generates, due to the appeal of the fairy-tale-like background story. Shanley wishes everyone could experience being moonstruck. It is interesting that director Norman Jewison has chosen *That's Amore*, performed by Dean Martin, as the theme song. Could he be more direct about the background story?

We have other screen stories, like *Moonstruck,* Sam Shepard's *Fool For Love,* and David Mamet's *Things Change,* in which background story not only dominates the film, but the interior lives of all the characters are more important than their actions. Noteworthy is the fact that all three films are written by playwrights. Indeed, Shanley, Shepard, and Mamet are probably three of the most interesting screenwriters of the '80s. We can look at the screen work of other playwrights—Paddy Chayefsky *(The Hospital, Network),* Peter Shaffer *(Amadeus),* and Herb Gardner *(A Thousand Clowns)*—and note that, in all cases, the background story is more important in their respective works.

As might be expected, stories with little foreground are accused of having no action and stories that are all foreground are accused of having no character. The type of story that balances foreground and background offers the opportunity for action and character. Harnessing that interplay, however, poses a very particular problem for the writer.

"The Moment" and Subtext

To set up action and character, particularly character with an interior dilemma, requires a strategy that we call *the moment.* The moment is the point at which we join the screen story. Needless to say, there are thousands of points at which we can join a story or enter a character's life. The moment we refer to, however, is the point that launches us into the story in a gripping fashion.

For example, we join *The Apartment* at the moment when C. C. Baxter has so overcommitted his apartment that he is crowded out and has to sleep on a park bench instead of in his bed. Clearly, the use of the apartment by corporate executives is out of hand. Does he want a personal life or not? In *Moonstruck,* we join the story at the point Loretta receives a marriage proposal. The engagement sets into motion the events that follow and illustrates the lovelessness in Loretta's life. The moment in *Something Wild* is the point when Charles meets Lulu. She has accused him of stealing and he is already on the defensive. The moment in *Mystic Pizza* is Jo's wedding. She faints and the wedding is called off. The rest of the story has to do with three young women and their quest for either marriage or independence.

The moment, then, can be called the critical moment, for in each case mentioned, the moment presents the character in a crisis—a marriage and engagement about which the characters are uncertain or a tactic for corporate advancement that has presented a housing crisis. The moment is a critical event as well for the main character. It highlights the nature of her dilemma and places the viewer right in the middle of the quandary.

It is important to note that no background or insight into the main character is necessary to interpret the problem. We may not fully understand, yet, why the main character behaves as she does, but we soon will. The problem is also presented in conflicting terms and a resolution is apparent. We have a sense of how the story could end. Will Baxter opt for a personal life? Will Loretta be happy when she marries Jerry? Will Jo ever marry? In each case, the answer is yes or no. When the question posed during the moment is answered, the screen story is over.

The moment, then, is critical in that it positions a main character in an untenable situation, given her interior life. The character's preferences become clear as the story unfolds, but the moment is used to intensify her tension and, consequently, quickly to involve us in the screen story.

■ ■ ■ A Case Study of "The Moment": *My Beautiful Laundrette*

My Beautiful Laundrette Kureishi, is about Omar (Roshan Seth), who lives in England and thinks of himself as a Briton, although the British think of him as a Pakistani. He is both and neither. The story begins (the moment) when Omar tells his father he doesn't want to continue in school and he will go to work for his father's brother, Nasser. His father thinks Nasser is a barbarian. Nasser puts Omar to work in a car wash. But Omar has plans; he wants to be a businessman on his own. He talks Nasser into allowing him to take over one of his laundrettes. This laundrette, located in a poor neighborhood, is destined for failure. But Omar has a strategy. He brings on Johnny who is a local citizen, and a former classmate and lover, to enforce and to help. Johnny's fellow thugs feel that one of their own has betrayed them and gone over to the enemy. It is only a matter of time until the laundrette is subverted by the new colonialism—the Pakistanis as imperialists and the Brits as the new natives.

Who is the colonized and who is the colonizer is very much at the heart of Kureishi's screen story. The plot line, a young man's embrace of capitalism and its swift kick back, isn't very revealing or gripping. The background story, however, of Pakistani vs. Briton, is a critical internal issue not only for Omar, but for all the other characters as well. Everyone, including Nasser and Johnny, deliberates on their identity. Nasser challenges his marriage by keeping a British mistress; Johnny challenges his friends by taking a Pakistani employer and lover. All three characters—Omar, Nasser, and Johnny—challenge the status quo and suffer for it in varying degrees. Nasser loses his mistress, Johnny loses his friends, and Omar loses his laundrette. But in the end, Omar and Johnny have one another; they are two outsiders taking solace from one another.

The moment unfolds two options—Omar will either succeed or fail. When one outcome occurs, the screen story is over.

Although the screen story becomes somewhat more layered, the story ends with Omar's failure as a Brit. However, his British identity is replaced by another identity—his homosexuality—thereby leaving Omar as Pakistani but capable of a loving relationship with a Brit. The resolution is not a failure for the main character, but is a new, different, and more complex identity. The outcome was considerably more positive than anticipated.

The vitality of *My Beautiful Laundrette* derives from the inner lives of these characters (the background story). The use of the moment helps to involve us at a critical point, particularly in the life of Omar. The result is a screen story with considerable subtext.

The purpose served by the moment is to propel the story toward conflict and dramatic action. The character's actions pit him against prevailing expectations and situate him in both the foreground and background stories. The objective is to begin the character-intensive story in a compelling manner. Characters, as they are introduced, present the issue in a surprising fashion. The result is that the background story is fleshed out fully, while the foreground story is no more than a continuing device.

Conclusion

Screen stories can exist without subtext, but if the scriptwriter wants to tell a story that involves the inner life of the main character, the story must have subtext. To illuminate the subtext, the foreground story (the action line) must interweave with a background story. The degree of subtext is influenced by genre and by the writer's disposition toward action or character. It should be clear to the scriptwriter that subtext evolves in tandem with character and she should look for events that define character. If external events involve relationships, a subtext beyond plot is an option. The result can be a more emotionally satisfying experience for the viewer.

References

1. I. A. L. Diamond and Billy Wilder, *The Apartment*, screenplay, reprinted in *Film Scripts Three*, George P. Garrett, O. B. Hardison, Jr., Jane R. Gelfman, eds. (New York: Irvington Publishers, Inc., 1989).

11

....

The Primacy of Character Over Action: The Non-American Screenplay

Part of the mission of this book is to contextualize screenwriting as a form of storytelling related to and growing out of early forms of storytelling. Another goal is to challenge the myth that a single formula or form or structure is sufficient in writing a good screenplay. In this chapter we challenge another myth—that European and Asian films are a different type of screenplay and that what we have implicitly ascribed so far in this book is only applicable to American screenplays.

It is not our goal to throw down the gauntlet on this issue but to bring some clarity to the discussion of the non-American screenplay and to understand how it is similar as well as different from the American screenplay. In order to do so, however, it is critical to put forward the rationale for this chapter.

The Rationale

The contentious issues about non-American screenplays vs. American screenplays are best characterized by the following five statements:

1. That European and Asian films are sufficiently different from American films to be considered a distinct form of storytelling. The observation is often made that European film is high culture and American film is pop culture. Another characterization is to see European and Asian films as cultural and to see American films as entertainment.

2. That ideas about screenwriting, particularly those developed in the U.S. in the past fifteen years, are not applicable to European and Asian films.

3. That both European and American films are forms of storytelling with more similarities than differences.

4. That where differences exist they are principally cultural and could be described as preferences among storytelling strategies rather than different forms of storytelling.

5. That the international dominance of American films in the last fifteen years can be attributed to a preference for action-oriented, foreground or plot-driven screen stories over background or character-driven screen stories.

By looking at European screen stories and by using case-study comparisons we will explore these five propositions to arrive at our assessment of how wide the difference is between the American and the non-American screen story.

Classical European and Asian Films

Across the breadth of classical European and Asian storytelling, the literary quality of the work stands out, whether the film under consideration is a Tagore adaptation by Sajajit Ray or Jean Renoir's rendering of Emile Zola. Indeed if we look at such writers as Dostoyevsky, we can readily find French, Japanese, and American adaptations of their work. And if we look at a popular American writer like Ed McBain, we can find Japanese as well as American adaptations.

Our point here is that whether looking at an American version, a French version, a Russian version, or a Japanese version, the literary qualities, the storytelling virtues that made the original endure, transcend national boundaries. They are great stories and in many cases have become fine film stories. To explore this notion of a close, literary cross-national boundary to classical stories, we need only look more closely at a number of great non-American writer-directors.

Beginning with Ingmar Bergman, we can discern certain storytelling characteristics to his work. Bergman has a propensity for domestic melodrama and moralistic fables, in essence life lessons. His style is very reminiscent of theater, in which he also works—his stories often have a dialogue-intensive quality. Referred to more than once as the spiritual descendant of Strindberg, Bergman is easily identified in the mainstream of storytelling. Like all the great storytellers, however, his passion and insight into human behavior is vivid and universal.

Federico Fellini, at least in the first part of his career, shared many of the same storytelling qualities of Bergman. Working most often with co-writers Tullio Pinella and Ennio Flaiano, Fellini was also influenced by theater, principally Pirandello. His screen stories can be viewed as an exploration of particular character types—the fool, the clown, the brute, the cynic—and through the character's relationships he attempts to explore the comedy and tragedy of everyday lives. His artistic point of view is unique but as a storyteller, Fellini, too, is part of the larger tradition of storytelling.

We can draw similar comparisons between Luchino Visconti and Leo Tolstoy, between Francois Truffaut and the great early French filmic storyteller Jean Vigo. And we can look at the relationship from another perspective—how such literary figures as novelists and playwrights have been the screenwriters of many of the most famous European films. Jacques Prevert, for example, wrote Marcel Carne's famous *Children of Paradise* (1944). Charles Spaak, working with Renoir, was responsible for *Grande Illusion* (1937) in the way Raymond Chandler later worked with Billy Wilder on *Double Indemnity* (1944). How would the later career of Luis Buñuel have differed without the storytelling skills of Jean-Claude Carrière? Would Volker Schlondorff have been as successful without the script collaboration of his wife, Margerethe Von Trotta? And what would Howard Hawks's *film noir* classics have been like without the novelist Leigh Brackett? Whether American or European, the classic filmmakers have aligned themselves with the best writers possible. And their great work stands out internationally in the transnational tradition of storytelling.

Perhaps no filmmaker has been as international in his work as Akira Kurosawa. As a writer-director, Kurosawa has adapted at least two Shakespearean plays: *Macbeth* became *Throne of Blood* (1957) and *King Lear* became *Ran* (1985). He also adapted Dostoyevsky's *The Idiot* (1957) and Gorky's *The Lower Depths* (1957). Kurosawa has also written original work and adapted the work of Japanese writer Ryonosuke Akutagawa's *Rashomon* (1950).

To restate, classic European and Japanese screen stories tend to be part of the broader panorama of storytelling. In this sense, the international fame of Bergman, Fellini, and Kurosawa is far easier to understand.

Exceptions

Although we could apply three-act structure, main character–secondary character, foreground-background strategies to classical European and Asian films and determine that there are more similarities than differences, there are exceptions. As with the examples of much of Spike Lee's work in the feature film and of Su Friedrich's work in experimental narrative, there are filmmakers who disregard three-act structure for two-act structure and who seek another vehicle for their voice than the main character.

Those filmmaker-writers such as Alain Resnais, Michelangelo Antonioni and Jean-Luc Godard attempt to tell their stories in unique ways. Some, like Godard and Buñuel, use the conventions of storytelling as their basis, although they subvert its methodology as much as they use it. Others, like Antonioni, subvert our notions about character and plot. Still others, like Eric Roehmer and Jacques Rivette, will challenge a single narrative strategy and focus on how dialogue subverts the visual action (or vice versa). Another approach, used by Rainer Werner Fassbinder in melodrama and Werner Herzog in the adventure films *Aguirre: The Wrath of God* (1973) and *Fitzcarraldo* (1982), is to subvert the form of the genre itself.

At the heart of these exceptions is an exploratory narrative intention—with structure in the case of Resnais (*Muriel*, 1963) and Antonioni (*L'Eclisse* or *Eclipse*, 1962), with irony as applied to structure and character in the case of Buñuel (*The Discreet Charm of the Bourgeoisie*, 1972) and Godard (*Weekend*, 1967), with character identification in the case of Nagisa Oshima (*In the Realm of the Senses*, 1976) and Alexander Jodorowsky (*El Topo*, 1971).

This impulse to experiment, to find interior stories, to contradict convention, is not exclusive to non-American film. It can be found also in much experimental American work.

European and Asian Experiments in Foreground Stories

In spite of the superficial impression that European and Asian films are principally character-driven, there have been many efforts in non-American films at foreground or plot-driven stories. A number of important writers and directors have tried their hand at foreground stories. Francois Truffaut made a thriller, *The Bride Wore Black* (1968); Akira Kurosawa made a gangster film, *High and Low* (1962) as well as two films later made into classic Westerns, *The Seven Samurai* (1954), (remade in 1960 as *The Magnificent Seven*) and *Yojimbo* (1961), (remade in 1964 as *A Fistful of Dollars*.) Philippe de Broca made the adventure film *That Man from Rio* (1964) and Luc Besson has even mixed genres in the thriller–police story *La Femme Nikita* (1990). Bo Widerberg made a straightforward police story, called *Man on the Roof* (1977). Well-known writers such as Jean-Claude Carrière have written gangster films such as *Borsalino* (1970). In fact, American genre films have been a mainstay in national European cinemas—the Western in Germany, the gangster film in Italy, and the situation comedy in France, all genres principally with foreground stories.

The point to remember here is that the foreground story hasn't been the exclusive domain of American writers nor has background storytelling been the exclusive domain of non-American screenwriters and filmmakers.

The Success of Old-Fashioned Storytelling: The Australian Case

Few countries have been as successful at exporting film talent and capturing international attention as Australia and New Zealand. Directors now working internationally include Phillip Noyce, *Clear and Present Danger* (1994); Bruce Beresford, *Driving Miss Daisy* (1989); Fred Schepisi, *Six Degrees of Separation* (1993); Peter Weir, *Witness* (1985); George Miller, *Lorenzo's Oil* (1992); Roger Donaldson, *No Way Out* (1987); and Jane Campion, *The Piano* (1993).

From 1974 to 1994, the outpouring of fascinating narratives from Miller's *Mad Max 2: The Road Warrior* (1981), to Fred Schepisi's *The Chant of Jimmy Blacksmith* (1978) to Vincent Ward's *The Navigator: A Medieval Odyssey* (1988), and Campion's *Angel at My Table* (1990) has been remarkable.

It is our contention that the success of these non-American films as a whole is due to the storytelling skills exhibited. In a sense these films and this movement represent storytelling at its old-fashioned best.

The virtues of storytelling can be grouped in three areas—character, structure, and voice. In all of these areas, the Australian and New Zealand films have shared a vision that is striking.

Three lieutenants are accused of murder during the Boer War in Beresford's *Breaker Morant* (1979). The drama is enhanced by the severity of the charges and by the fact that the men are Australians fighting as part of the British forces in South Africa. This tension between British politics and Australian principle and sacrifice are also explored in *Gallipoli* (1981). The subject is played for adventure in *The Lighthorsemen* (1987), but more often British wars and the Australian role in them provide a layer of drama that strengthens the viewer's sense of the characters. Not only do they have the Germans or Boers to contend with, they also have the British! The resulting drama makes for a heroic sense of character, and the Australian main character is individualistic and strong-willed but generous, certainly appealing. The same sense of character infuses the female protagonists in *The Piano* (1993) and *My Brilliant Career* (1979). Australian main characters in these films are goal-directed, willful, and energetic. In short, they are appealing.

Background stories such as *The Piano* exhibit in their structure, a boldness of character polarities as much as the plot development of foreground story does in *The Chant of Jimmy Blacksmith* (1978). *Breaker Morant* moves between past (the events) and the present (the trial) of the three soldiers in a dynamic and urgent manner. Few foreground stories unfold as boldly as the adventure form does in *Mad Max 2: The Road Warrior.* As with character, there is a confident utilization of classical dramatic structure in these films. Attention is paid to joining the story at a useful critical moment.

Finally, these films have a tone that marks them as unique. Beginning with a respect for genre, writer-directors such as George Miller bring an over-the-top zeal to making *Mad Max 2: The Road Warrior,* an adventure story to top all other adventure stories, and Jane Campion brings a poetic, complex feminism to the melodrama in all of her work, especially *The Piano.* Whether the racial rage in *The Chant of Jimmy Blacksmith* is due to Thomas Kenneally's original novel or to Fred Schepisi's passion, there is a definite point of view that drives the narrative.

Other countries deal with such issues as racism using irony and metaphor; not so the Australians. They have a directness that makes the narrative credible. Tone, structure, and character are all used in the old-fashioned or classic sense to tell familiar tales that are retold in such a way that we don't forget them. This immediacy, passion, and storytelling strength explains the success of the Australian and New Zealand films. It also explains why so many veterans of that movement are now prominent Hollywood filmmakers.

Success of Personal Storytelling: German, French, and Hungarian Examples

The reputation of European and Asian films rests on the intimate storytelling identities of filmmakers such as Bergman, Fellini, Renoir, Mizoguchi, Ozu, and Ray. This tradition, call it personal vision, is so marked that in the minds of many in the audience, and many others in the business of film art and its expression, European and Asian filmmaking is associated with personal filmmaking.

This reputation is the context in which to consider a number of current European writer-directors, who are very much in the mold of the personal tradition. Although many of the German filmmakers are essentially genre filmmakers (Fassbinder: melodrama; Wenders: the road sub-genre of melodrama), there are also writer-directors such as Werner Herzog, who falls into the category of personal filmmaking. The result from a narrative perspective is that Herzog is likely to make an adventure film with considerable background story (*Aguirre: The Wrath of God,* 1973) and melodramas with considerable plot (*The Enigma of Kaspar Hauser,* 1974). In this sense, Herzog follows a different artistic tradition, that of breaking the rules, challenging the conventions, and creating an artful alternative.

Like Herzog in Germany, Louis Malle and Eric Rohmer in France push the classic parameters of storytelling. In *Lacombe, Lucien* (1974), Malle is as interested in the negative main character as he is in *Le Feu Follet* (*The Fire Within*, 1963). In *Atlantic City* (1980), he challenges the story form and produces a gangster film with considerable background story and a motif twist when the gangster not only survives but thrives. In *Murmur of the Heart* (1971), he challenges the conventional melodrama resolution and in *Au Revoir les Enfants* (1987), he challenges the narrative tone of the classic war film. Malle makes his films his own by challenging narrative convention.

A similar pattern characterizes the moral tales of Eric Rohmer. In both *Claire's Knee* (1971) or *Summer* (1986), Rohmer uses irony to probe the behavior of his characters in a series of melodramas he calls his moral tales. Whether the issue is sexuality or the permanence of relationships, Rohmer uses irony of structure, character, and dialogue to probe the behavior of his characters. More difficult to identify with, his characters nevertheless have enough determination to keep us curious about whether they will succeed or fail.

Finally, in Hungary, Istvan Szabo has maintained a singularly personal view of life. As with Rohmer, there is an irony in Szabo's approach to character. In *Father* (1966), the concern is personal relations in a Communist period; in *Mephisto* (1981), his concern is personal relations in the Fascist period; in *Colonel Redl* (1985), his concern is personal relations in an anti-Semitic period; and in his English-language film *Meeting Venus* (1991), his concern is personal relations in an artistic period. Szabo, as you can assume, is always fascinated by the irony of human behavior, in the will to survive no matter what, and in the will to find love, no matter what. His is an ironic approach to narrative but as with his spiritual mentor, Luchino Visconti, Szabo is capable of great feeling and empathy. In both cases he follows his own personal direction in the tradition so well identified with Bergman and Fellini.

▪ ▪ ▪ A Case Study of Classic Storytelling: Kusterica's *Time of the Gypsies*

Emir Kusturica and Bohdan Mihic have written a classic melodrama in *Time of the Gypsies* (1989). The interesting notion about exploring the film is to see where it is different from and where it is similar to North American screen melodrama. In scale, *Time of the Gypsies* is more comparable to the great novelists Dickens, Tolstoy and Dreiser. A young boy, Pheran, is brought up by his grandmother. He wears thick glasses and looks sickly. His mother died giving birth to his physically disabled sister. Only a vagrant uncle provides a perspective on the gypsy adult male and family life. The story follows Pheran through his youthful romanticism to his adult paranoia. He joins a local gypsy criminal as he travels to Italy to make money. En route they drop off his sister for medical treatment. Pheran leaves the girl whom he loves in the village. Her family totally rejects him.

Later, prosperous, he returns and marries her. When he discovers she is pregnant, he does not believe it is his child. His wife dies in childbirth. He also discovers that he has been deceived by his criminal patron. His sister was never medically treated but used instead as a beggar on the streets of Rome. He sends his sister and his son back home and seeks out his former patron. He kills him and then he himself is killed. At Pheran's funeral, his son, now 4, steals the gold coins that cover Pheran's eyes.

This brief synopsis cannot do justice to the richness of the narrative of *Time of the Gypsies*. The detailing of the script creates a sense of the gypsy subculture and of the male character Pheran, who starts out optimistically but is doomed. He is doomed because he cannot accept his wife as faithful and as the mother of his child. This paranoia seems endemic among the men, who change wives as readily as North Americans change jobs. But there is another unique quality to Pheran and to his culture—he not only is superstitious, he believes in superstition. Consequently, in his world the will, divining, and magic all play an active part. As a result, the gypsies' world is religious but also animistic.

As with classic melodrama, there are characters, principally women, who help Pheran, and there are characters, mainly men, who oppose him. The power structure that Pheran tries to challenge is the economic power structure of his village. The criminal is on top with most of the villagers eking out a living. Only by establishing his base in Italy, that is, outside Yugoslavia, can the criminal enjoy prosperity. When Pheran attempts to join this power structure, the poison of deception infiltrates his ideology and he believes he has been deceived by his wife. He has been deceived by his patron but not his wife. Once he has crossed over to the model of his patron, Pheran is doomed.

As in classic melodrama, *Time of the Gypsies* has a strong background story. How it differs is in two areas—its plot is a far more elaborate plot than is usually found in melodrama, and it spends a great deal of Act I acclimatizing us to the gypsy culture before it introduces the main character. This latter decision may not be so much cultural as necessary, given the importance of gypsy culture to the story and the lack of audience knowledge about it.

In tone, the film shares the irony so often used in Central Europe. Consequently, humor plays a very important part in drawing us into what is essentially a tragic melodrama. Even after the death of Pheran, Kusturica uses humor in the last scenes—the stealing of the gold coins and the hasty leavetaking of Pheran's uncle.

Summing up, *Time of the Gypsies* is a classic melodrama with modifications in tone and in the pace of the story, particularly in Act I.

■ ■ ■   ## A Case Study of Ironic Structure: *The Double Life of Veronique*

As with so many other Central European directors and writers, Krzysztof Kieslowski and Krzysztof Piesiewicz have deployed an ironic structure to explore the life of a contemporary young woman. Far more subtle in irony than either Kusturica or Szabo, Kieslowski and Piesiewicz sidestep the political possibilities for the psychological.

The Double Life of Veronique (1991) is about two young women, Veronique in France and Veronica in Poland. Both were born at the same time and grew up to look alike but do not know each other, at least not consciously. Veronica is a musician, a gifted singer who dies in the midst of a performance. At that moment, Veronique is making love and suddenly feels a sense of loss. She also gives up her voice lessons, without understanding or explanation. The story that ensues is about Veronique falling in love with a man who is a puppeteer and writer. She seems to know what he will do to reach out to her, even though she has only seen him once at a school performance for children. As the relationship develops, Veronique is aware of a level of knowing, of consciousness that anticipates emotion and events. It's as if a link to Veronica remains and that her need for this relationship relates to the loss of the other, Veronique. Near the end, the puppeteer finds a picture he believes to be of Veronique from her visit to Cracow. But it is not her. Finally a conscious acknowledgment of the other, Veronica. The writers connect the two women beyond appearances. Each is very close to her father. Each lost her mother at a young age. And each has a musical talent.

In terms of the structure, the notion of having a dramatic double invites the character and the viewer to reflect on the character. The double is the distancing device. The question in *The Double Life of Veronique* is, irony to what purpose? The young woman is lively, beautiful, appealing, an example of a positive life force. And yet the double, Veronica, dies suddenly in Cracow. It's as if Kieslowski and Piesiewicz are exploring the loss, the fear of loss, and inevitably the fear of dying through a young, attractive woman. By giving her a double, the writers explore the dialectic between living and dying and in the course of doing so comment upon the quality of life. For Veronique to live means to love and to remember, to remember the other, Veronica, who represents the cumulative losses in life.

Another reading of the structure is to view the other as a way of controlling events. When Veronique knows what will happen via the other, Veronica, she can anticipate and protect herself. This more cautious view of living is reflected in the puppeteer as well—he makes puppets of Veronique and Veronica but tells Veronique that he uses the double only if injury or destruction occurs to the first during a performance. The artist, in this case, the puppeteer and writer, is as cautious as Veronique.

The Double Life of Veronique provides but one example of ironic structure, for Kieslowski's work is often ironic in its structure. *White* (1994) and *A Short Film About Love* (1986) are more powerful for their use of ironic structure, but again, Kieslowski uses it in a more delicate and subtle manner than many of the other Central European writers and directors.

■ ■ ■   ## A Case Study in Foreground-Background Variation: *Ghost* and *Truly Madly Deeply*

Comparing American and non-American treatments of the same subject yields other insights into the mix of narrative strategies. Ghost (1990), written by Bruce Joel Rubin, and *Truly Madly Deeply* (1991), by Anthony Minghella, are both stories of relationships where the man dies unexpectedly. A major part of the story is how the woman copes with the loss. In both stories the supernatural is invoked and the dead male plays a significant role; the relationship continues in spite of death.

In *Ghost*, a man (Patrick Swayze) is killed in a robbery. Unsatisfied with his departure, he hovers between worlds, in essence a ghost. He tries to communicate with his wife (Demi Moore) but only when he uses a medium (Whoopi Goldberg) does he communicate successfully with her. Before he goes to the other world, however, he must protect his wife from the advances of his best friend, and he discovers it was his friend who had him killed. Once he has settled the score, he can say good-bye and move on to the other world. In *Ghost,* the man is the main character and his goal is to move on with his house in order. By doing so his love (life) is confirmed in the person and future of his wife.

The main character in *Truly Madly Deeply* is a woman (Juliet Stevenson) who has lost her husband (Alan Rickman). Her goal is never to give up her grief at the loss. All men, including her landlord and her boss, seem to love her, or at least want to protect her. But her grief is so deep that her lover returns as a ghost, and she is happy. At the same time, a teacher who works with limited young adults falls in love with her. He is the opposite of her lover—unsure, but startling in his honesty. Now she lives with a ghost and is pursued by an earnest mortal. Which she chooses is the subject of the second half of the script.

One clear difference between the two story treatments is the main character. *Ghost* is told from the point of view of the ghost; *Truly Madly Deeply* is told from the point of view of the survivor, the one who has to go on living despite of the loss. This choice of main character puts the British film in the more realistic camp, while the use of a ghost as a main character makes *Ghost* principally a fantasy. We will return later to this issue of tonal difference.

Another difference between the stories is their emphasis. *Ghost* is plot-intensive, while *Truly Madly Deeply* is character or background-story-intensive. In fact, *Ghost* has considerable foreground. The plot focuses on the killing of the main character, his own investigation of the killing, and the resolution of the foreground story, the killing of the best friend, who is the antagonist. The background story of *Ghost* focuses on love and loss in the relationship between husband and wife. The believability and emotional complexity of the background story is seriously eroded by the dramatic device of a comic medium, which allows the dead husband and living wife to communicate with one another.

Truly Madly Deeply, on the other hand, has very little plot. The background story unfolds after the level of the main character's grief and longing are revealed. By Act II, when her lover returns as a ghost and the teacher begins to pursue her, we proceed along the classic relationship triangle: Which will she choose? Once she has made her choice for life, a choice to bear a child, her ghost lover recedes and she begins her life again. The entire story has been, in essence, the main character's mourning over her loss. The resolution of the background story, her choice for life, ends this deeply emotional, painful story on an upbeat note. *Ghost,* on the other hand, ends with the admission of loss and the transcendence of the relationship beyond mortality into that realm best described as foreverland. *Truly Madly Deeply*, having moved into the fantastic in Act II, ends as it began, realistically, whereas *Ghost* ends reaching romantically for new heights in fantasy.

Thus, the two films differ considerably. Not only is the point of view chosen by Minghella in *Truly Madly Deeply* more realistic, so too is the resolution of the story. By using background story over plot, Minghella creates more complex, believable characters and he explores a difficult interior issue, loss. Rubin, on the other hand, has written a romantic fantasy about loss. *Ghost* is plot-intensive and its tone never veers from the fantastic. *Ghost* consequently requires an antagonist whereas *Truly Madly Deeply* needs no other for the antagonist. The main character is both protagonist and antagonist. When she lets go of her grief, she is victorious over her loss.

Ghost and *Truly Madly Deeply* provide useful examples of American and non-American treatments of a similar subject. To explore more differences it is necessary to look at other comparable films.

■ ■ ■   ## A Case Study of the Position of the Main Character: *Dances With Wolves, Black Robe,* and *Close to Eden*

Generally a main character sits in the middle of the screen story. The screen stories in this case study, however, differ. All three films—*Dances With Wolves* (1990), *Black Robe* (1991), and *Close to Eden* (1992)—position their characters differently. Each could be called an East-meets-West story. The first, written by Michael Blake, is set in the post-Civil War West. The main character,

Lieutenant John Dunbar (Kevin Costner) is a white man assigned to an abandoned fort. We sense he is fed up with war and the white man. He is first curious about and eventually utterly taken with his neighbors, the Sioux. The story is essentially about the clash of native culture with the dominant Eurocentric white culture. Dunbar clearly comes to admire and imitate the native culture. As a main character, he is an outsider who comes as close to being an insider as possible. The foreground story follows Dunbar the soldier; the background story follows Dunbar the individual in search of his humanity. He finds that humanity in the Indian culture.

Black Robe is set 250 years earlier. The central character is a French priest and, as in *Dances With Wolves*, the story deals with the clash of religions. The priest's religion is spiritual without the physical; the Indian religion is physical, spiritual, and animistic. In this story, the priest holds to his position. He does not enter the Indian culture but instead attempts to alter it. In terms of the story, since so much is taken up with articulating and validating the Indian culture, the priest remains an outsider. Consequently, we stand aside from the story, not quite in an ironic position, but far more distanced from the story than was the main character in *Dances With Wolves*. The result is that we don't see a victor in *Black Robe*. Whether this is more realistic or ascribable to cultural differences is worth considering. *Black Robe*, written by Brian Moore, is an Australian-Canadian co-production directed by Bruce Beresford, one of the exceptional filmmakers from Australia. Is the narrative distinctly non-American? The fact that almost all the Indians (except Chomina and his family) are distinct threats to the priest's survival in *Black Robe* positions the main character on the periphery of the narrative. John Dunbar in *Dances With Wolves*, on the other hand, is a white man in a film about a culture dying because of the white man. Only when we turn to the third example, Nikita Mikhalkov and Roustam Ibraguimbekov's *Close to Eden* do we see a story of East meets West told entirely from the native's point of view.

In *Close to Eden*, the main character is a herdsman in modern Mongolia. He lives with his family on the steppes. He rides a horse and when he wants to have a child, he follows a ritual of chasing his wife on horseback, staking a suitable hill, and displaying his banner, the equivalent of a do-not-disturb sign. A Russian trucker gets lost, and the Mongol helps rescue him. The herdsman feeds him and the ensuing contact between the European Russian and the Asiatic Mongol grows. The Mongol visits the Russian in the town. There, more trucks and the trappings of civilization make the Mongol look ridiculous. But he is not embarrassed and he does make his way. In fact, he proves to be a man of means and he purchases a television and other gifts for his family. On the steppes, he stares at the television, clearly considering its usefulness or uselessness. He brings the gifts, but in the end he is unsullied in his true interests in his family and in increasing the size of his family. But we are left with the sense that the next generation will not be able to resist modern life as well as he has.

As in *Black Robe*, the Mongol is spiritual, physical, open. He is not a fool but he does seem a naif next to the white man, and as in *Black Robe*, the gulf between the two cultures is enormous. The key difference between *Dances With Wolves*, *Black Robe*, and *Close to Eden* is that only *Close to Eden* tells the native story from the perspective of a native; the story is told from inside rather than from outside.

It is also notable that both *Black Robe* and *Close to Eden* do not seek the kind of narrative closure used in *Dances With Wolves*. The shape of the story is more open-ended, a rarity in the Western, a genre often defined by the closing gunfight or battle.

Finally, the tone of *Black Robe* and *Close to Eden* is far less romantic than *Dances With Wolves*. Irony in both cases distances us enough to consider the actions and the fate of the main character.

■ ■ ■   ## A Case Study of Mixing Genres: *Schindler's List* and *Europa, Europa*

Few movies have been as quickly acclaimed as *Schindler's List*. The Steve Zaillian script, the Thomas Kenneally book, the Steven Spielberg direction each has been lauded. We would like to look at *Schindler's List* (1993) as an American war film and it is our goal to look at another recent war film from Eastern Europe, Agnieszka Holland's *Europa, Europa* (1991). Both are films about the Holocaust, but for the purposes of our discussion we will consider both as war films. Both are also mixed-genre films.

Zaillian's *Schindler's List* is a war film and a melodrama. The war film follows the events in Nazi-occupied Kracow from 1942 to 1945. Through that period, Jews were first placed in a ghetto and then the ghetto was exterminated with the survivors shipped to concentration camps. In *Schindler's List*, the German industrialist Oscar Schindler uses Jewish labor in his factories. Those who work for him are in the end saved because he retains the permission of the authorities to use Jews as labor. The result is that those 1,000 to 2,000 Jews who work for Schindler survive the war. In the war story, the protagonist does all he can to survive. In *Schindler's List*, the Jews as a group are the protagonist, and the antagonist is the Nazi commandant in charge of the labor camp in the Kracow area. He kills randomly, without pity. And for all the Jews he represents death.

In the melodrama, Schindler is the main character. He challenges the power structure of the Nazis by choosing to save Jews. Schindler's tragedy is that he can only save a handful out of the thousands who are killed.

Schindler's List uses the war story as foreground, the plot to kill the Jews, and the melodrama, the struggle of Oscar Schindler, as the background story.

The result is a realistic, powerful story that takes advantage of the strengths of each story form: plot and character. The tone of the film is serious and earnest.

Europa, Europa is strickingly different. It tells the story of a single Holocaust survivor, Solly Perel. He is a young adolescent, a German Jew who does not look Jewish. His parents send him east when the war breaks out. He is separated from his older brother and taken into a Soviet boys' school. As the Nazis move into the U.S.S.R., he flees further east but is captured by the Germans. He makes a decision to pose as a Russian of German descent. He is accepted and survives. He travels with an army unit where a homosexual sergeant befriends him and discovers he is a Jew. The sergeant promises not to betray him, and Solly finally feels he has a friend, but the sergeant is soon killed. The captain of the unit, an anti-Semite, is taken with Solly and offers to send him to the Hitler Youth in Germany. He will also adopt him. Back in Germany, Solly strives once more to survive, knowing that his identity as a Jew will be apparent if his friends see him naked. He takes on elaborate measures to avoid detection. He seems a model young Nazi, as even his teacher, another anti-Semite, claims in front of his classmates.

The next threat to Solly, however, is love. He falls in love with a young German girl but arouses suspicion when he is unable to consummate the relationship. Overwhelmed with adolescent feeling and anxiety, he confesses his identity to the girl's mother. But again, he is not given away.

He eludes detection until the end of the war. About to be shot by the Russians and the Jews they have released, his brother, a survivor of a concentration camp, recognizes him and he is saved. Together they have survived the war.

Europa, Europa follows a chronology from Krystallnacht in Germany, 1938, to April 1945. A postscript shows the real Solomon Perel in Israel in 1990. As in the war film, there is a great deal of plot, foreground story. Solly is clearly a protagonist trying to survive, and the many settings and events suggest how dangerous the war is for him. His sister and later his parents and oldest brother are killed. Only his other brother survives. The war is presented in a surrealistic sense; however, since he is a non-combatant, there is a surreal quality to how relentless and eccentric death is to a boy so young.

The other genre deployed by Holland, however, is far less realistic and tends to exaggerate the surrealism of the story. The second layer of the film is a satire on race. Since Solly looks non-Jewish, he passes as an Aryan. His encounters with the captain and the teacher are deeply ironic for each man professes an insight into who is a Jew and yet both mistake him for a German. Satire also allows Holland to be playful about Nazism. Solly is practicing the Nazi salute, which devolves into a jig. What is menacing to so many is amusing to him. We are reminded that he is a young man, barely more than a child. Finally, the satire allows Holland to explore his fantasies, including his thoughts about Stalin and Hitler.

The playfulness of the satire is totally different in tone than the war film. Indeed, the jarring shifts in tone are unsettling. Are we to believe this surreal tale, or is it a nightmare, imagined, not real?

As we discovered with Szabo, Kusturica and Kieslowski, irony is an important distancing device, used to reflect upon the fate of the character, the nature of events. The satire distances us from Solly and allows us to consider the Holocaust as experienced by this one person.

Summing up, Zaillian's script for *Schindler's List* mixes compatible genres for a realistic presentation of the Holocaust and of Schindler's role in saving Jews. Holland's script for *Europa, Europa* uses satire to undermine the sense of realism in the war story and to consider Solly Perel's struggle for survival a nightmare on the level of Jerzy Kozinski's *The Painted Bird*, a totally irrational experience modified by the will of one individual to do anything to survive. The experience of *Schindler's List* is dominated by realistic story forms; the experience of *Europa, Europa* becomes more complicated as Holland using satire, distances us from the fate of her main character.

Conclusion

We cannot be definitive about storytelling strategies in non-American film. But we can point out their linkages to storytelling in general and we can discern preferences in the narrative strategy mix.

Just as plot or action over character seems to be currently dominant in American film, we can see a clear preference for background story, character over plot, in many European films. This primacy is neither good nor bad; it simply appears to be the current preference.

Also discernible is the use of irony in many Central European films; given the history of the region, that choice seems understandable. We also note, as in the comparison of *Ghost* and *Truly Madly Deeply*, a preference in the United States for fantasy over realism and the reverse, the choice for realism over fantasy, from the perspective of the British example.

American, European, and Asian films have much in common, but they also have distinctive qualities. Understanding these distinctive narrative qualities may help the storytellers, the screenwriters, learn more readily from one another.

12

......

The Subtleties and Implications of Screenplay Form

It is sometimes said that a screenplay has the same relationship to a finished film that a blueprint does to a completed building. While this relationship may be true for the final shooting script, most screenplays lack a clear one-to-one correspondence to the finished film. Instead of being a precise list of specifications, screenplays have a language that suggests, but does not lay out, the actual shot structure of the film. A good screenplay must first succeed in evoking a strong emotional response from the reader.

Shots and Scenes

To understand the distinction between a screenplay and a shooting script, we need to review a basic distinction in filmmaking—the difference between shots and scenes. A shot is a continuous strand of film. During the shooting process, a shot begins when the camera is turned on and ends when it is turned off. During the editing process, a shot is the space between cuts. Thus, assuming the camera is running at normal speed, a shot inscribes and relates real time and space. Revealing a different space within a shot always takes time, because the camera must be moved physically (e.g., tilted, panned, dollied) to get to the new space.

A scene, on the other hand, is made up of one or more shots and is defined as *implying*, rather than inscribing, continuous time and a contiguous location. A scene takes place in one room, on one baseball field, in one car. However, within that space, the camera may cut to any angle or perspective without implying a lapse of time. The eyeline-match shots that make up many dialogue sequences are a good example. In this type of scene, the camera cuts back and forth from close-up to opposing close-up without any appreciable break in time to account for the change in angle. Of course, a scene may be made up of only one shot; in that case, it is inscribed with continuous time and space.

Shooting Scripts and Screenplays

Since the addition of sound, the primary technical problem of screenwriting has been the integration of image and dialogue. Later in this chapter we show that this is, in fact, a false distinction, because in a well-written mainstream script, both image and dialogue function in the same way—as dramatic action or intention. But, for a moment, let's use the distinction between image and dialogue to help us understand the difference between a screenplay and a shooting script or, more specifically, between a scene-based and a shot-based script.

Let's start with what comes last in the production process—the shooting script. Based on the completed screenplay, a shooting script is a shot-by-shot breakdown of what the finished, edited film will look like. In theory, it is possible to film a shooting script exactly as it is written, cut the shots together as planned, and have a complete, coherent film. The following is an example of a shooting script from the 1958 film *I Want To Live!*, written by Nelson Gidding and Don Mankiewicz and directed by Robert Wise.

```
23.  INT. LIVING ROOM—CLOSE ON THE BONGO PLAYER
now beating up a storm on his skins. He's a real
cool type—faded blue jeans, sandals.

24.  ANGLE ON PEG
By the open window. She's brooding about her split
up with Barbara. She belts down half a tumblerful of
whiskey, then walks over to the bongo player and
stares at his flying hands.

                         PEG
           Give it some head, Joe.

The tattooed noncom grabs her and they join the wild
dance. The party is really getting into high gear.

25.  OMIT

26.  MED. SHOT
Barbara, ringed by an excited GROUP of men, dances
almost frenzied to the driving rhythm of the drums.

27.  CLOSE SHOT
The drummer's hands flailing the skins faster and
faster.
```

```
28.   HEAD CLOSE-UP—BARBARA
reacting more and more excitedly to the increasing
tempo. In a sudden crash of abrupt silence, we ...

                              STRAIGHT CUT TO¹
```

The first and most important element of a shooting script is that the slug lines, the numbered lines of uppercase text that organize the flow of the script, describe shots rather than scenes. The example from Gidding's script is actually the continuation of a party scene that runs several pages. Within this one scene, the slug lines indicate many camera positions. Since these numbers refer to the shooting schedule and script breakdowns, the script is not renumbered after a rewrite; rather, numbered slug lines are indicated as omitted.

The dramatic tension between Barbara and Peg is clearly marked off by the slug lines. Both characters never appear in the same shot, and the alternation of shots focusing first on Peg and then on Barbara heightens this sense of separation.

A screenplay, on the other hand, is a more broadly visualized rendering of the film, which emphasizes the emotional and logical flow of the story over the breakdown of shots. Frequently called the *master scene-style*, slug lines in a screenplay indicate scenes rather than shots and are generally unnumbered. Even within a scene, the screenwriter rarely, if ever, indicates specific shots. Rather, a form of language has developed (we look at this in more detail later) that allows the writer to imply a pattern of shots, while still concentrating on the dramatic progression of the scene.

The following example is from Billy Wilder and I. A. L. Diamond's screenplay of *The Apartment*. We pick up the story at the scene in which Sheldrake asks to borrow Bud's apartment key so that Sheldrake can take Miss Kubelik, with whom Bud is in love, to Bud's apartment. Bud owes his rise to the executive suite to his willingness to lend out his apartment. This is the obligatory scene.

```
[Picks up in middle of scene]

INT. SHELDRAKE'S OFFICE—DAY

                    SHELDRAKE
          I'm not bringing anybody—I'm
          bringing Miss Kubelik.


                    BUD
          Especially not Miss Kubelik.
```

                    SHELDRAKE
          How's that again?

                      BUD
                (flatly)
          No key!

                    SHELDRAKE
          Baxter, I picked you for my
          team because I thought you
          were a bright young man. You
          realize what you're doing?
          Not to me—but to yourself.
          Normally it takes years to
          work your way up to the
          twenty-seventh floor—but it
          takes only thirty seconds to
          be out on the street again.
          You dig?

                      BUD
                (nodding slowly)
          I dig.

                    SHELDRAKE
          So what's it going to be?

Without taking his eyes off Sheldrake, Bud reaches
into his pocket, fishes out a key, drops it on the
desk.

                    SHELDRAKE
          Now you're being bright.[2]

In this example, the slug line marks the scene, not the shots. Yet, if
we look carefully, we suspect that there must be more than one shot in
this scene. Let's see if we can construct a shooting script from this screenplay.

Before we do, let's think about the turning point of the scene—the moment when Bud gives Sheldrake the key. Clearly, this is not merely an un-
considered action on Bud's part. The fixedness of Bud's glance ("Without
taking his eyes off Sheldrake . . .") suggests that something more is going
on. Sure enough, in the next scene, we learn that Bud gave Sheldrake the
key to the executive washroom instead of the key to his apartment. Based
on this knowledge, we know that the pivotal moment in the scene is when

Bud, backed into a corner and deciding what to do, regards Sheldrake before giving him the key.

One of the most useful guidelines for the writer is the principle of reaction that comes from the theater. It suggests that we tend to respond to something in a specific order—by looking, moving, and, finally, by speaking. Generally, by the time we speak, we have made our decisions. Thus, the reactions that precede speech, the looking and moving, are critical for the writer to capture, because this is where we see the character thinking.

In order to underscore this moment's importance, the shot must stop the action. This can be done by a close-up of Bud, intercut with his point-of-view shot of Sheldrake, followed by a return to the close-up in which Bud decides to move, and a match cut to a wider shot of Bud taking his key out of his pocket. From here, we can fill in the rest of the scene. Sheldrake's long speech, his ace in the hole, probably will be in a close-up, possibly cut with a reaction shot of Bud as he starts to weigh his decision. These shots will not break the flow of the action, nor will they be as tight as the decisive close-up on Bud. Somewhere at the beginning of the scene illustrated here, there will be a two-shot, not so much to set the spatial relationship between the two men (most likely that's already been set), but to relax the scene before its build to the final beat.

We have constructed a shooting script even though no actual shots were mentioned in the screenplay. Of course, our construction is really an interpretation. We have no confidence that these shots are exactly what the screenwriter had in mind. So does the screenwriter have the final say in how the film actually looks? Can a screenplay instruct the director in what to do? The answer is no. A screenplay exists to be interpreted.

However, screenplays have a connotative, expressive freedom that, we would argue, more than makes up for the proscriptive loss of the shooting script. Instead of being limited to describing the concrete details of individual frames, contemporary screenplays have developed a rich language that connects details to emotional impulse, pictures to feelings, and the rhythm of prose to the flow of the dramatic line of the film. The trick is to learn how to use the logic and structure of language to imply the logic and structure of the scene.

We said previously that shooting scripts are shot-based while screenplays are scene-based. We can take this a step further and say screenplays are not merely scene-based, but beat-based. Beats are the smallest unit of coherent dramatic direction. They change when a character either succeeds with or gives up a line of pursuit, when another character takes over dominance of the scene, or when something new is introduced. In the scene from *The Apartment*, Sheldrake's attempt to convince Bud to loan out his apartment constitutes one large beat (this may be made up of a number of smaller beats in which they argue back and forth, or where Sheldrake changes strategy). The beat changes when Bud makes up his mind to give him the wrong key. Beat changes are marked in screenplays by stage directions and changes in rhythm.

Wilder and Diamond could have written the scene from *The Apartment* in the form of shooting script, detailing each shot so that the section we reviewed would run a number of pages. However, here is the key: Even though they would have more control over each shot, they would lose the impact that their screenplay conveys. In the shooting script, the shape of the scene, the rhythmic acceleration of the dialogue preceding the pause, and the change of beat when Bud makes up his mind would have been lost in the details. In the screenplay, the moment where Bud hesitates and then makes up his mind is inescapable—as it is in the film. Rather than convey technical details, the screenplay dramatizes the line of the scene and the progression of the beats, so that its impact hits the reader. It is the director's job to find the exact visual equivalents for that impact.

The Basics of Screenplay Form

It is time, now, for details. We will start with a scene of pure whimsy. The numbers listed above the script excerpt correspond to the margins and tab stops in Pica and Elite, although Pica is the standard choice in screenwriting. Pica and Elite correspond to 12- and 10-point type, respectively; Pica has 10 characters to the inch, Elite has 12. Thus, a 20 space Pica indentation corresponds to a 2-inch margin. When you print out the text, your page appears skewed to the right as it does in our example. In fact, a screenplay page is always printed with an additional inch of binding margin to the left of the text, so that the script may be fastened with copper brads along the left edge and still be readable. The bracketed numbers that appear in this excerpt refer to specific features of screenwriting that will be noted in the following pages. They should not appear in the script.

```
20   Pica   30      36      40

24   Elite  36      42      48

FADE IN[1]

[2]EXT  [3]  OPIUM HEAVEN[4]—DAY[5]

[6]GEORGE[7], an ageless hippy, and WILLIE, 30[8]
```

with the largest pupils you ever did see[9] are
[10]
puffing on a SEVENTEEN FOOT WATER PIPE[11]. The
very clouds that waft past their heads reflect the
state they are in.

George passes the mouthpiece to SUSAN, late twenties,
who is not too happy.[12] She inhales, then coughs
and grimaces. This is supposed to be heaven, but the
weed just doesn't smoke as sweet. Susan looks[13] at
her friends. Their bodies are already in seventh
heaven. Who knows where their heads are.[14]

Suddenly Susan rises and punches her fist through a
cloud.[15]

                    SUSAN[16]
              (Whining)[17]
         What fun is it to be high
         when everyone else is?

She lifts the filter from the waterpipe and drops it
off the cloud.[18]

EXT. SHEA STADIUM—DAY
The PITCHER is in the middle of his windup when the
MANNA FROM HEAVEN lands at his feet.[19] He freezes.

                    UMP
         Balk!

The pitcher ignores the UMP, picks up the filter,
wets a finger, and then tastes it. He smiles. Looks
up at heaven. Some of the fielders move in to see
what it is about.

Now the opposing dugout empties. The first fans climb
onto the field. The organist begins playing "Happy
Days Are Here Again."[20]

EXT. OPIUM HEAVEN—DAY
The commotion can be heard, however faintly, even up
here in heaven.[21]

                         IRIS IN ON[22]

    1.   Fade In—The traditional screenplay beginning; it no longer means
a literal fade. Use it if you wish; it is useful if you don't like staring at a
blank page.

2.   Each master scene starts with a slug line that indicates INTerior or EXTerior, location, and DAY or NIGHT. The slug line is in uppercase letters and never underlined. Leave three line spaces between the end of the previous scene and the slug line. Leave two line spaces between the slug line and the start of a new scene. Generally, there is an em dash (—) between the location and DAY or NIGHT.

3.   EXT.—Outside.

4.   OPIUM HEAVEN—The location, wherever it might be.

5.   DAY or NIGHT—Even if there are no windows in an interior scene, it is important to know this to clarify the time flow of the script. You can indicate TWILIGHT or DAWN if we can see evidence in the sky. But you cannot put 3:42 P.M. because the slug line is what you want the viewer to be able to infer when she first looks at the scene. If you want the viewer to know that it is 3:42 P.M., you must explicitly indicate that in the body of the scene.

6.   Use a single space setting on your typewriter or word processor. Use double spacing to separate paragraphs.

7.   GEORGE—Type the first introduction of each character in uppercase letters. From then on, only capitalize the first letter.

8.   Get in the habit of anticipating the kinds of questions you imagine your viewer will ask the first time the character appears on the screen. Generally, after determining gender, the first thing a viewer will seek to determine is age. You can answer this in a script with a newspaper-style age citation or a descriptive phrase (e.g., an ageless hippy).

9.   "The largest pupils you ever did see"—Try to limit your descriptive details to brief fragments that serve to place your characters in the reader's mind. Never indicate a precise, specific detail that doesn't pay off in the script.

10.   Everything must be written in the present tense. Describe only what the viewer will be able to see at a given moment. There is no direct equivalent to a linguistic past tense in film.

11.   Capitalize the first introduction of major props, especially those that are unusual.

12.   "Not too happy"—How do we know she is unhappy? Purists prefer to state a physical, external indication of her unhappiness, such as "Susan frowns" or "Susan kicks rocks" and let the viewer infer her state of mind. This is entirely a matter of taste and learning to traverse the two dangers of screenwriting prose.

The first danger is that you overdescribe an emotional state or some form of abstract knowledge that cannot be externalized and made visible on the screen. Screenwriting must dramatize. You cannot reveal information or moods in stage directions that are not implied in the drama, such as, "Susan thinks about her first date."

The second danger is that you will use of a lot of physical description that means nothing. Like all evocative writing, screenwriting works by combining event and meaning, the concrete and the inferential. Nothing should be on the page that does not contribute to the reader's sense of meaning.

13. Looks—The word *looks* establishes point of view within a scene. It suggests some variant on a sequence that begins with a close shot of Susan's head turning, a longer shot of her friends that shows us what she sees, and a return shot of Susan for her reaction. It tends to make us regard the scene through the eyes and attitude of the character. We'll talk more about this later.

14. Again, some screenwriters would find this paragraph too descriptive of internal state. But there is nothing described here that you cannot infer from the action. This is the test you want to apply to determine whether a particular descriptive phrase is filmable.

We encourage you, particularly in early drafts, to overdo the emotional content of stage directions. More screenplays don't succeed because of a lack of emotional charge to their stage directions than because their scenes cannot be visualized. Put another way, it is almost impossible to visualize a scene that does not have an emotional charge. A scene with such a charge can almost always be brought to the screen. It is easier to cut a few lines in a later draft than to give life to meaningless movement.

15. Beat change. Use movement to articulate beats. Stage directions are the screenwriter's best tool for dramatizing thought and change.

16. SUSAN—The name of the person speaking is indicated in capital letters. There is no space between the name and the parenthetical notes or dialogue that come after it.

17. (Whining)—Instruction to the actor. It does not indicate a beat change. Keep these to a minimum. The character's attitude and intention should be inferable from the dramatic line of the script.

18. It is what she *does*, not what she *says*, that makes the scene. In classic mainstream dramatic writing, the old cliche holds—action is character. Movement is what brings this style of filmmaking to life (this is also true in most, although not all, independent films). You want to top dialogue with movement. The inference in this excerpt is that Susan has complained for a long time, but this is the first time she has done anything about it.

19. These three scenes inscribe continuous time. We indicate this by picking up the action in the previous scene (the dropping of the filter) and carrying it over to the next scene (the Manna from Heaven landing at the pitcher's feet).

20. Capitalize the introduction of any major sound effect.

21. When you return to the same scene, you want to come in with action. Remember, in most cases, film is a medium of images first and dialogue second. Always reestablish the physical layout; do not use, "Same as Scene 1."

22. You may choose to connect scenes using optical effects. These may include LAP DISSOLVE TO:, FADE OUT:, FADE IN:, FADE TO BLACK:, WIPE TO:, etc. You may also connect scenes by using the transition, CUT TO:. However, since the lack of any indicated transition implies CUT TO:, we suggest that you use it only between scene sequences (see next excerpt).

Scene Sequences and Transitions

When a group of scenes implies continuous action, as do the three scenes in the previous excerpt, we call them *scene sequences*. Within scene sequence, the cuts between scenes are sometimes called *non-nodal*, because our eye continues right through them, usually following a movement or sound cue. Scene sequences are frequently terminated by a nodal cut or transition. Such a transition serves as a marker, releasing us from one line of dramatic development and positioning us somewhere else. While non-nodal transitions suggest that the characters are carrying us from place to place, nodal transitions feel as though the filmmaker is picking us up and placing us down somewhere else. To continue using the previous excerpt, an example of nodal transition is as follows:

```
Now the opposing dugout empties. The first fans climb
onto the field. The organist begins playing "Happy
Days Are Here Again."

                                             CUT TO:


EXT. THE RUSSIAN STEPPE DAY
The vast expanse of Mother Russia. Nothing much grows
in these parts. We move down until we reach:


EXT. SOCCER FIELD—DAY
Or at least, what passes for one. The wind blows
the sandy soil. A lone BOY stands near a broken
goal and practices heading the ball. Nothing else is
around.
```

```
Suddenly a huge image of a grinning STALIN appears
in the sky.
```

Notice the use of the word *we* in the stage directions. It implies the presence of the narrator or the filmmaker moving the camera. If we say, "Susan races along the cloud tops," we are implying that the camera is traveling invisibly with her. Our sense is that she is moving the camera—nothing calls our attention to the fact that a narrator outside the scene is responsible for this movement. However, if we say, "We move down until we reach:", we are implying some form of crane shot that is overtly controlled by the director. Although the shot may be so smooth that it doesn't call attention to itself, this phrasing brings us into or out of a scene in a manner that a shot motivated by character does not.

Notice how we indicate the nodal transition by stipulating "CUT TO." Although the transition between Scene 1 and Scene 2 is also made by a cut, we have used the direction "CUT TO" only to articulate the end of the scene sequence.

One more thing. We talked about using action as expressed through stage directions to articulate beat changes. Beat changes that take place within stage directions (i.e., the appearance of the vision of Stalin) are indicated by paragraph breaks.

Language

A screenwriter is an expressive writer, which means that like all expressive writers she uses language not only to describe but to evoke. Evocation means allowing the reader (and the viewer) to draw as many inferences and connections as possible from the events you describe. While the screenwriter is limited to describing scenes that can be visualized, such scenes can imply all kinds of unspoken details about the character's life and the screenwriter's attitude toward the issues of the screenplay.

The previous example, set in Opium Heaven, is a flip scene. Descriptive lines like, "This is supposed to be heaven, but the weed just doesn't smoke as sweet" or "Their bodies are in seventh heaven" do not so much convey information as evoke the tone of the scene. "This is supposed to be heaven, but the weed just doesn't smoke as sweet" implies something of the author's playful attitude toward the scene. Clearly, this is not a serious polemic on drug abuse. Since the line "Their bodies are in seventh heaven" comes after Susan's look, we assume that it represents her thoughts. Without having to say so explicitly, we imply a great deal about her attitude. By contrast, the following excerpt is a much more dead-on, serious scene.

INT. MATTHEW'S ROOM—NIGHT
WILLIAM, 39, darts a peek at his son MATTHEW, 14,
who lies silent, brooding next to him, but Matthew
won't meet his eyes. Instead, he stares up at the
stars, hundreds of them, projected from the small
planetarium ball in the center of the room.

                    WILLIAM
          Okay, so you won't tell me.

Giving up, William starts to his feet when Matthew
finally asks.

                    MATTHEW
          Dad, you can't catch AIDS
          holding a girl's hand?

Surprised by the question, William studies his son
below him.

                    WILLIAM
          No.

                    MATTHEW
          Just wanted to be sure.

The reflections of the stars in the dark room make
Matthew's eyes so unnaturally bright and clear that
for a precious moment, William believes he can see
all the way into them. Moved, he reaches to touch
him.

Matthew relaxes. He takes a lighted pointer and
points to a cluster of stars.

                    MATTHEW (CONT'D)
          Look at that. The Keyhole
          Nebula.

Buddies again, William slides down next to his son.

                    WILLIAM
          What's her name?

                    MATTHEW
          Who?

                    WILLIAM
          The girl.

```
                    MATTHEW
          You're grilling me, Dad.

                    WILLIAM
          We're buddies, aren't we?
          There's Eta Argus up in the
          corner.

                    MATTHEW
          Eta Cerinae. We're close.

                    WILLIAM
          Damn close.
```

Matthew jumps up and flicks on the hall light behind him.

```
                    MATTHEW (CONT'D)
          I've had it with stars.
```

William looks up at Matthew who stands with the light behind him, outlined, dark, and now totally inaccessible.

The prose of this scene is no longer flippant nor unreliable, as evidenced in the direction

The reflections of the stars in the dark room make Matthew's eyes so unnaturally bright and clear that for a precious moment, William believes he can see all the way into them. Moved, he reaches to touch him.

Unlike Susan's reactions, Matthew and William's reactions seem closer to our own. The expression "precious moment" implies sympathy with the character's desire. If the scene works, then we will see what he sees, and, more importantly, it will mean the same thing to us as it does to him. Without having actually to say so, we know how much this father wishes to communicate with his son and how difficult it has become. We also know that the screenwriter is asking us to take the father's desire for connection seriously.

Who Is Seeing?

One of the critical differences between theater and film is the fact that the camera position changes, positioning the viewer within a spectrum that runs from the objective position of the theatrical seat to the highly subjective point-of-view shot. Even when an actor in the theater reacts to a situation, we still see that situation through our own eyes. Film, however, places us so we see the situation unfolding in much the same way that the character does. These situations can be subjective to such an extent that the character appears to be describing or narrating the scene for us—the scene takes on the inflection or coloration that corresponds to the character's attitude. One of the major functions of screenwriting is to articulate the modulation from an objective to this more subjective point of view.

Once again, we can control this modulation through language. The use of the terms *we* or *the camera* in phrases like "The camera moves in on JOHNNY, the young man in the group" or "We see the gun before Marji does," suggests an omniscient point of view. Sometimes it implies dramatic irony, a situation in which the audience knows more than the character. At other times, the camera might be expressing the character's state of mind (e.g., "The camera pushes in on Max as he looks desperately from one to the other, searching for a clue."), but still implying a narrative emphasis that comes from outside.

However, if we describe a character's action directly (without identifying the camera or our, the viewer's, position) as in "Delighted, Mary smiles as she skips across the room," we are implying that we are seeing the character with the minimum of narrative intervention. This means that if the camera moves, its movements will be timed to correspond to the character's. Such movements pass invisibly on the screen.

The use of the words *looks* or *watches,* as in "Johnny watches Jennifer take tiny bites of the steak," suggests some form of point-of-view sequence. There are many technical alternatives to point-of-view sequences, but they are all built around the same notion of replacing the omniscient narrator with a character narrator.

The most common point-of-view structure is made up of three shots. For example, the character turns her head and looks; we cut to what she is looking at from an angle that matches (or nearly matches) her eyeline; and we return to a shot of the character (usually a reverse shot close to the eyeline) for her reaction. The effect of the reaction shot is to color what we see in the point-of-view shot with her attitude.

Technically, when a character in one location sees something in another location, we indicate it by using the acronym *POV* as illustrated in the following example.

```
INT. LORI'S BEDROOM—DAY
In disgust, Lori flings herself around only to freeze
when she catches sight of something out the window.
```

```
EXT. LORI'S FRONT YARD—LORI'S POV—DAY
Jacob looks uncertainly at the house. He is about to
turn away when he notices a baby robin squawking on
the grass. He bends down and tenderly holds the
robin in his hand. Then he starts toward the house.

INT. LORI'S BEDROOM—DAY
For a moment, Lori watches fascinated. Then quickly
she strides over to her vanity, picks up a tissue,
and starts wiping off her make-up.
```

The indication, "Lori's POV," specifies precisely how we see Jacob. It functions exactly like the direction, "Lori looks at Jacob," would function if they were both in the same location.

Since POV functions by putting us in the character's position, it is important that there be some rhythmic or visual indication to take us from the more omniscient position we usually occupy. This is marked off by the change of rhythm in the stage direction, "In disgust, Lori flings herself around only to *freeze* when she catches sight of something out the window."

Dramatic Action

In the beginning of this chapter we said that one of the problems that usually confounds beginning screenwriters is relating dialogue and stage directions. We suggest that this problem is ultimately superficial, because dialogue and stage direction must function in the same way—as dramatic action. That is, every line of dialogue, like every movement, must come out of some need that can't be expressed any other way. Dialogue becomes movement, it becomes an expressive act. The content of the words is less important than the need to speak.

The trick to good evocative writing is to make everything mean something. Everything you put down (or leave out), every change in rhythm (or its continuation), and every choice of word, sentence structure, descriptive detail, and character nuance conveys a point of view and is fair game for the audience entering your story. The more the readers feel they can ferret out, the more elements to which they respond, the more intrigued they will be, and the better chance the script has of being made into a film.

If you are able to write a script in which characters do not move or speak and the camera does not reveal anything unless there is a reason, then when your characters do move or speak or when we are shown something, we will pay particular attention. We will trust your screenplay and make the effort to respond to everything that is there.

We are not saying that before you write anything down you must understand exactly what it means. Many times an experienced writer will add things to the script, apparently without thinking, that end up being very important to the finished film. Instead, we are talking about a critically important writers' habit—one a writer develops by constantly asking herself, "Do I see it?" If you see it, and if what you see is consistent with your story and your characters, then your staging automatically begins to have meaning.

Also, we are not saying that a character has to know the meaning of everything he does. Much of the movement of stories, in particular restorative three-act stories, centers around the character's gradual awareness of his motivations. Prior to this, the character acts more reactively, sometimes blindly. However, what the character knows has nothing to do with what you, as the writer, must know. We all do things in particular ways that define who we are, without being conscious of them. But a writer works to orchestrate this meaning.

Okay, now how does all this relate to the specifics of writing stage directions? Too often, writers lay out a scene entirely in dialogue. Only after the scene is spelled out, do they add stage directions as sort of obligatory filler to keep their scene visual. No matter how visual the details, no matter how full of action, the scene is not visual or active in the dramatic sense, unless the stage directions serve the story. Suppose we write the following dialogue fragment.

```
INT.  STEAM BATH—DAY

                    SAUL
          And then it would take the
          burden off of you.

                    JAKE
          No.

                    SAUL
          Suppose, just suppose, I told
          you that I had made up with
          my father.

                    JAKE
          Is that a possibility?

                    SAUL
          We had dinner last night.
```

                         JAKE
          I see.

Now, let's throw in some stage directions and description.

INT. STEAM ROOM—DAY
A luxurious steam bath, at least twenty feet long,
with gold towel fixtures on one wall, a rack of
newspapers on the other. The whole room is full,
mostly with older men, but here and there we see a
smug young face. JAKE and SAUL enter. The steamer is
bubbling, but hasn't yet emitted much steam.

                         SAUL
          And then it would take the
          burden off of you.

Before we go farther, let's look at what is implied by this description.
First, it is omniscient; that is, it is shown to us independently of any characters in the scene. Second, it is indiscriminately descriptive; that is, the
camera would need to pan the whole room, taking note of all the details
mentioned in the description but giving weight to no detail in particular.
While one might want to set the location like this, there are several consequences to such omniscience. The first is that the description takes us out
of the scene by transferring the reaction to the steam room from the character to the audience. By the time the character comes in and reacts, we are
already a beat ahead of him. The second consequence of this description is
that it slows down the story. If we give such a grand introduction to each
location, all scenes will appear nodal, announced like chapter headings. What
we need, here, is a point of view to organize the way in which the opening
is written and by extension, the way the camera sees.

INT. STEAM BATH—DAY
SAUL, a young man clearly out of his depth, follows
the older man, JAKE, into the steam bath. While
Jake, at home in his club, waves to his cronies,
Saul pauses in the doorway and stares in awe at the
sheer grandeur of the place. Gold towel fixtures and
a newspaper rack in a sauna! Then he pulls himself
together and hurries over to Jake, who turns away as
he calmly spreads out a towel. Saul finds himself
speaking to the older man's back.

                         SAUL
          And then it would take the
          burden off of you.

```
          Satisfied that the towel is even, Jake sits
          emphatically on the bench, puts his head back, and
          places a rolled-up towel over his eyes.

                              JAKE
                    No.


                              SAUL
                    Suppose, just suppose, I told
                    you that I had made up with
                    my father.

          Jake raises the rolled-up towel slightly and casts a
          withering glance at Saul.

                              JAKE
                    Is that a possibility?


                              SAUL
                         (Trying to hold up under Jake's glance)
                    We had dinner last night.

          Dropping the rolled-up towel now altogether, Jake
          slides over on the spread-out towel and motions for
          Saul to sit next to him.

                              JAKE
                    I see.
```

Okay, now we are beginning to have a point of view. We start with Saul's awe as he looks around the steam bath, go to Jake as he emphatically shuts off Saul by putting the towel over his eyes, and then stay with Jake as he begins to respond to Saul's gambit. Description becomes a means of dramatizing Saul's state of mind rather than a catalog of details.

This fragment of scene starts out as Saul's and ends up as Jake's. There is nothing wrong with such a change in perspective except that in this case, it seems to dilute the intensity of the scene. Let's limit our focus to Saul.

```
          INT. STEAM BATH—DAY
          SAUL, a young man clearly out of his depth, follows
          the older man, JAKE, into the steam bath. While
          Jake, at home in his club, waves to his cronies,
          Saul pauses in the doorway and stares in awe at the
          sheer grandeur of the place. Then he pulls himself
          together and hurries over to Jake, who turns away as
          he calmly spreads out a towel. Saul finds himself
          speaking to the older man's back.
```

> SAUL
> Then it would take the burden
> off of you.

> JAKE
> No!

Saul watches as, discussion over, Jake spreads
himself out regally on the bench and takes a section
of newspaper from the pile on the bench. Saul
doesn't quite know what to do. Seeing that Jake's
towel is wrinkled, Saul bends down to straighten it
up. Without daring to look up, Saul mumbles.

> SAUL
> Suppose, just suppose, I told
> you that I had made up with
> my father.

> JAKE
>   (After a pause—behind the paper)
> Is that a possibility?

Now that he's finally gotten Jake's attention, Saul
takes his time. Casually, he unbends and flicks some
water on the coals. A great cloud of steam hisses
up, obscuring the older man.

> SAUL
> We had dinner last night.

> JAKE
>   (From somewhere in the steam)
> I see.

This version is focused entirely on Saul. We are with him as he is overcome by the steam bath, as he is brushed off by Jake, and finally when he
enjoys himself after gaining Jake's attention. Notice several things. There is
an unrelenting feeling to this version that we don't get with any of the others. This is achieved purely by the focus that staging brings to the scene.
This focus is achieved by changing the rhythm and the emphasis of the previous version. Our movement from Saul to Jake in the earlier version is
shown by the fact that Jake becomes the subject of the stage directions—
e.g., we go from "Saul pauses in the doorway" to "Jake sits emphatically."
In the later version, Saul remains the subject of the directions—e.g., "Saul
pauses in the doorway," "Saul watches as ... Jake spreads himself out,"

"Saul takes his time." Notice how a sentence like the one that starts "Saul watches" uses point of view to keep the beat focused on Saul (his watching) even though Jake is doing the action (spreading himself out).

Note also the importance of the moments of the transitions. Saul, unable to approach Jake head-on, bends down to straighten the towel and only in the subservient position can bring himself to speak. When he's finally gotten Jake's attention, he unbends and takes his time before speaking. Such transitions include us in the preparation for the character's action and bring us into the scene. It's as though we, along with Saul, look at Jake lying in front of us and don't know what to say. Looking around for any sort of connection with the older man, we see the towel needs straightening. Finally, feeling momentarily protected by looking down at the towel, we venture another request.

Staging for Beats

Dramatic actions are given shape by a progression of beats, for example, the movement of Saul from when he has difficulty approaching Jake to taking his time before speaking once he has Jake's attention. This progression must be articulated in the staging.

Alternating dialogue sequences without stage directions are generally shot in some variant of eyeline matches; that is, in alternating reverse two-shots or close-ups. A sequence like this implies a single continuous beat. Character movement (indicated in the script by stage directions) or a new shot pattern breaks us out of these tight shots and causes a reframing. Such reframing indicates shifts in beats.

Alternatives to Screenplay Form

There are, of course, many other ways to organize written material to be turned into a film. Some screenwriters eschew the master-scene technique and go directly to a shooting script, arguing that this gives them more control over the final film. Others use a half-literary, half-visual form of stream of consciousness to present a profusion of images that the viewer must reassemble. Other writers use a variation of the live-television, two-column script that has a column of visuals down the left side of the page opposite a parallel column of audio cues on the other side.

If you are producing and directing your own project, then you will be free to come up with whatever notational combination is useful to you. For instance, filmmakers making dance films have come up with a variation of the Laben dance notation to visualize their finished films. However, most of the independent, narrative films of which we have spoken in this book were written using conventional screenplay form. Unless you absolutely can't live without some hybrid form, we recommend that you stick to the conventional style. It's a matter of picking your battles. Since the process of supporting and producing independent films is so difficult, it is usually not worth putting the additional obstacle of a "badly" formatted script in your way. Screenplay form frees you from the nuts and bolts of shots and editing sequences and allows you to evoke in your audience the most vivid mental images of the film you want made.

Conclusion

To write screenplays, you do not need to know a whole list of abbreviations for the technical details of filmmaking. In fact, the constant use of such details is the sure mark of an amateur writer. What you do have to understand is something that is ultimately much more difficult and more powerful. You need to know the way dramatic filmmaking articulates and controls the dramatic line of the story. To do this, you have to learn to see and to write about what you see. Once you've learned this, everything else is just typing.

References

1. Nelson Gidding, *I Want To Live* (from the Shooting Final Draft, March 14, 1958), p. 15.
2. Billy Wilder and I. A. L. Diamond, *The Apartment* (MGM, 1960), p. 135.

13

● ● ● ● ● ● ● ●

Character, History, and Politics

In Richard Leacock's 1964 documentary, *Campaign Manager*, a heated, meal-time strategy session slides into an equally intense argument over who ordered the medium-rare steak. A similar scene is dramatized in Michael Richie's 1972 feature film *The Candidate*.[1] Because these two films have virtually identical content, they enable us to study how mainstream scripts have traditionally transformed historical and political material into fiction. We pay particular attention to three transforming techniques—the filling in of missing spaces, the use of rhythm to heighten articulation, and the personalization of decision making. We then look at how these techniques serve to diminish the historic overview that makes *documentary realilty* so powerful. Finally, we examine some alternative transformations that, while dramatizing the tension within individual personality, still affirm documentary reality.

We now accept it as a critical commonplace that the traditional distinction between documentary and narrative—articulated as truth versus fiction—is problematic. However true the events of a documentary may be when they are filmed, the act of filming transforms them into recorded, mediated, formally constructed representations. Such representations necessarily convey an interpretative meaning independent of their subject. All the filmmaking choices—selection, framing, focal length, photographic quality, editing sequence, shot length, sound mix—inscribe such a point of view.

Rather than looking at the question of truth, we, instead, approach the distinction in terms of the representation of individual motive. Restorative three-act structure locates the source and the meaning of action within the psychology of character. All else is subordinated to this. Documentary, on the other hand, deals with the material world's resistance to such a clear-cut sense of individual causality. This may be acknowledged or not, but while both fiction and documentary construct their representation to reveal, a documentary is always constrained by the fact that it must recognize that its subject has an existence independent of the film. Of course, it is such limitation, such a sense that meaning is not fully accounted for and contained within the film, that brings documentary closer to history. We must recognize this limitation if we are to make fictional films that speak to the interactions between the individual and the larger world.

▪ ▪ ▪   A Case Study of Form: *Campaign Manager* and *The Candidate*

Mainstream films have certainly represented the larger world, but by and large they have addressed it on the level of content rather than of form. In other words, the subject is made overtly political or social, but the means and manner of storytelling remain located within character. This suggests that history, politics, and society are primarily individual problems. We can clearly see this when we look closer at the *Campaign Manager* and *The Candidate* scenes.

Shot in black-and-white, direct-cinema style, the scene from *Campaign Manager* (mentioned above) feels fragmentary, incidentally observed—voices come from off-screen, images linger behind the overt content of the scene, and the camera concentrates on details, like the way a man listens, and the way his fingers play across his cheek while another man shifts restlessly in his seat. The scene captures the behavior of a body of men rather than any particular personality. We do not see the food cart being rolled in; instead, it is revealed when the film cuts to a wider shot. Voices overlap so that the debate on campaign strategy, someone offering the Black waiter a tip, and the discussion about how the steaks are cooked all run together. The rhythm is continuous, moving without a break from the Virginia primary to who ordered what. The scene ends in a disquieting manner, by focusing in on a man who grins and shakes his head as he looks self-consciously at the camera.

By contrast, *The Candidate* personalizes this scene by setting up a spatial and dramatic tension between the campaign manager and the other members of the campaign staff. Presenting strategy, the manager stands alone in front of the others who are seated below him. The food cart defines the space between them as it is rolled into the room. While the waiter tries to get the food orders right, the manager keeps up the campaign discussion until he is finally interrupted by someone who asks whether they can get this thing straightened out. There is a dramatic pause, a threatening silence, a series of expectant shots, and then, in close-up, the character asks, "Who has the medium-rare?" Merely a joke.

Campaign Manager reads like a parody of the political personality in general, rather than a comment on a specific group of individuals. This focus is reinforced by the casual overlapping of dialogue, the camera's interest in character quirks at the expense of the action line, the sense of seeing events that have been discovered rather than set up, the suspicion that important moments might have been missed, the lack of rhythmic articulation of beats, the equality in the way the participants are presented, and the participant's awareness of the camera at the end of the scene. *The Candidate* reads more like a personal dispute, the embodiment of a power struggle between a dry campaign manager and one of the campaign workers—the group's clown. While *Campaign Manager* seems casual and haphazard in its design, *The Candidate* is rigorously and obviously structured. The character of the campaign manager is set against the other characters through staging and dialogue, the speed with which everyone else turns to their food, the fact that the food cart is rolled between them (prefiguring the dispute), and the rhythmic articulation (the expectant pause) that leads to the final humor of the last beat.

What difference does all this make? Only one, but it raises a series of questions critical to any film that attempts to deal with social and political issues. Is history made by individual conflict or by larger and more impersonal forces that in some way act on individuals? Are stories about what we can control or what is bigger than we are? Can power be fully explained by personal quirks? Experience suggests a very complex and ever changing interaction between these two perspectives. The problem with fully personalized, mainstream filmmaking is that its very technique, its means of involving us in and explaining the story, simply does not speak to this tension.

Filling in, Rhythmic Articulation, and Personalization

To demonstrate why mainstream screenwriting does not speak to this tension, we will show what happens when you use three techniques— filling in missing spaces, heightening articulation through rhythm, and personalizing decisions—to transform historical material into fiction. Transcribed below is a section of documentary footage taken from the fifth episode of the PBS documentary on the civil rights movement, *Eyes on the Prize: Mississippi, 1962–64*. The scene is from the training camp for the Mississippi Freedom Summer, run by veteran civil rights workers at Miami (Ohio) University in Oxford, Ohio, during June 1964.

```
M.S. of African-American man speaking left to right
across the frame. He is identified by supered title
as JIM FORMAN of SNCC. Other civil rights organizers
stand behind him. Hand-held, black-and-white, news
footage.

FORMAN: We're going down there, trying to face a
real situation that will occur; mainly there'll be a
mob at the courthouse. And we want you to get used
```

to this, used to people jeering at us, and we also
want the white students who will be playing the mob
to get used to saying things, calling out epithets,
calling people niggers and nigger lovers.

CUT TO LATER. A paper sign reading "Courthouse" taped
to a tree. Jeering over. Camera zooms out between
two lines of white students standing on either side
of the tree, yelling and gesturing toward camera.

CUT TO LATER. White students now gathered around and
pushing civil rights leaders to the ground. Jeering
continues. Camera seems to be on edge of crowd,
looking up and over. Hand-held.

CUT TO LATER. Some confusion. The African-American
leaders seem to be standing up. Camera is walked
around an arc so we move from behind James Forman
until he is once again in profile. Laughing.
Embarrassment. Ends similarly to first shot.

FORMAN: Okay, that was very good. (Laughter) Because
that happens . . . (drowned out)

(Pause)

FORMAN: That was very good because you all got
carried away, see. I mean you were just supposed to
yell and you started hitting us and you got out your
frustration. But that's what happens, you know.

WHITE STUDENT: Isn't that the way it really happens
down there?

FORMAN: Hey it happens, you know, people begin
shouting, then somebody lurches forward, and then
everybody begins to lurch forward so that was even
better than we had anticipated.[2]

Does this scene illustrate a residual racism lingering in America so that
even America's apparently most liberal white children are susceptible to it?
Or is it a moment where one individual, for whatever personal reason, gets
angry (we don't see this, but we can imagine it) and starts pushing and pro-
voking everyone else? Or is it just an accident of confusion, without any
meaning beyond the event itself? There is, of course, no single answer, but
the open-endedness that characterizes this direct-cinema documentary technique allows—even more than that, it forces—a number of interpretations.

Even if we finally reject those interpretations that suggest a disturbing and ironic indictment of racism in American society, we must at least consider them as possibilities.

We are now going to rewrite the previous transcript into a mainstream fictional scene, by centering our attention almost exclusively on character, in order to show how such rewriting restricts our range of interpretation. Normally when rewriting, we would first ask ourselves, What effect do we want to achieve? Once we answer this, we would know what to change. However, for purposes of illustration, we are going to work backward—making changes and then analyzing their effects.

When we look at the previous transcription, we see that two important stretches of time are not represented. The transition between Forman asking the students to role-play and their presumably subsequent gathering by the mock courthouse has been cut out (or more likely, not filmed), and, although we see the crowd beginning to collapse around the civil rights leaders, we do not actually observe the leaders being knocked to the ground. The fact that they stand up and brush themselves off in the next sequence allows us to assume that this happened.

Let's now reconstruct this scene in screenplay form, filling in these missing moments with imagined transitions. This filling in of transitions is one of the ways we traditionally transform fragmented historical material into fiction. Six beats have been marked for subsequent discussion.

Version #1

```
EXT. COLLEGE CAMPUS—OXFORD, OHIO, JUNE 1964—DAY
A bucolic college campus on a lovely summer's day. A
group of white college-age students cluster
reverently around an African-American civil rights
LEADER. Several other African-American leaders stand
with him.

                         LEADER
                 We're trying to give you
                 experience with a real
                 situation that will occur
                 when you get down to
                 Mississippi. We'll do a
                 little role-playing, see.
                      [Beat #1]

LEADER #2 slaps a scribbled sign that says
"Courthouse" on the trunk of a large oak tree that
dominates the campus.
```

                         A WHITE STUDENT
          Hah. Hah. "Courthouse."

                         LEADER #2
          You're the mob, you got it.
                 [Beat #2]

The students play at being the bad guys while Leader
#2 retreats to join the other African-American
leaders.

                         A WHITE STUDENT
          You catch any Neeeeegroes in
          your cotton fields? Hah. Hah.

                         2ND WHITE STUDENT
          I get my hands on one of
          them agitators, I'll rope 'em
          to my plow.

                         A THIRD
          Hah. Hah. Draw and quarter
          'em.

                         LEADER
          Now yell.
                 [Beat #3]

The students cut loose, yelling insults at the
African-American Leaders watching them.

                         WHITE STUDENTS
          Hey idiots. Fools. Your
          mother sucks tomatoes.

                         LEADER
          Louder. You've got to get
          used to saying things.

                         WHITE STUDENTS
          Assholes. Mother fuckers.

                         LEADER
          Niggers! Nigger lovers!
          Things you wouldn't say in
          your worst dreams.
                 [Beat #4]

The white students go silent. They giggle, but they
can't begin to say it.
                    [Beat #5]

Finally, one of them whispers.

                         STUDENT
               Nigger.
                    [Beat #6]

The earth does not open under their feet. Still
hesitating, the others pick it up.

                         WHITE STUDENTS
               Nigger. Nigger lover.

                         LEADER
               Alright. Now here we come,
               just like it'll be for you
               when you're trying to
               register a few voters.

The Leader and the other African-Americans begin to
move toward the "Courthouse." The white students yell
louder, their voices growing.

                         WHITE STUDENTS
               Nigger lover. Nigger. Coon.

The African-American leaders push through the
students who refuse to give them room.

                         WHITE STUDENTS
               Darkie. Nigger. Boy.

The students begin to push back. For a moment, there
is a standoff as the two groups shove against one
another.

Suddenly, the white students burst forward,
collapsing in on the African-American leaders. With
unexpected viciousness, they knock them to the
ground. The Leader's voice calls out, sharp,
commanding.

                         LEADER
               Hey. Hey.

Stung, the white students freeze, then step back. The

African-American leaders break free. For a long and uncomfortable moment, the two groups eye each other suspiciously. Then the Leader laughs.

> LEADER (CONT'D)
> You all got carried away,
> see? I mean you were just
> supposed to yell and you
> started hitting us. But
> that's what happens, you
> know.

Relieved, everyone begins to joke. The camera is quick, hand-held. It moves over faces, vital, alert, but nervous in their grinning, everything just a little too fast.

> WHITE STUDENT
> That's the way it's supposed
> to happen, right?

Without personalizing the group of white students any more than is strictly necessary (we will do that in the next section), we have fleshed out, or "milked," the transitions merely implied by the documentary footage, shaping them by rhythmic articulation. Let's look closely at how the first transition works.

In Beat #1, Leader #2 slaps the "Courthouse" sign on the tree without telling the students what they are supposed to do. Figuring it out, the students play (Beat #2) at being southern rednecks. A general trick is used here. A tight script avoids doubling; that is, it avoids an explanation followed by an action played out precisely to the specifications of that explanation. Rather than have Leader #2 tell the white students what to do and then show the students doing it, we achieve a tighter scene by having Leader #2 hint and then having the students show us, as they (and we) figure it out. If you *do* place the explanation first, you will want to show us something that does not go according to plan.

In the third beat, the Leader challenges the white students to cut loose, then in the fourth beat, he ups the ante by asking them to yell the word "nigger." They go silent. Note the use of contrast here. The silence after the Leader asks them to say the word "nigger" becomes much more powerful, because the intensity of the white students yelling has been jacked up by the previous beat. Only in the fifth beat can one person finally step forward and say it; and only in the sixth beat do the rest of the students dare to join in.

The beats were written to create a logical momentum that leads the white students to break their taboo and say the one word that is most difficult for them to say. The logic builds like this. Beat #1—The civil rights leaders are asking the students to lean forward by hinting at what they want the students to do, but not telling them outright. Beat #2—The students figure it out and play at being bad guys. Making the leap on their own to playing rednecks establishes the eagerness of the students to do what is expected of them. It suggests an energy and a willingness to throw themselves into childlike game-playing that will be intensified by Beat #3 and will ultimately lead to Beat #6. After the boisterous acceleration of Beats #2 and #3, Beat #4 closes in silence. The silence inscribes a space, a clear moment of expectation that not only fills in the transition, but directs us to its most important moment. When the white student finally says "nigger," the importance of this action has already been carefully framed.

In the transcription of the actual film, we saw how the sense of historical inevitability developed, in a large part, due to the omissions of the transition scenes. Lacking their particularity, we are led to generalize and fill in on our own. Rather than focus on character for motivation, we look to the historical situation.

By dramatizing the omitted transitions, we begin to reduce the sense of historical inevitability in favor of narrative causality. Something specific happens, events evolve from that, and this specificity makes us less confident about the kind of historical generalizations we can make.

We have added detail to the script, but we have not yet tied it to a specific personality. Although we have filled in the transition, the movement toward the fight remains completely impersonal. The white students act, but we do not know why. The motivation comes rhythmically from the previous beats; the buildup of excitement and anticipation in Beats #2 and #3 generates a momentum that is irresistible, if uncharacterized. We have no idea why one specific student volunteers and the rest do not.

Now we'll go deeper into the screenplay and lay in a specific character motivation. As you no doubt can guess, this takes us even farther from historical representation.

Version #2

EXT. COLLEGE CAMPUS—OXFORD, OHIO, JUNE 1964—DAY
A bucolic college campus on a lovely summer's day.
DAVID, 21, a white student, intense and eager, his
hair buzzed down to a crew cut, scurries to keep up
with JOHN, 24, who coolly saunters through the

campus, almost oblivious to the younger man at his
heels.

>   DAVID
>   That bad?

>   JOHN
>   Worse.

>   DAVID
>   I can't believe you want to
>   go back.

>   JOHN
>   (Flat)
>   A man has to do what needs
>   to be done.

David nods in respect at the older man's cool, then
follows him into a group of white college-age
students clustered near a dorm. They greet John
enthusiastically while paying no attention to David.

>   STUDENT
>   Hey, John.

>   ANOTHER STUDENT
>   How's it going?

Before John can answer, an African-American civil
rights LEADER, along with several other African-
American leaders, struts out from the dorm.

>   LEADER
>   Okay, listen up.

Not wishing to miss a word, the students go dead
silent. David pushes to the front of the group where
he gazes at the Leader in awe.

>   LEADER (CONT'D)
>   We want to give you
>   experience with a real
>   situation that will occur
>   when you get down to
>   Mississippi. We'll do a
>   little role-playing, see.
>   [Beat #1]

One of the other African-Americans slaps a scribbled sign that says "Courthouse" on the trunk of a large oak tree. Confused, David looks at John, who laughs.

> JOHN
>
> Always the bad guys?

> LEADER #2
>
> I ain't gonna play no redneck.

> JOHN
> (With an exaggerated drawl)
> You catch any Neeeeegroes in your cotton fields? Hah. Hah.
> [Beat #2]

David turns to the others who don't seem to know what to do.

> JOHN (O. S.)*
>
> I get my hands on one of them agitators, I'll rope 'em to my plow.

Then David looks back to John who continues to play at his notion of southern redneck behavior. Now David turns the words in his mouth.

> DAVID
>
> Hah. Hah. Draw and quarter 'em.
> [Beat #3]

The Leader steps forward.

> LEADER
>
> That's right. Now yell.

---

*The parenthetical phrase O. S. stands for Off-Screen. It is used to show that a character within the scene is speaking but is not currently on camera. This is distinct from the parenthetical indication V. O. which stands for Voice-Over. V. O. means that the character speaking is either not physically present in the scene, or that the dialogue is a rendering of the character's internal voice. O. S. is a useful designation if you want to keep the beat focused on the character reacting (the one described by the stage directions) rather than on the character speaking (the one whose dialogue is off screen).

Encouraged, the others pick it up.

                              WHITE STUDENT #1
                Hey idiots. Fools.

                              DAVID
                Your mother sucks tomatoes.

                              LEADER
                Louder. You've got to get
                used to saying things.

                              WHITE STUDENTS
                Shit heads. Mother fuckers.

                              DAVID
                Assholes.

                              LEADER
                Niggers! Nigger lovers!
                Things you wouldn't say in
                your worst dreams.
                     [Beat #4]

The white students go silent. Nervously David looks
at the others. All they can do is giggle; they can't
begin to say the word.
                     [Beat #5]

Finally John steps forward.

                              JOHN
                   Nigger.
                     [Beat #6]

But no one picks it up. The word itself overwhelms
them. David looks between his tongue-tied peers and
John who casually stands alone between the two
groups, apparently not bothered.

                              DAVID
                It's only a game, isn't it?

                              JOHN
                Only a game.

                              DAVID
                   (Experimentally)
                Nigger.

                              JOHN
          That's it.
                [Beat #7]

David beams. The others look at him with new respect
as he struts out to join John.

                              DAVID
              Nigger.

                              JOHN
              Nigger lover.

                              DAVID
              Polak.

                              JOHN
              Kike.

They clasp hands in newfound solidarity.
                [Beat #8]

Seeing that, the others finally pick it up.

                          WHITE STUDENTS
              Nigger. Nigger lover.

The Leader and the other African-Americans begin to
move toward the "Courthouse." The white students yell
louder, their voices growing firm.

                          WHITE STUDENTS
              Nigger lover. Nigger. Coon.

The African-American leaders push through the
students who step back gingerly under their pressure.
Only John refuses to give them room. For a moment,
there is a standoff as John shoves against the
African-American leaders.

                              JOHN
              Darkie. Nigger. Boy.

When David sees this, he lunges forward again to
join the fray. But just at this moment, John and the
African-American leaders ease off, giving up the
role-playing. The force of David's lunge knocks the
unprepared Leader back against another African-
American who falls to the ground.

In what seems to be a reflex action, the Leader's
hands come up and knocks David back against the
group of white students, toppling one of them. The
other students burst forward. For a moment, all we
see are flailing bodies. Then the Leader's voice
calls out, sharp, commanding.

> LEADER
>
> Hey. Hey.

Stung, the white students freeze, then step back.
With David stuck between them, the two groups eye
each other suspiciously. Finally David breaks the
standoff.

> DAVID
>
> That's the way it's supposed
> to happen, right?

The Leader looks at him for just a moment too long,
then grins.

> LEADER
>
> You all got carried away,
> see. I mean you were just
> supposed to yell and you
> started hitting us. But
> that's what happens, you
> know.

Relieved, everyone begins to joke. The camera is
quick, hand-held. It moves over faces, vital, alert,
but nervous in their grinning, everything just a
little too fast, until we reach David. He is still
somber, stunned by what happened. We pass over his
face, then reverse direction and come back on him as
he finally lets the giddiness wash over him and
breaks into a grin.

By opening the scene on David's attempt to get a reaction from an indifferent John, this new version immediately frames the issue in terms of
character. While our interpretative position in the first dramatized version
remains ambiguous (we see the transitions, but we do not understand individual motivation), this version leaves us with little doubt about how we
are meant to enter the scene. In the first version, we wonder what will happen between these groups of whites and blacks given the history of American

race relations and the lack of anything turning us in other directions. In the second version, we wonder why David is so eager for affirmation and how this eagerness will condition his subsequent actions in the context of this moment in the history of American race relations.

This difference in focus serves to change the location of the meaning. In the first version, our initial interest is in the content of the Leader's words. The opening shot holds our attention even though it runs much longer than we would expect in a narrative film. But in the second version, the words are less important than the physical relationship of David trailing after John, all the while seeking his recognition. In the documentary, we would be lost without dialogue, while the opening beats of the fictional screenplay would be quite intelligible without sound.

The first beat dramatizes John's cool familiarity with the role-playing. He is the only white student to know what Leader #2 is suggesting. When David picks it up in Beat #2, he plays off John, not off the Leader. This is a critically important transformation—the Leader has been reduced to the "other," the unknown character who remains in the background. The force that David responds to is no longer the African-American man, but John, a potential white friend. The unspoken implication is that, while intellectually David might be here for the racial equality of the civil rights movement, emotionally he is still more eager for approval from the older white man he understands, rather than from the African-American leaders he apparently has come to work with. This relationship is reinforced in Beat #6 during which David seeks permission to say the word "nigger" ("It's only a game?"), not from the African-American Leader who has asked him to say it, but from John.

The cumulative effect of this is to give a public act a private meaning. We have personalized David's decision to say the "nigger"—we have given it subtext. The paradox is that, normally, subtext is a sign of the writer's success; it implies there is more to the character's private life than meets the eye. But if we want to maintain focus on more abstracted social issues, on historical perspective, we cannot explain everything in terms of the character's personal life. We must suggest that larger, more impersonal circumstances have something to do with the outcome.

We have taken a documentary scene that we are inclined to read as an expression of a moment of racial intolerance and have turned it into a personal story about an insecure character, named David, who is seeking approval through his involvement in the civil rights movement. Of course, we have no way of knowing what really happened in Oxford, Ohio, that day in June 1964. The issue, though, is not what actually happened, but what is suggested by different forms of representation, because it is these forms of representation that we can control. By using the mainstream model and placing the character story in the foreground, we bring a greater individual specificity to this event that may involve us more in the story, but the cost is considerable. History becomes secondary to personal will. The possibility that this scene might represent anything greater than David's psychological needs is diminished. Far from being indifferent or cruel, the world becomes highly responsive to our individuality. It becomes expressive of an internal state. If we want to maintain historical causality, that sense that at times we are moved by forces larger than ourselves, we have to find some way to flatten the story, to diminish character motivation and create some space for a broader range of motivation.

Before we go on, we need to add one more thing. A fictional film that maintained the distance of this documentary segment for its whole length would bore the most discriminating viewer. Storytelling assumes modulation of distance to achieve its effects. An indiscriminate use of such distance would be read as a lack of filmmaking control. However, used selectively, the flattening, the sense of inevitability suggested by the documentary, is a tool that the fictional filmmaker can use for considerable effect.

Using Narrative Distance to Suggest the Impersonality of History

To control narrative distance, we have to find a means to establish tension between the personal and the more formal, distant voice characterized by the documentary. One way to bring about tension is to account for the narration by presenting the scene as though it were actually a documentary seen by a character within the story. This is very useful because it can suggest two, apparently simultaneous, orders of reality—the documentary itself and the dramatic space in which the documentary is viewed. Framing the event as a documentary within a dramatic film also frees the camera to assume a more open, documentary form without having to account otherwise for the radical change in style. Holes do not have to be filled in, rhythms do not have to be articulated, the documentary scene does not have to be personalized, while at the same time, the framing dramatic scene can serve all three techniques without disturbing the fragmentary quality of the documentary. The following is an example of a scene in which a middle-aged man, having used the memories aroused by looking at a tape of himself as a young man to revive his own sense of social commitment, begins to realize that the moment in Mississippi was not as clearcut as he remembered. The content mixes in another documentary scene from the same episode of "Eyes on the Prize."

Version #3 (Picks up a section of script in progress.)

INT. DAVID'S OFFICE—DAY
DAVID, 42, enters the office. The videotape hasn't been touched since the day he first received it. The tape itself lies on his desk. He puts it in the VCR and turns it on.

The screen breaks up for a moment, then settles down to grainy black-and-white documentary footage. Under the supered title *Mississippi Delta*—1964, the camera pans over flat bottom land and a wide swollen river until it finally settles on a boy-man, intense and eager, his hair buzzed down to a crew cut, his surprisingly innocent face leaning determinedly toward the camera. David Fish at 21.

> YOUNG DAVID
> I'm down here because I
> believe that my freedom is
> very much entangled with the
> freedom of every other man.

The older David watches intently.

> YOUNG DAVID (CONT'D)
> And that if another man's not
> free, then I'm not free. So
> I'm fighting for my own
> freedom down here.

> REPORTER
> Are you scared?

The young David hesitates.

> YOUNG DAVID
> Yeah, I'm very much afraid.
> Everyone here is.

In perfect solidarity with his younger self, David raises his fist.

> DAVID
> Yeah.

David turns away from the monitor and picks up the phone. Behind him, the video goes to snow. Then something else comes up.

A college campus, Oxford, Ohio, 1964. A group of
white college-age students cluster around a large oak
tree and yell at several African-American civil
rights leaders.

> WHITE STUDENTS
> (Faint)
> Hey idiots. Fools. Your
> mother sucks tomatoes.

David begins to dial, paying no attention to the
TV.

> LEADER
> Louder. You've got to get
> used to saying things.

> WHITE STUDENTS
> Assholes. Mother fuckers.

> LEADER
> Things you wouldn't say in
> your worst dreams. Niggers!
> Nigger lovers!

Phone in hand, David turns on the word and stares at
the TV.

The white students go silent. They giggle, but they
can't begin to say it. The young David is among
them. He whispers.

> YOUNG DAVID
> Nigger.

Still hesitating, the others pick it up.

> WHITE STUDENTS
> Nigger. Nigger lover.

> LEADER
> All right. Now here we come,
> just like it'll be for you
> when you're trying to
> register a few voters.

The Leader and the other African-Americans begin to
move toward the "Courthouse." The white students yell
louder, their voices growing firm.

                              WHITE STUDENTS
                    Nigger lover. Nigger. Coon.

The African-American leaders push through the
students who refuse to give them room.

The older David watches, the phone still in his
hand. We can hear it ring.

                              WHITE STUDENTS
                    Darkie. Nigger. Boy.

The students begin to push back. For a moment, there
is a standoff as the two groups shove against one
another.

                              VOICE ON PHONE
                    Hello? Hello?

But David ignores it.

On screen, the students suddenly burst forward,
collapsing in on the African-American leaders. With
unexpected viciousness, they knock them to the
ground. The Leader's voice calls out, sharp,
commanding.

                              LEADER
                    Hey. Hey.

Stung, the white students freeze, then step back.
The African-American leaders break free. The two
groups look at one another, stunned.

Still staring at the tape, David replaces the
receiver without answering.

There is another technique that can be used to distance the viewer from
a scene without actually throwing the scene into the past. We can play it
almost exactly as before, but, by exaggerating the pattern of the scene, we
call attention to its formal qualities, to the fact that it is not quite natural.
This conscious lack of naturalism suggests that there is more going on here
than a specific character's story.

Version #4

COLLEGE CAMPUS—OXFORD, OHIO, JUNE, 1964—DAY
A bucolic college campus on a lovely summer's day. A

group of white college-age students clusters
reverently around an African-American civil rights
LEADER. Several other African-American leaders stand
with him.

> LEADER
> We're trying to give you
> experience with a real
> situation that will occur
> when you get down to
> Mississippi. We'll do a
> little role-playing, see.
>> [Beat #1]

LEADER #2 slaps a scribbled sign that says
"Courthouse" on the trunk of a large oak tree which
dominates the campus.

> A WHITE STUDENT
> Hah. Hah. "Courthouse."

> LEADER #2
> You're the mob; you got it.
>> [Beat #2]

The students look at each other now uncertain what
to do, while Leader #2 retreats to join the other
African-American leaders.

> LEADER
> Hey, come on now.

Finally one of them volunteers . . .

> A WHITE STUDENT
> You catch any Neeeeegroes in
> your cotton fields? Hah. Hah.
>> [Beat #3]

The others pick it up.

> 2ND WHITE STUDENT
> I get my hands on one of
> them agitators, I'll rope 'em
> to my plow.

> A THIRD
> Hah. Hah. Draw and quarter
> 'em.
>> [Beat #4]

LEADER
Now yell.

The students cut loose, yelling insults across at the black leaders watching them.

WHITE STUDENTS
(Faint)
Hey idiots. Fools. Your
mother sucks tomatoes.

LEADER
Louder. You've got to get
used to saying things.

WHITE STUDENTS
Assholes. Mother fuckers.
[Beat #5]

LEADER
Niggers! Nigger lovers!
Things you wouldn't say in
your worst dreams.

The white students go silent. They giggle, but they can't begin to say it.

LEADER (CONT'D)
Hey, come on.
[Beat #6]

Finally, the same person who volunteered before whispers.

STUDENT
Nigger.

Still hesitating, the others pick it up.

WHITE STUDENTS
Nigger. Nigger lover.

In Beat #1, Leader #2 slaps the "Courthouse" sign to the tree, leaving the white students uncertain about what they are to do. Only after the Leader's encouragement does one student tentatively take a stab at it (Beat #2). The Leader affirms the student's action. Because it is okay, the other students join in (Beat #3), pretending to be southern rednecks. In the fourth beat, the

Leader challenges the white students to cut loose; in the fifth beat, he ups the ante by asking them to yell "nigger." They go absolutely silent. Only after almost identical encouragement in the sixth beat can the same white student finally step forward and say it.

Notice the intentional repeating of motif in Beats 1–3 and Beats 5–7. These two sets of beats stop the action and focus on the same individual who hesitates, receives identical encouragement, and finally acts. The success of that individual's action then frees the others to follow. But there is no explanation for this repeated interplay between the individual and the Leader. By repeating it a third time, the repetition of the motif moves to the foreground so that the viewer's attention is unconsciously taken from the question of individual motivation to the broader sense of a patterned or formal motivation. The scene will begin to seem artificial, intentionally stagy. Such artificiality displaces the motivation. The scene will seem to come not from the story world (i.e., a character's specific motivations), but from some imposed outside world. Because the scene is so distant, this outside world may supply the necessary perspective without consciously breaking the immediateness of the story.

We will end with a few examples of films that use these techniques.

The film *Swoon* gets its historical perspective not by updating the case of Leopold and Loeb or presenting it as though we were there, but by foregrounding the distance between then and now by introducing into the story a number of historical anachronisms that emphasize the difficulty in an historic recreation. It starts and ends with a scene of recreation in which actors circle around one another in front of a backdrop while we see modern film equipment at the edges of the frame—the whole thing is a performance. Sometimes, the performance comes from the script as in the choice of framing the story with these two scenes. Sometimes, it comes from the directing. As Leopold waits in the car, Loeb draws the boy they will kill into the car. The camera remains with Leopold in the car, but not with his point of view. Instead, it twice slides over to a lake and goes out of focus. The feeling it conveys is not only a lyric expression of what the character is feeling (an out-of-focus dizziness), but also an acknowledgment of the act of narration (the movement is independent of the character), which distances the scene and reminds us that it is an historic recreation. Instead of seamlessly appearing to enter history, we are constantly aware of the tension between our perspective today and the not fully explainable quality of this moment in our past.

Daughters of the Dust achieves its historic perspective in a number of ways. By opening with a title that sets the historical situation and its outcome, much like the titles in Brecht's *Mother Courage* which tell us exactly what will happen in each scene, the film becomes a meditation on the pull of history or the individual. In one critical scene in *Daughters of the Dust*, Nana Peazant, the island's matriarch, confronts her great-grandson, Eli. After Eli turns away, Nana begs him to return. At first, he does not and a series of cross-cuts builds the tension between them. However, as this scene reaches what seems like a climax, we cut away from it altogether to a group of women dancing on the beach. This imagery becomes processed and slowed down so we read it not as emphasizing individual characters, but the dance, the act and joy of ritual, itself. We cut back to Nana Peazant as she holds her hands out to Eli. After a beat, he comes back on-screen and takes them.

A character changes, but we do not see the moment of change. Instead it happens while we watch the dancing women. The motivation for the change does not come at the individual level, but rather is relocated to the interaction between the individual and his history. Eli's decision is motivated by some combination of his own circumstances and the history of his people. His actions become more than just his own.

Conclusion

As we move beyond the simple truth/fiction distinction, we can see that documentary approaches open up subjects and forms that may be borrowed by fictional filmmakers. At the same time, documentary filmmakers' increasing awareness of the constructed nature of their work has led them to appropriate devices that had been traditionally limited to narrative films. It is important for filmmakers to realize that while the old truth/fiction distinction is no longer automatically applicable, there is a sense in which documentary suggests a very different world view than mainstream fictional films. To truly use documentary as a source for fiction, we not only have to appropriate its content, but we have to think about using its form to expand the possibilities and range of fictional filmmaking.

References

1. We would like to thank Professor Warren Bass of Temple University for calling this to our attention at the 1990 Symposium on Screenwriting and the Academy in New Orleans.
2. *Eyes on the Prize: Mississippi, 1962–64*, Transcription of fifth episode.

14

· · · · · · ·

Tone—
The Inescapability
of Irony

In Chapter 12, we established the relationship between screenplay form and dramatic intention. In this chapter, we look at dramatic intention and examine how it is presented through character, dialogue, atmosphere, and narrative structure.

The screenwriter uses tone to imply directionality. Generally, in the treatment phase, the writer is faced with pinning down many dimensions of the story, a process that continues into the first draft and perhaps the second. (Events subsequent to this phase are the subjects of Chapter 15.) In further drafts, the writer or writer, producer, and director introduce the directionality (voice) that leads the reader, and later, the viewer to interpretation. Of course, interpretation is not singular; there are many ways to construe material. Each yields a different interpretation. The recent screen versions of the modern play and 18th-century novel *Les Liaisons Dangereuses* *(Dangerous Liaisons* and *Valmont)* are good examples of differing interpretations.

The principle of interpretation is carried forward by the director and actors in the production phase of the script, and later by the editor in the postproduction phase. It is critical to the film's viability that the various phases mesh smoothly, that further development and maturation of the ideas and intentions of the screenplay take place. When the process works well, it results in a film like *The Godfather;* when it doesn't, there are many participants to whom to apportion blame.

In this chapter, we concern ourselves with the early phase of the screenplay, between treatment and the first few drafts, the phase in which tone is a critical factor in rooting the screen story. When writing a screenplay, the writer is faced with many hurdles. The first is credibility. Do I, the reader, believe this story (no matter the genre used)? Second, do I care what happens in the story? Third, am I stimulated by the story? All these issues—

credibility, involvement, and stimulation—are strongly influenced by the tone of the screen story. Here, we examine how character, dialogue, atmosphere, and narrative structure are used to establish the tone of the story, and how looking for alternative options inevitably takes the writer to an ironic mode or approach toward the material.

Character

The primary question of character, as it influences the tone of your screen story, is the relationship of your main character to the screen story. The choice of a character is not simply a question of a suitable main character; you must ensure that the screen story amplifies and breathes life into his central conflict. It's not enough that the main character as observer becomes involved in a series of events that constitute the plot line; a more symbiotic relationship must exist between character and plot. If this relationship does exist, your task as a writer is to flesh out both character and plot in ways that amplify that symbiotic relationship. Dominant physical and behavioral characteristics help create a more three-dimensional character. If these qualities are relevant to the plot line, you are making choices that help foster credibility and involvement with your character and your story.

For example, Steve Martin's *Roxanne* is a modern version of Edmund Rostand's classic *Cyrano de Bergerac*. Although Martin's screenplay is a situation comedy, rather than a melodrama (as was the original), the basic story line remains the same. Fireman Charlie Bales, complete with lengthy proboscis, loves Roxanne (Darryl Hannah). He is poetic and romantic, but he has no confidence. He helps a better-looking, but verbally inept, coworker win over Roxanne. The only modification to the original version is that Charlie survives and wins the hand of Roxanne.

The key to the relationship of Martin's character and the screen story is to project Charlie's physical shortcoming (the length of his nose) with his behavioral passion—he is both a romantic and a poet. When Martin's character helps the other fireman, the story takes on a poignancy that forges an even stronger link between us and the Martin character. When the most beautiful woman in town, Roxanne, returns his love, the goals of the character and the screen story are synonymous. For the audience, the sense of satisfaction is pervasive.

Dialogue

The language that you use may reflect character function, but it is important for you, the writer, to realize that dialogue can create credibility for your character, a credibility every bit as great as the techniques of dominant characteristics and function-oriented actions. Regionality, culture, class, profession, as well as personality and disposition all color what a character says.

Part of your task at this stage is to use dialogue to make your character credible. Your choice of words can reflect the idiom of a region, and the complexity of the idiom can tell us the speaker's class. Finally, the balance of emotion and socialized (sanitized) language tells us about the nature of the speaker. Power implications also are reflected in the choice of words and how they are put together. All of these elements—regionality, culture, class, status—build a grid that supports or undermines a particular character's image. The dialogue you choose helps set the tone of the script and supports characterization.

The next film we discuss as an example is neither over-literary nor memorable in terms of the language, but it is an effective classical use of dialogue. Howard Franklin's *Someone to Watch Over Me* tells the story of Detective Mike Keegan (Tom Berenger). Keegan, a Brooklyn-bred policeman, has just been promoted to detective and is assigned to the Upper East Side in Manhattan. His first job there is to protect Claire Gregory (Mimi Rogers), a material witness to a murder. Since she has been sighted by the murderer, Joey Venza (Andreas Katsulas), Keegan and his colleagues have to provide her with 24-hour protection. In the course of his duties, the married detective falls in love with Claire and has to decide whether he will remain in his own culture (Queens) with his wife and son, or whether he will leave it for the other woman and the other world, the Upper East Side. In the foreground, the story of murder-protection-capture unfolds.

The element critical to the tone of the story is the use of dialogue to help create the two worlds in which Keegan lives. In the world of Queens, intensity and violence are key. Swearing, explosive dialogue, as well as a kind of lower-class simplicity to the language contrasts sharply with the quiet, controlled, cerebral language of the Upper East Side. Since Keegan lives in both worlds, he can swear like a trooper or be as sensitive as a psychoanalyst. Franklin's dialogue is consciously class-driven. He makes very clear the origins of each character. As is so often the case, the dialogue helps develop a core of believability that supports the central issue for Keegan. Who do you want to be, Queens or Upper East Side?

Atmosphere

If dialogue provides the verbal cues to support character, atmosphere provides the nonverbal equivalent. In *Someone to Watch Over Me*, the atmosphere is the two worlds—Queens and the Upper East Side. It is critical for the credibility of the main character that these two worlds be visually articulated. We have to sense the world from which Keegan comes, his home and his neighborhood. In this film, the key atmospheric elements are the blue-collar class together with the potential for violence. Color, furnishings, noise are all referred to in the script to highlight the characteristics of Queens, as they are useful to the screen story. Later, the art director, director, and cinematographer articulate the nonverbal vision for viewers. It is equally important that the affluent, opulent, high-technology life of Claire Gregory be clearly articulated for Mike Keegan. The Upper East Side has to be strongly presented so that the alternative is credible and understood. Interestingly, the first few times we see Keegan in this milieu, he is either lost or burning toast. This is how far Franklin wants to go to illustrate how Keegan is out of place in Claire's apartment, her world.

Similarly, in *Roxanne*, it is critical that the setting (Nelson, British Columbia) is conducive to a romantic fairy tale. In fact, Martin goes to great lengths to ensure that the only challenge to Roxanne's beauty is the beauty of the town. We believe that this story would occur in such a setting!

Critical, then, to the credibility of the story is the nonverbal building of visual evidence. Just as dialogue makes a character credible, atmosphere helps make narrative credible.

Narrative Structure

When a writer chooses to write a screen story in a particular genre, she is making a choice that elicits particular viewer response. When Howard Franklin chooses to write a police story, the viewer expects an urban crime-and-punishment tale. In *Someone to Watch Over Me*, Franklin adds a love story, but we know that a solution to the crime will be found. The class dimensions of the story are very much in keeping with the classic gangster story (the basis for the development of the police story). When Steve Martin chooses situation comedy, we understand that the story will work out to the protagonist's advantage (thus challenging our expectations that *Roxanne* will be a repeat of the Rostand original).

Narrative structure affects the tone of the screen story to the extent that the viewer has particular expectations about the antagonist, the nature of the protagonist–antagonist relationship, and how their struggle relates to the resolution of the story. In both genres (gangster and situation comedy), these relationships are developed with the expectation that realism, as opposed to fantasy, is the modus operandi. People and events seem real. If they are not, the genre expectation is broken.

At this point, we are concerned with the classic case, where the genre expectation is not broken. This is critical to help the writer understand how narrative structure helps set the tone for the screen story. Until this point, the emphasis has been on the classic relationship of character, dialogue, atmosphere, and narrative structure, and how they influence the tone of the screenplay, particularly in the early writing phase. But what if the writer wants to create a different kind of story, a story that opts to challenge the conventional approach?

When the writer does attempt to alter tonal expectations, inevitably she begins to write more ironically. Irony is a writing style that, in its farcical description, is tongue-in-cheek, but in its more serious manifestation is profound.

According to literary theorist, Northrop Frye, "irony never says precisely what it means."[1] It often presents a content that is undermined or contradicted by its style. The same principle can be applied to a character that functions against our expectations in a role, or a character speaking in a manner that undermines his authority or credibility or that of the person to whom he is speaking. Irony, when applied to realistic genres, implies what is underneath the realistic veneer. Inevitably, one person is designated to seek out what is underneath. In its extreme, comic irony becomes satire. Ironic writing, according to Frye, also has implications for how we use the main character. Often, the main character is the innocent victim and the events that happen to him are far greater than anything he has provoked. We suggest that as you move against conventional writing, you begin to write ironically. Our task for the balance of this chapter is to illustrate how this manifests itself.

The Ironic Touch

Particular screenwriters have become known for using a pronounced sense of irony in their writing. Samuel Raphaelson's work is a good example *(Trouble in Paradise)*, along with Ben Hecht *(Design for Living)*, and Billy Wilder *(Ninotchka)*. Interestingly, all three screenwriters wrote for the great German-American director, Ernst Lubitsch. Lubitsch was the master of having his characters speak and project a meaning that was quite different from the literal meaning of the dialogue. He was also known for staging visual action that had a meaning somewhat different from its most superficial meaning. This tendency of distancing meaning from content, the ironic mode, was taken up by writer-director Billy Wilder in his work with I. A. L. Diamond *(The Apartment, Some Like It Hot)*, by writer-director Joseph L. Mankiewicz in his late 1940s and early 1950s films *(A Letter to Three Wives, All About Eve, 5 Fingers)*, and by writer Herman J. Mankiewicz *(Citizen Kane)*. This tradition has been explored most recently by David Lynch *(Blue Velvet)*, David Hare *(Strapless)*, Harold Pinter *(The French Lieutenant's Woman)*, and Hanif Kureishi *(Sammy and Rosie Get Laid)*, among others.

To exemplify how irony works in setting the tone through character, dialogue, atmosphere, and narrative structure, we use the work of two writer-directors and one director. Until this point, we have emphasized scriptwriters by quoting films with reference to their writers rather than directors. At this point, we are going to emphasize works by directors and writer-directors, such as Preston Sturges, Stanley Kubrick, and Jonathan Demme. Sturges is the sole writer of the films he directs. Kubrick is often the cowriter and, in some films, the sole writer of the films he directs. Only Jonathan Demme does not receive writer credit on his films.

The Ironic Character

There are a number of ways to use an ironic character. The most obvious is the sidekick role performed by so many comedians and character actors. From Stan Laurel to Jerry Lewis, the idiot savant commenting on the serious endeavors of his partner provided the viewer an instant alternate insight into the unfolding dramatic situation. This tradition, in numerous films, manifests in the characters played by such character actors as Tony Randall or Donald O'Connor, who is the quintessential ironic character in *Singin' in the Rain*. More recent manifestations include Mary Stuart Masterson in *Some Kind of Wonderful* and Nick Nolte in *Down and Out in Beverly Hills*.

The ironic main character is more of a challenge and less of a tradition in screen stories. According to Northrop Frye, the ironic character is something of an innocent who unleashes a course of events that "punish him or her" far beyond what we might expect, given their actions.[2]

What makes the ironic main character interesting is that her positioning in the story is so important that her ingenuousness as a character leads us to ask naturalistic questions: Is she for real? Is she mad? Can anyone truly be as innocent or as ingenuous as she is? Think for a moment about the Keith Carradine character in Alan Rudolph's *Choose Me* or the Burt Lancaster character in John Guare's *Atlantic City* or Paul LeMat as Melvin in Bo Goldman's *Melvin and Howard*. They seem too honest or naive to be believable. They must be deceptive or manipulative. This first impression is wrong; they are precisely what they present. What is notable about ironic main characters is that their very nature can shift our perceptions from viewing *Atlantic City* simply as a gangster film or *Choose Me* as a melodrama, to fantasy. As Frye claims, the story is then pushed toward myth.[3]

The ironic main character is somewhat different from the conventional main character. Whereas the traditional main character is someone we are visually encouraged to identify with, the ironic main character is somewhat distanced from us. She may seem likable, but her actions convince us that she is also foolish. The ironic main character acts opposite to the traditional heroic action of the main character (even main characters who are not necessarily likable or empathic). She unleashes action that, in its results, undermines her intentions, with results that are often closer to tragic than to heroic.

In the work of Preston Sturges, Charles Pike (Henry Fonda) is the ironic main character in *The Lady Eve*. Woodrow (Eddie Bracken) is the central character of *Hail the Conquering Hero*, and John L. Sullivan (Joel McCrea) is the ironic central character in *Sullivan's Travels*. Although we can also highlight the Barry Lyndon (Ryan O'Neal) character in *Barry Lyndon* or Alex (Malcolm McDowell) in *A Clockwork Orange* or Joker (Matthew Modine) in *Full Metal Jacket*, we will concentrate on the Sturges characters for the moment.

Charles Pike in *The Lady Eve* is a naive, rich young man who would rather affiliate with snakes than women. On a sea cruise, Jean, a professional gambler (Barbara Stanwyck), prepares this lamb for slaughter, but she inadvertently falls in love with him. He, meanwhile, has discovered what he considers her true intentions—to marry him for his money—and he breaks off the relationship. To avenge herself, she visits his family pretending to be British nobility. Pike falls for the transparent ruse and once again proposes. This time, she confesses a history of marriages (on the wedding night) that, in its extensiveness, insults his masculinity. Again, the relationship is off. But Charles, a true innocent, takes another cruise and falls in love with the same woman, Jean, who now claims to be the original gambler. The film ends with Pike taking a third stab at this relationship. We can only hope for the best. In quintessential fashion, Sturges has created an Adam and Eve story that maintains the illusion of the Garden of Eden but admits some contemporary qualifications—that money skews vision and perception.

Pike moves from innocent to wronged young man, to a spiteful and then naive young man, with abandon. As the main character, he seems remarkably unaware and impulsive, and he does not have a very clear goal. Nor is he a pillar of strength; he is a flawed innocent.

The same type of description can be claimed for John L. Sullivan (Joel McCrea), the main character in *Sullivan's Travels*. Sullivan is a very successful film director whose success is based on his comedies. However, Sullivan doesn't feel directing comedies is appropriate during the Depression. He wants to do a serious film based on an important book. As he knows nothing about the down-and-out people in society, the subjects of the book, he goes out into the world to do research. The studio, to protect its investment, sends a team of public relations and medical people to look after him. In order to lose them, Sullivan hops a southbound train. Aroused from sleep by a train guard who takes him for a hobo, he is arrested and imprisoned. A real hobo is killed by the train and the body is presumed to be Sullivan's. Sullivan, now in a southern prison, is mourned by his friends and employers.

The film turns very serious and Sullivan suffers as a prisoner. He only regains his perspective on himself when, one night, with the other prisoners, he watches cartoons in the local church. He laughs and he realizes the importance of laughter. When he is released from prison, he acknowledges his inability to make serious films and celebrates the importance of laughter.

Sullivan functions as a stand-in for Hollywood success stories that don't relate to the world outside of Hollywood. They take themselves seriously—often too seriously—elevate superficially important things, and downgrade ordinary life. Just as Sullivan doesn't have a good grasp of the reality in society, neither does Hollywood. In many ways, Sturges is poking fun at himself and Sullivan's character is the means to do this. Again, the ironic character is far from heroic.

In *Hail the Conquering Hero*, Woodrow (Eddie Bracken) can't get into the army (he has allergies), but his father was a World War I hero. Now that World War II is upon him, it's his turn. He can't face telling his mother or his sweetheart the truth, so he begins a deception. He works in a military plant a few hours from his hometown, but has soldiers, who are shipping out, mail letters home from Guadalcanal for him. His family thinks he is a soldier.

One night, he meets a group of Marines with very little spending money and buys them a drink. The Sergeant (William Demerest) knew Woodrow's father in World War I, and vows to make the situation better. He telegraphs Woodrow's family to notify them that Woodrow has been discharged due to a war wound and will be coming home. The Marines will go home with him.

An elaborate deception ensues, which Woodrow resists. He becomes, to all concerned—town and companions—a war hero. Some people in the town want him to become the new mayor. Woodrow's original deception has grown so elaborate that the family's reputation, not just his own, is at stake. When he finally confesses the truth, he faces his humiliation squarely. But the town needs a hero and they claim him as one in spite of his lack of a military war record. Whether the ending of the film comments on war, small towns, heroism, the issue of deception in public life, or on all of these things, Woodrow is as far from John Wayne in *The Sands of Iwo Jima* as he can get. As an ironic character, Woodrow is an innocent who is deceptive to prevent hurting his loved ones, but in the end, he humiliates them and himself.

No matter the outcome of the narrative ending, the ironic character plants doubt in our minds and we are left with a sense of unease. We are also as far from identifying with the character as we would be if the main character was unsympathetic. The ironic main character is quite far from the conventional main character.

What we have described so far are essentially unusual characters who are positioned in the story in such a way that they are ironic. Another approach to ironic character is to allow for less identification with the character because of the nature of the character. For example, Janet Frame, a writer, is portrayed as unattractive and disturbed and at all times eccentric in Jane Campion's film of the Laura Jones screenplay, *An Angel at My Table*. This intense portrayal of the early life (leading up to her commercial success) of the writer is troubling in the frequency of rejection of Janet by almost all of the characters. The consequence of these rejections and of her behavior, Janet is positioned as an ironic character.

Rejection also plays a role in how we view Forrest Gump (Tom Hanks) in Eric Roth's screenplay, *Forrest Gump* (1994). He is both an influence on events because he was there but he also seems to be out of touch with those events. The consequence of his interactions and the death of characters who tolerate him is such that he seems detached from those events and people. It is the ultimate irony of the story that he has such an impact on people and events because of that detachment. Forrest Gump is certainly an ironic character.

Finally we turn to an unusual example of an ironic character. Bruno Ramirez and Paul Tana have used the striking device of shifting main characters at the end of Act I in order to reflect on the fate of both main characters. Their film, *La Sarrasine* (1991) is a Canadian film set at the turn of the century. An Italian immigrant in Montreal is a successful tailor, and he is very paternal about his employees, fellow immigrants. Intimidated by a local Quebecker, an argument between one of those employees and the Quebecker escalates into violence. And it is the conciliatory tailor who acts. He kills the Quebecker. The resulting trial confirms the guilt of the tailor.

At this stage the story shifts to his wife. She too wishes to survive but as her husband struggles for dignity she is the person who insists on fighting. She will not return to Italy. She will fight for her husband's life. But she fails. The tailor commits suicide in jail and she decides to stay and to make a life for herself.

The shift from one character to the other at the end of Act I works because both characters share the same goal—to survive. However, because we shift from one character to the other we are distanced from the tailor and we can reflect on the implication of the cultural, social and legal struggles of both the tailor and his wife, indeed of all Italian immigrants in Quebec. The shift allows husband and wife to become icons of the immigrant experience. The result is a power unexpected in the story. The use of the ironic character, once again, has made more complex our response to the screen story.

Irony and Dialogue

Dialogue often relates to the function of the character speaking in the screenplay. It can be used for purposes of characterization or plot advancement, or it can be used simply as humor to alleviate the tension in a scene. When dialogue is used ironically, it draws attention to itself as does the ironic character. It distances us from the unfolding story and, by taking us out of the scene, makes us think about the contents of the scene or about the dissonance between character and language, character and character, or what the characters know and what we know.

Perhaps the best way to study ironic dialogue is to look at it in its simplest form. In *The Lady Eve,* everyone on the ocean liner is aware that Charles Pike is very rich. Consequently, every woman on the ocean liner (and in the film) is consumed with trying to marry Charles Pike. In the rush for bar orders for dinner, the following brief conversation takes place between the bartender and a steward:

```
            A STEWARD
      (coming up to the bar)
  Six more Pike's Pale, and
  snappy, my lad.

            BARTENDER
  What are you trying to do,
  embarrass me? We're all out
  of Pike's. Work something
  else off on them.

            THE STEWARD
  They don't want nothing else.
  They want the ale that won
  for Yale . . . rah, rah, rah!

            BARTENDER
  Well, tell them to go to
  Harvard.[3]
```

It is clear that the bartender is not suggesting his recommendation literally. In fact, his response suggests his loss of patience with the patronizing efforts of the shipmates trying to ingratiate themselves with an indifferent Charles Pike. The request is ruining the bartender's ability to serve and his professional pride requires the ironic comment about Harvard.

Moving to a more complex use of dialogue, the relationship of function to character, we turn to *Sullivan's Travels*. The following exchange takes place between Sullivan and his butler:

                    SULLIVAN
        I'm going out on the road to
        find out what it's like to be
        poor and needy . . . and then
        I'm going to make a picture
        about it.

                    THE BUTLER
        If you'll permit me to say,
        Sir: The subject is not an
        interesting one. The poor
        know all about poverty and
        only the morbid rich would
        find the topic glamorous.[4]

The function of the butler is to serve his employer, Sullivan; but in this scene he challenges Sullivan's goal to make a serious film. The butler suggests Sullivan is one of those morbid rich people who find poverty glamorous and he goes on to lecture his employer about poverty. The exchange points out Sullivan's naivete and sets up a pattern in which all of Sullivan's expectations are undermined (as they are in the narrative).

Another purpose of dialogue is to characterize. In the excerpt that follows, a fledgling actress buys breakfast for a hobo in Hollywood. The hobo is John L. Sullivan, a Hollywood director, but she doesn't know it yet:

                    THE GIRL
        Say, who's being sorry for
        who? Are you buying me the
        eggs or am I buying them for
        you?

                    SULLIVAN
        I'd like to repay you for
        them.

                    THE GIRL
        All right, give me a letter
        of introduction to Lubitsch.

                    SULLIVAN
I might be able to do that
too . . . Who is Lubitsch?

                    THE GIRL
Eat your eggs.

                    SULLIVAN
          (with his mouth full)
Can you act?

                    THE GIRL
What did you say?

                    SULLIVAN
          (swallowing)
I said, can you act?

                    THE GIRL
Sure I can act. Would you
like me to give you a
recitation?

                    SULLIVAN
Go ahead.

                    THE GIRL
          (not expecting to be taken seriously)
Skip it. My next act will be
an impersonation of a young
lady going home . . . on the
thumb.

                    SULLIVAN
In that outfit?

                    THE GIRL
How about your own outfit?

                    SULLIVAN
          (after a moment)
Haven't you got a car?

                    THE GIRL
No. Have you?

                    SULLIVAN
Well . . . no . . . but . . .

                              THE GIRL
                    Then don't get ritzy. And
                    I'll tell you some other
                    things I haven't got. I
                    haven't got a yacht, or a
                    pearl necklace, or a fur
                    coat, or a country seat, or
                    even a winter seat. And I
                    could use a girdle, too.

                              SULLIVAN
                    I wish I could give you a
                    few of the things you need.

                              THE GIRL
                    You're not trying to lead me
                    astray, are you? You big, bad
                    wolf!
                         (Sullivan laughs sheepishly)

                              THE GIRL
                    You know, the nice thing
                    about buying food for a man
                    is you don't have to laugh at
                    his jokes. Just think, if you
                    were some big shot like a
                    casting director or
                    something, I'd be staring
                    into your bridgework . . .

In this sequence, we get a sense of the girl's generosity, as well as her spirit. Another level of meaning is added because the girl doesn't know Sullivan's true identity. Ironically, she can be herself and Sullivan, also, can be himself, rather than a director auditioning an actress. Consequently, the dialogue shifts from emphasizing the relationship between director-actress to man-woman, and keeps shifting. The relationship advances much more rapidly than it would otherwise. It's as if both characters dropped their public personalities for their personal ones. The result is an intimate feeling between them.

Finally, dialogue is used for plot advancement. The following excerpt from *The Lady Eve* characterizes the first meeting of Jean and Charles Pike, and also reflects the primacy of Jean. Jean is looking into her mirror as women all over the room are attempting to command Pike's attention. He is oblivious or indifferent.

JEAN'S HAND, A MIRROR. SHOT OF CHARLES IN MIRROR.

JEAN

That's right . . . pick it up
. . . it was worth trying
anyway, wasn't it? . . . Look
at the girl over to his left
. . . look over to your left,
bookworm . . . there's a girl
pining for you . . . a little
further . . . just a little
further, there! Now, wasn't
that worth looking for? See
those nice store teeth, all
beaming at you? Why, she
recognizes you! She's up . . .
she's down . . . she can't
make up her mind. She's up
again! She recognizes you!
She's coming over to speak to
you. The suspense is killing
me. "Why, for heaven's sake!
Aren't you Fuzzy Oathammer I
went to manual training
school with in Louisville?
Oh, you're not? Well, you
certainly look exactly like
him . . . it's certainly a
remarkable resemblance, but if
you're not going to ask me to
sit down; I suppose you're
not going to ask me to sit
down . . . I'm very sorry. I
certainly hope I haven't
caused you any embarrassment,
you so-and-so. . . . " So he
goes back to the table.
Imagine thinking she could
get away with anything like
that with me. I wonder if my
tie's on straight . . . I
certainly upset them, don't
I? Now, who else is after me?
Ah, the lady champion
wrestler, wouldn't she make
an armful . . . Oh, you don't
like her either. Well, what
are you going to do about it?
Oh, you just can't stand it
anymore . . . you're leaving

> . . . these women just don't
> give you a moment's peace, do
> they? Well, go ahead! Go sulk
> in your cabin! Go soak your
> head and see if I care.

CLOSE SHOT—CHARLES
He rises, places a finger in his book and starts for
the door of the main dining room. The CAMERA PANS
with him. As he gets a little distance away from
Jean and her father—

POINT-OF-VIEW SHOT
Jean and her father watch us rigidly. Suddenly, Jean
gets lower in her seat as she stretches out under
the table. Charles goes hurtling PAST THE CAMERA and
we hear a frightful crash.

> JEAN
> (half-rising)
> Why don't you look where
> you're going?

Charles being helped to his feet.

> CHARLES
> Why don't I look . . . ?

He walks toward Jean.

> JEAN
> Look what you did to my shoe.
> You knocked the heel off.

> CHARLES
> I did? Well, I'm . . .
> certainly very sorry.

> JEAN
> You did and you can just take
> me right to my cabin for
> another pair of slippers.

> CHARLES
> (slightly rattled)
> Oh . . . well . . . certainly
> . . . I guess it's the least I
> can do . . . by the way my
> name is Pike.

                    JEAN
          Everybody knows about that
          . . . nobody's talking about
          anything else. This is my
          father, Colonel Harrington.
          My name is Jean. It's really
          Eugenia.
                    (she takes his arm)
          Come on.[6]

In this scene, the dialogue suggests a passive viewer, at best, editorializing about the efforts of the women in the room to meet Charles Pike. Toward the end of the excerpt, when Jean trips Pike and blames him for the fall, not only does she move from passive commentator to participant, she actually moves into command of the situation. He will, of course, take her to her cabin for a change of slippers. She not only meets him, she isolates him, a man who has been in the jungle for a year, and gets him alone with her in her cabin.

We, in the audience, are privileged. We know things that Charles does not. The irony is that Jean is totally controlling the situation. Her dialogue does not convey her true intentions. We understand her intentions, but Charles does not. He remains the innocent and is about to be victimized by Jean. In this scene, the plot is advanced to the next phase of the relationship.

Irony and Atmosphere

If nonverbal detail creates a sense of atmosphere that supports the credibility of the narrative, the use of detail in an ironic manner subverts the most obvious direction of the narrative. The result is to alter meaning through a tonal shift. Irony widens the gap between the foreground and background stories. We have no choice but to adjust our interpretation of the screen story.

Few writers or directors use irony as deftly as Stanley Kubrick. In *2001: A Space Odyssey*, Kubrick presents a future world in which a computer, Hal, exhibits more humanity than the two astronauts who are his masters. Indeed, when he senses their distrust will lead to his destruction, Hal sets out to destroy his destroyers.

This role reversal, the humanizing of the machine and the dehumanization of man in this futuristic setting, is rife with irony. What is critical for the credibility of both perceptions is the presentation of the spaceship. Its interior, as well as the behavior of the astronauts, has been stripped of feeling. The cool white planes of the ship contrast sharply with Hal's red eye, his operational light, and the voice that acknowledges that Hal is in operation. Kubrick contrasts the antiseptic world of the humans with the passion of the computer. Hal's sound and visual dimensions are both limited, but they allow our imagination to conjure up the degree of Hal's humanity.

In *Lolita*, Kubrick uses irony to portray the two worlds of Humbert Humbert and America. Humbert is a guest to America and a lecturer in poetry at an American college. When he stops at a guest house to vacation prior to the school year, he falls in love with Lolita, the 15-year-old daughter of the guest-house owner. Humbert is a man consumed by his obsession and his passion. All the while, the place and the people (including Lolita) are somewhat sterile. The clash between Humbert's feelings and the character's milieu is so great that we are left wondering about the reality and meaning of his passion for a nymphet. Without this clash, the irony of Nabakov's screenplay wouldn't resonate with such powerful commentary about sexuality in post-war America.

Irony and Genre

As suggested in Chapters 5 and 6, genres lend themselves to consistent narrative structures. What happens when a writer sets out to alter a motif or challenge a convention? Whether this occurs through mixing genres or altering a single motif, the resulting genre violation is similar to the result of using an ironic character or dialogue. Meaning is altered. At times, this enhances the richness of the genre experience. At other times, it can depreciate the experience. In all cases, the viewer is moved away from the expectations that genre films imply.

Genre violation is probably the most typical ironic challenge to narrative structure. Jonathan Demme seems very attracted to this approach. In his film of Max Frye's script for *Something Wild*, Demme mixes *film noir* with screwball comedy. The result is both more and less than the sum of the two parts. The main character, as victim (a characteristic of *film noir*), does reconcile with the ironic main character; but after the midpoint of the film, the main character begins to entertain heroic action. The result is inconsistent; we don't know whether to admire or pity him. In the end, we have a mixed feeling for Charles Driggs and, as a result, his heroic efforts in the second part of the film don't yield the results for which Demme may have hoped. However, the film does have the patina of freshness for having attempted to mix genres.

Demme has more success with Bo Goldman's *Melvin and Howard*. This story, about the consequences of an encounter between Melvin, a simple Westerner, and Howard Hughes, is rife with irony. Melvin, in possession of what he views to be the Last Will and Testament of Howard Hughes, attempts to become what society suggests is the pinnacle of success—to be rich and, therefore, happy. But Melvin's efforts are those of an innocent. Where money is concerned, happiness proves elusive. There are a lot of people who want Howard Hughes's legacy. Melvin has neither the guile nor the resources to be rich like Howard Hughes.

In this film, Demme and Goldman portray Melvin as the ironic character and achieve a feeling for the mythology that made America until recently the richest nation in the world. In *Melvin and Howard*, we feel for the myth and the man. But in the end, Melvin is the tragic main character of the melodrama. Because of the use of ironic main character, the film moves in the direction of satire. The dissonance between the two genres, melodrama and satire, elevates the film beyond melodrama, but not quite as far as the aggressive aftertaste of satire.

It is useful to explore this notion of irony and genre further by focusing on genre violation at the level of the nature, goal, and fate of the protagonist. When the expectation that Bill Mooney will be a classic Western protagonist is upset in *Unforgiven* (1992), we are distanced from him and we reflect upon his goal, financial gain, in the light of the Western hero's classical goals of moral equilibrium and an individualistic sense of freedom. Mooney's goal debases his character in our eyes and dims the sense of pastoral myth with it; thus our experience of the story form, the Western is altered.

This is the pattern of irony when applied to genre. In melodrama, the classic character challenges the authority of the power structure and is punished accordingly. Good examples of this kind of character are the Donald Sutherland character in Euzhan Palcy and Colin Welland's *A Dry White Season* (1990) and the Richard Gere character in Nicholas Meyer and Sarah Kernochan's *Sommersby* (1993). In *A Dry White Season*, the Sutherland character challenges apartheid in the South Africa of the 1970s and is killed, and in *Sommersby* the Richard Gere character challenges the power of property and marriage when he pretends he is another man. Both characters suffer the classic fate of the main character in the melodrama.

But in Steven Soderburgh's *King of the Hill* (1993), the young man who is its main character will do anything to survive the travails of the Depression in St. Louis in the 1930's—and he does survive. By layering the fate of this main character, Soderburgh subtly shifts our attention to the unfairness and the cruelty of this period. He makes something of a hero out of the boy by celebrating his survivalism. Many who were kind or helpful to him are not so lucky in this grim portrait of the time and place.

Similar results occur in Alison Anders's *Gas, Food, Lodging* (1992). This story of survival focuses on a single mother's attempt to raise two daughters in the modern West. The mother's ability to survive against a power structure that is skewed against women makes the story more poignant and more believable than Callie Khouri's *Thelma & Louise* (1991). The melodrama is far more suited for such a message than the mix of road film (adventure) and melodrama allow for. And again the survival of the protagonist in this melodrama poses a wish for a better life for the 3 women in this story.

A more distanced and complex alteration of the fate of a main character occurs in John Guare's *Six Degrees of Separation* (1993). A young black man pays a visit to a wealthy older married couple. He claims to be the son of Sidney Poitier and a friend of their son. He is soon all but adopted into the family. When they find out he is an impostor, they turn against him although the wife wants to rescue him. She feels a loyalty to him totally absent from the relationship with her own children.

The main character in this Upper East Side New York melodrama is the wife. Her goal in the earlier part of the story is a status most clearly associated with great wealth. Having passed through the phase of wanting to associate with Sidney Poitier, she transcends her disappointment and sense of betrayal and works toward a relationship with the young impostor. Whether this is another deception or a liberal feint at race and age reconciliation is unclear.

What is clear is that the main character does not suffer the classic fate of the main character in melodrama. The distancing poses reflective questions about economic, social, and political standing in the community. Irony is not deployed critically here, but more as a conciliatory device. And the results are surprising.

The fate of the protagonist is also surprising in Don McKellar's *Highway 61* (1992). A gentle mix of melodrama and road movie (adventure), *Highway 61* tells the story of a young, rural Canadian barber (Don McKellar) who is convinced, without much pressure, to drive a young woman (Valerie Buhagiar) and her "dead brother" to New Orleans for burial. What he doesn't know is that she is using the body to transport drugs across the border. They meet an assorted and sordid group of characters. The emphasis on the journey is on eccentricity (the tone is definitely ironic).

The main character, the barber, a man with musical aspirations, succeeds in transcending his own meekness. Borrowing from the fate of the heroic character in the adventure film, McKellar allows the contradiction between the melodramatic main character and the adventure main character to indicate that melodrama does not have to be tragic when leavened by adventure. The result is an ironic meditation on the fate of the main character in melodrama. Funny, surprising, *Highway 61* is in every way fresh. Irony succeeds in the breech of genre expectation.

Three-Act Structure

In *Full Metal Jacket,* Stanley Kubrick challenges the traditional structure by presenting the story in two acts. Act One is basic training; Act

Two is the battle in Vietnam. By moving away from introduction–confrontation–resolution to introduction–confrontation, Kubrick opts for an open-ended ending to the film. There is no catharsis. This troubling result is compatible with the use of ironic secondary characters—the drill sergeant in Act One becomes the enemy, rather than the father figure generally portrayed by the character, and the sniper in Act Two proves to be a slight woman who is near death. She is not presented as the enemy usually is. Given the death the enemy has inflicted, we expect her to be an invincible, larger-than-life force. But, ironically, the enemy is this woman. In both cases, the characters subvert our expectations and support a structure that offers no resolution.

Woody Allen, as mentioned earlier, chooses to subvert structure and genre in *Crimes and Misdemeanors*. Two stories, each written in three acts, intertwine freely, the point of view of one undermining that of the other. Although melodrama and situation comedy are flip sides of the other, the happy ending to the melodrama (when our genre expectation is tragedy) and the tragic ending to the situation comedy (when our genre expectation is a happy ending) subvert each other and make the final scene, the meeting of Cliff and Jonah, ironic.

Woody Allen uses, as Kubrick did in *Full Metal Jacket*, structural and genre violations in order to produce the ironic tone that unsettles the viewer to reflect upon issues beyond genre—war, morality, the quality of life. Both *Crimes and Misdemeanors* and *Full Metal Jacket* are serious films that use tone and irony to invite meaning beyond what is apparent in the narrative.

Recently, a number of writers have experimented successfully with structure. The most commercially successful experiment is Richard Curtis's *Four Weddings and a Funeral* (1994). An argument can be made that this film actually follows conventional three-act form—boy meets girl, boy doesn't want girl, boy finally decides he really does want girl. But we suggest that on another narrative level, Curtis does organize the entire story around a series of special events—weddings, proposed weddings, and a funeral. By doing so he has contextualized the personal issue (commitment to a relationship) into a social context, that is, the weddings and the funeral.

As a genre, *Four Weddings and a Funeral* is clearly a situation comedy with the main character challenging the values of marriage. The story has a clear protagonist, the male (Hugh Grant). The challenge to storytelling conventions of structure comes from the theatrical device of organizing the entire story around five social events. Superficially, the implication is five acts, but actually the film neatly divides into three acts with turning points just after the two have slept together for the first time, when she (Andie MacDowell) poses the issue of commitment and he rejects it. The next turning point occurs after her marriage. He confesses his love for her, but now she is married and the possibility of a relationship has never seemed more distant.

The dissonance between the possible structure of the film (five acts) and the dramatic structure (three acts) make the film seem novel and inventive. The dissonance between the two structures also allows the audience to consider more powerfully the clash of personal and social goals as represented principally by the Hugh Grant character.

Another recent experiment with structure is Don McKellar's *32 Short Films About Glenn Gould* (1994). This unusual mix of recreated dramatic episodes together with documentary segments are thirty-two episodes about the life of the great Canadian interpreter of Bach, Glenn Gould. The film for the most part follows the chronology of his life and career. Particular episodes, such as his decision to stop performing live and his last concert, are much longer than other episodes.

By mixing documentary and drama, by altering lengths, by shifts in tone in thirty-two self-contained films within a single story, *32 Short Films About Glenn Gould* becomes an example where rules are broken in the name of creating a complex, creative, bold pastiche of a man who defied categorization. Because of the structural violation, McKellar and director Francois Girard force us to consider the undefinable nature of genius and the playful core of creativity. The film undermines structural expectation and creates its own structure in order to move us beyond convention.

Jean-Claude Lauzon in *Leolo* (1992), his meditation on the limits of family and the opportunity of art, travels further down a path marked out by McKellar and Girard. *Leolo* tells the story of a young boy growing up in Quebec in a family that is limited both mentally and spiritually. Consequently, the young boy conjures up a new identity for himself. He is really an Italian born out of an unusual alliance. In Sicily, a young Italian masturbates on a fresh shipment of tomatoes. In Montreal, his mother falls on those same tomatoes, and Leolo, as he calls himself, is born of this union. He denies he is his father's son. Faced with a primitivism, emotional violence, and illness, and a sterility of life he cannot accept, Leolo imagines another life, a better life, an artistic effort to escape the physical realities of his life.

Lauzon has structured his film along a foreground story that highlights the physical realities of Leolo's life, and a background story that reflects his artistic efforts at a rich spiritual life. The dissonance between the two story lines, between fact and fiction, between reality and fantasy is so great, so vivid that we enter a relationship with Leolo's hopes and dreams. Lauzon manages to use the ironic shifts in tone between the two to create a rich interior life for the boy, a world where dreams can overcome despair.

Our involvement becomes so visceral that it is quite a shock when *Leolo* ends with the boy being hospitalized for the same schizophrenia that afflicts his siblings. It is a remarkable creative achievement that Lauzon's structural violation and contradictions are as effective as the thirty-two short films used by McKellar and Girard in creating a complex, rich, creative inner life in the main character.

A similar range of tonal shift for purposes of satire can be found in Robert Altman's *Short Cuts* (1993). This meditation on the urban nightmare, set in Los Angeles, attempts to underscore the cost to one's humanity. No one is immune. A mother diapers her child while dispensing phone sex. A policeman harasses a young woman driver with the threat of fines; he will dispense with the fine in return for sexual favors. Mothers are indifferent to their daughters, and fathers are self-serving and narcissistic. The sons will clearly pay a price in the future. Alternating between humor and emotional violence, Altman creates an equivalent to Hieronymous Bosch's hell in today's Los Angeles.

It is useful to contrast Altman's effectiveness in *Short Cuts* with a less extreme presentation of humanity in the urban context—John Sayles's *City of Hope* (1992). Because Sayles does not use extreme tonal shifts in order to present a more realistic portrait of personal and political corruption in an unnamed eastern city, the effectiveness of *City of Hope* is blunted when it is compared with *Short Cuts*. As with the work of Lindsay Anderson and Stanley Kubrick, satire applied to a critical social issue can be a remarkably powerful story form.

Satire

Perhaps no genre offers more freedom to the writer than satire. Satire is the extreme case of deploying irony in the screen story. The writer is free to use an ironic main character, but beyond the characters the writer can move as far from realism as she desires. In the work of two film satires, Terry Gilliam's *Brazil* and Stanley Kubrick's *Dr. Strangelove or: How I Learned to Stop Worrying and Love the Bomb*, the healthy irreverence of the writers is generated from their passion about the issues—the future, and nuclear bombs—and from their ferocious use of humor.

Satire affords the writer with the ultimate opportunity for irony in a screen story. The tonal violation is so great that satire shakes the viewer's sense of security.

David Sherwin's *O Lucky Man!* is the story of Mick, a young coffee salesman, interested in getting ahead. He is earnest, but the barriers that prevent him from getting ahead include friends, lovers, employers, and total strangers. He is almost killed on a highway and in a hospital. He is arrested for the malfeasance of his employer, and when he tries to reform himself after prison, he is attacked by the very homeless he helps feed. The world is more than cruel, it's lethal. Naturally, Mick decides to become an actor and there the story ends.

This brief description doesn't do justice to this modern *Candide* with musical interludes. The story is savage in its portrayal of the alienating forces active in our modern lives. Although not Luddite in its goals, it's certainly a modern equivalent. Sherwin uses Mick as an ironic main character, the innocent victim of an economic system determined to exhaust him, but more likely to destroy him.

The narrative structure of *O Lucky Man!* is constantly challenged. Seemingly spontaneously, the story line breaks away to a musical interlude. Eventually, the musician who performs the interludes, Alan Price, is introduced as a character in the narrative. Transgression follows transgression and the narrative progresses readily away from realism. Satire is the extreme case of tonal violation and its primary quality is its use of irony.

Conclusion

Tone is a crucial factor for the screenwriter to consider and should concern you early in your writing. In the treatment-to-first-draft phase, your attitude toward the characters, their language, and the narrative structure will prompt you to make choices about the tone of your script. These choices are critical signposts for the viewer, although they don't fully interpret the story, they point in the direction of the interpretation of the story.

As a writer, you can create a conventional tone—the classic empathetic main character, functional dialogue, and the expected three-act structure, including the use of genre. Or, you can challenge those notions, in which case the use of irony comes into play.

In the extreme case, you can use satire, the ultimate genre application of irony. You can challenge our expectations by using an ironic main character. The use of this type of character will result in a more distanced relationship between viewer and character. Whether the result is to reflect upon the actions of the character or to seek out alternate meaning for his role in the narrative, the use of the ironic main character yields very different, often more complex, results than the use of the conventional main character.

Additional meaning can also result from the use of ironic dialogue. Ironic dialogue is the result of genre violations and mixed genres, rather than conventional narrative patterns. In all cases, tonal shifts alter meaning and alter the audience's experience of the screen story. Whether the shifts are verbal (dialogue) or nonverbal (atmosphere), both point out the critical role tone plays in setting up the relationship between the audience and the screen story.

References

1. Northrop Frye, *Anatomy of Criticism* (Princeton: Princeton University Press, 1957), p. 47.
2. Ibid.
3. "The Lady Eve" in *Five Screenplays by Preston Sturges*, ed. Brian Henderson (Los Angeles: University of California Press, 1985), p. 362.
4. "Sullivan's Travels" in *Five Screenplays by Preston Sturges*, ed. Brian Henderson (Los Angeles: University of California Press, 1985), pp. 552–553.
5. Ibid., pp. 589–590.
6. "The Lady Eve," in Henderson, pp. 364–366.

15

....

Dramatic Voice/
Narrative Voice

One definition of mainstream cinema is that it subordinates everything to narrative cause and effect and character motivation. "In Hollywood cinema, a specific sort of narrative causality operates as the dominant, making temporal and spatial systems vehicles for it."[1] These subordinated temporal and spatial systems, the actual elements of film language, are rendered transparent by the functioning of a conventional structure creating the illusion that the story would happen exactly the same way whether the camera were there or not. Most of our dramatic concerns—the plausibility of motivation, the consistency of character, the avoidance of overt coincidence, the construction of a believable back story—come out of the conceit that we are spying on a pre-existing event. As we discussed in Chapter 2, this conceit is deeply embedded in 19th-century notions of realism and naturalism and, like restorative three-act structure, can be traced back to the well-made play.[2]

For our purposes, we identify a scene that seems to tell itself, that plays without making us conscious that it is being narrated, as a scene that is working in the dramatic voice. But as we said earlier, even a scene using the dramatic voice must be given shape by some form of narrating agency that organizes the presentation of events. No matter how realistic the representation, we are not watching reality—the act of representing the world implies narration. The narrating may be overt or virtually invisible, but it is always present.

The use of the terms *narrator* and *narrative voice* in film is problematic. First, a narrator in film is most often understood as a voice-over narrator. Relatively few films use such voice overs and, if our comments pertained only to them, we would be addressing a very narrow concern.

The second reason that narrative voice is problematic in film is that it is deeply embedded in literature and refers to the manner in which the writer speaks directly to us. Such simple and direct address is not possible in most films because there are too many intermediary agencies in the mass media production process to speak of a unified, singular filmmaker's voice. Also, in most films, the articulation of the narrative voice is much less direct than in literature.*

However, even given these reservations, we find the notion of voice or narration to be the only terms that speak to the independent filmmaker's desire to be heard, to express a personal vision while still using the story-telling power of narrative (as opposed to experimental) filmmaking. Thus, we use these terms to refer to the agency that communicates the story to us, whether overtly or not. In fact, the literary antecedents are useful to us, because we can understand the development of narrative voice in main-stream film by looking at the movement from the classic 19th-century omniscient narration to the limited, three-person narrator of Henry James and Gustave Flaubert.

The classic omniscient 19th-century narrator was not only all-knowing, but all-judgmental; not only able to spy on all aspects of this pre-existing world, but also capable of commenting and evaluating. For instance, George Eliot opens *Middlemarch* with this sentence,

> Who that cares much to know the history of man, and how the
> mysterious mixture behaves under the varying experiments of
> Time, has not dwelt, at least briefly, on the life of Saint Theresa,
> has not smiled with some gentleness at the thought of the little
> girl walking forth one morning hand-in-hand with her still
> smaller brother, to go and seek martyrdom in the country of the
> Moors?[3]

Not only does this sentence serve to introduce Theresa, but also to introduce a style of narration in which the narrator is willing to admit to a clear sense of what is important. This is evident in the flat declaration that Theresa is a saint going out to seek martyrdom.

Today, we probably find such prejudgment by the narrative voice old-fashioned, preferring instead to make our own judgment as the story plays out. In effect, we would rather infer the quality of the character by the dramatic voice, rather than be told by the narrator. Even if we wanted to, it

---

*In *Narration in the Fiction Film* (Madison, University of Wisconsin Press, 1985), David Bordwell has an interesting set of chapters which contrast dramatic and narratives analytic approaches to narration. He concludes that neither model is theoretically satisfactory, a conclusion with which we agree as applies to pure theory. However, we still find this distinction extremely useful in describing different modes the writer has at her command.

would be very hard to communicate this omniscient judgment directly in film. How would we show Theresa as a saint? With the superimposition of a statue, church music, an animated halo? All these expressionistic devices have been tried and, for the most part, were found to be heavy-handed and literal. Eisenstein's mocking of the pompous Kerensky by superimposing his walk with the strut of a cock has historical interest, but does not suggest much of a practical alternative to us today. Does this mean, then, that a filmmaker cannot suggest a point of view without being so mannered? No. The late 19th-century development of the narrator within the story provides an analogy for the classic film style.

Reacting against the overt authorial presence of writers like Charles Dickens and George Eliot, many novelists (foremost among them, Gustave Flaubert and Henry James) looked for another way to narrate stories. They shifted their interest from the question of what we know, to how we know it, and, as a result, they saw the omniscient, judging narrator as problematic, asking: Where did this voice of God come from? What explained the certainty with which an omniscient narrator created and claimed to know the fictive world? Though it was possible for a reader to judge the characters' trustworthiness (based on their actions, about which we could form an opinion), how could we possibly engage the narrator who injected a point of view, but stood outside the text?

Thus, instead of commenting directly on the action, Henry James came up with the notion of the reflector character or the narrator within the story—a character who is presented quite neutrally by the writer, but who is allowed to recount and make judgments about the events in which she was involved. This character narrates in place of the writer, but since she exists in the fictive world of the story, it is possible for us, as readers, to engage with her even as she is presenting information to us.

We can see how this works when we contrast this sentence of Henry James's *The Ambassadors* to the *Middlemarch* section quoted above: "Strether's first question, when he reached the hotel, was about his friend; yet on his learning that Waymarsh was apparently not to arrive till evening he was not wholly disconcerted."[4] Notice, immediately, how little authorial judgment this sentence makes (of course, there are implications of narrative voice in the syntax, word usage, length of the sentence, etc.). The emotion directly described is Strether's, an emotion that we take to be one of which he is fully conscious. By contrast, in *Middlemarch* the judgments are the author's; nothing there allows us to assume that the young Theresa regards herself as a saint.

Strether's being not "wholly disconcerted" is taken up over the next few pages, developed, as it were, through Strether's consciousness, so that we learn as he figures out the reason for being "not wholly disconcerted."

... the fruit of a sharp sense that, delightful as it would be to find himself looking, after so much separation, into his comrade's [Waymarsh's] face, his business would be a trifle bungled should he simply arrange for this countenance to present itself to the nearing steamer as the first "note" of Europe.[5]

Strether is, in effect, setting (narrating) his own situation—we enter the dominant voice of the book with his plotting his own expectations of how he wants to first meet Europe.[6]

The classic film style draws on this idea of allowing the character to, in effect, narrate his or her own story, without forcing the filmmaker to comment overtly. For instance, there is a scene in *The Verdict* in which Galvin enters the victim's hospital room with the intention of taking Polaroid pictures that he can use to get more money from the out-of-court settlement. As he takes the pictures, however, he moves slower and slower until finally he stops altogether, staring at one picture of the victim as it develops in front of his eyes. We know that this is the important moment of the scene, the moment where he begins to realize he must take the case to trial. But how do we know? Without in any way calling attention to them, the narrator employs a number of devices (rhythm, lighting, cutting pattern) that emphasize the importance of this decision, but because they all seem to be at the service of Galvin's realization, we get the sense that Galvin is not only making a decision, but he, not the narrator, is directing our attention to its importance.

Henry James was quite strict in staying with one particular consciousness, while mainstream film generally uses a combination of omniscient narration and various narrators within the story. Very few films use systematic control of point of view as part of their narrative strategies. Those films that do, *Rear Window* for instance, derive considerable formal power by their control of this device.

Hiding the narrator agent behind the character explains one of the paradoxes of the classic style—that, although the story appears to be driven by character, the camera expresses very little of the character's emotion on its own. The lens is almost never distorted by subjectivity, and rarely do we see extreme angle interpretative shots. Rather the narrative agency sets the stage for the character perspective by its use of point-of-view and eyeline-match sequences, structuring a series of neutral shots and reverse shots that are carefully tied to the line of the character's emotion. Our movement through the film is made up of our progressive awareness of the character's (as opposed to the filmmaker's) attitude toward the action. It's as though the filmmaker, much like Flaubert or James, is unwilling to say anything directly, preferring instead to let the characters tell their own story.

This method of storytelling, during which the narrator apparently cedes emotional control of the story to his character (remember, the outside narrator never disappears; he only appears to), raises a major obstacle for the independent narrative filmmaker. Independent films are made out of the desire of the filmmaker to speak in his own voice (whether this is possible or not is another topic). But, by emphasizing the dramatic voice over the narrative, by concealing the filmmaker's voice behind the character's, the effaced narrator of the classic film style restricts direct lyrical expression. The independent filmmaker who is seeking her own voice must find a way to assert the narrative voice over the dramatic pull of events. This may be harder in film (and video) than in all other arts because of the inherent naturalism and apparent transparency of the camera's image.[7]

Voice and Structure

Clearly, much of what we are calling *voice* in film is under the control of the director. Things like the relative realism of color scheme, the lighting contrast ratios, the set design, the casting, the balance of ambient sounds to dialogue, and the final editing pattern are beyond the realm of the writer. Still, it is possible to construct a script that emphasizes the narrative voice at the level of the story. As before, we have to start with structure.

We said that in classic film style, overt narration tends to be hidden behind a structure that functions to organize the meaning of events without calling attention to itself. If we want to place the narrative voice in the foreground, we must reduce the primacy of this unacknowledged structural drive. However, if we reduce the dependence on restorative three-act structure, we must find other ways to supply a narrative voice.

To simplify, we might say that structure is a pattern designed to focus the questions we want the viewer to ask as the story unfolds. Although structure is tied up with character-driven plot in classic Hollywood films, it does not necessarily have to be used that way. Structure is pattern. It may be made of anything that organizes our attention—a repeated line of dialogue, a recurrent situation, a musical theme, an external historical moment, a radio in the background, a return to the same location. The less structure relates to plot, the more formal it seems to be. The more external it is to the action, the more structure reads as the filmmaker's voice.

The realistic use of patterns, which we identify as mainstream structure, functions in two distinct and apparently self-contradicting ways. Structure tells us what is necessary for the movie to come to an end, while at the same time it must not call attention to itself. We know, for instance, that in *Wall Street*, Bud must come to terms with his father before the movie can end; when he does, we must feel that this is an inevitable outgrowth of character, not an overt manipulation by the filmmaker giving order to what would otherwise be an ambiguous circumstance.

To play against the structural dominance of mainstream film, then, we have to uncouple plot structure from simple story closure (or at least twist it) and find a way to call attention to its patterning. This sounds like it requires a radical approach to filmmaking, but is not necessarily so, as evidenced in an apparently mainstream example, Alfred Hitchcock's *Vertigo*.

Scottie, a former police lawyer, falls in love with Madeline, the woman he has been employed to protect. Obsessed by bizarre suicide fantasies, she apparently kills herself by jumping from a church bell tower. Overcome by guilt, Scottie breaks down and is unable to pull himself together until he sees a woman who reminds him of Madeline. We are told that this new woman, Judy, actually had disguised herself as Madeline to cover up a murder plot. Scottie doesn't know this and proceeds to make Judy over to recreate an image of Madeline. When Scottie finally realizes what has happened, he takes Judy back to the bell tower where, after having it out, she convinces him that she loves him. As they begin to kiss, a nun, having overheard them, suddenly appears and causes the startled Judy to step back and fall to her death, mimicking the bell tower "suicide" earlier in the film.

The film is divided in half, which suggests a kind of oppositional binary structure (action in the first half, reconstruction of the action in the second) so different from traditional three-act structure. Scottie's recreation of Madeline seems to succeed. The traditional pattern of transgression, recognition, and redemption has been overturned—Judy looks like she will get away with murder and Scottie with his obsessive remaking. Then the nun appears and Judy tumbles to her death. The nun's appearance seems both realistic and self-consciously tacked on to the film. Although the death from the bell tower has certainly been set up, the dominant dramatic force throughout the second half of the film is the question of Scottie's relationship to Judy. Their final embrace seems to resolve this relation, but this would be a disorienting resolution. If they make it together, how are we to take the murder and the illicit perversity of Scottie? Does crime actually pay? But suppose we don't read the nun's appearance with the same sense of realism as the rest of the film? Suppose we have a sense that some agency outside of the fictive world told her to come in, as if Hitchcock quite boldly is saying, "It is time to end the film now and to restore order." Then would the message of the film be that crime does not pay? Or would we be getting a much richer, more self-conscious, and fascinatingly ambiguous message that seems to be primly acceptable, while at the same time winks at the simple morality of more traditional endings? Such a possibility takes us out of the realm of mainstream story closure and leaves us with a lingering, overt, and much more bitter perception of the decorative veneer of story closure and its attendant romance.

Psycho, too, provides an interesting example of what happens when the apparent structural pattern is turned around. Much has been written about how Janet Leigh's murder gains particular power because it breaks the genre expectation that the main character will survive. But the murder does something else. By breaking the apparent dramatic drive of the story, it leaves us confused, uncertain what to look for or whom to follow. Left on our own, the dark tonalities of the film rise to the foreground and we feel a loss of direction that makes us even more anxious than the murders themselves would warrant.

Although he twists our expectations, Hitchcock still works within (and at times against) classic narrative cinema. A much more extreme example can be seen in Antonioni's *Eclipse*. This film, which charts a skittish love affair between Vittoria, a nervous woman played by Monica Vitti, and an unimaginative stockbroker, is more about urban space and how it distorts intimacy than it is about character and relationships. The lovers meet twice at the same suburban intersection. Both times, nothing appears to happen between them; instead, the camera seems more interested in the surroundings—a race horse trotting by, the emptiness of the streets, the permanence of the physical location in contrast to the tentativeness of the characters. The camera, far from being neutral, regards the lovers with the same sense of formal distance it regards everything else and hence the dominant emotional force, this cold formal distance, comes from the camera, not from the characters. By the second visit, Vittoria senses that there is a relationship between this desolation and her own life. It's almost as if she is becoming aware of the camera's distance.

Toward the end of the film, the lovers agree to meet at the intersection for a third time. They never show up, but Antonioni does. In a famous eight-minute sequence, he films the intersection as it appears without the lovers. It slowly darkens and the street lights come on (representing an actual eclipse or merely dusk, we never know). Over the sparse electronic music, the shots become increasingly abstracted and fragmentary until the sequence ends with an extreme close-up of a light bulb going on, which then dissolves into the grain of the film.

The characters have disappeared; they are not important anymore. What had been a narrative film becomes an experimental one—the dramatic voice is completely taken over by the narrative. The only logic informing the shots is the filmmaker's. There appears to be no fictive world, only a lyrical documentary of the street.

Yet this ending is surprisingly powerful. Although the characters do not appear, somehow the filmmaking has taken on the characters' feelings. Or, more accurately, the characters have taken on the feelings expressed all along by the filmmaking. The devolution of image in the last sequence seems to be a direct personal expression of the filmmaker's sense of the ineffability of emotional experience against the mass meaninglessness of the landscape. The character and the narrator have merged.

Conclusion

We have used the distinction between dramatic and narrative voice to talk about the relative foregrounding of the organizing agency in the story. We note that all films use a combination of these two voices. Mainstream filmmaking tends to follow Henry James's edict for literature—"Dramatize, dramatize, dramatize"—and particularly emphasizes the effaced narrator and the character's narration of his own story by using the point-of-view sequence and the eye match.

We suggest that the independent filmmaker who wants her voice to be heard tip the scales back toward emphasizing the narrative voice. This requires finding ways to uncouple traditional structure's one-to-one linkage with plot. We end by demonstrating that such uncoupling requires only the slightest shift in balance, as in Hitchcock's *Vertigo*, or a great commitment to almost lyric experimentation, as in Antonioni's *Eclipse*. In the next chapter, we talk about making the shift.

References

1. David Bordwell, Janet Staiger, and Kristin Thompson, *The Classical Hollywood Cinema, Film Style and Mode of Production to 1960* (New York: Columbia University Press, 1985) p. 12.
2. Of course, it can be traced back to Aristotle, but as Auerbach points out in *Mimesis* (Translated from the German by Willard Trask. Garden City, NY, Doubleday, 1953), the combining of "low mimetic forms" and tragic forms, which define what we call realism, comes after the French revolution.
3. George Eliot, *Middlemarch* (New York: Penguin Books, 1979), p. 25.
4. Henry James, *The Ambassadors* (London: Penguin Books, 1974), p. 5.
5. Ibid.
6. We repeat again, we are simplifying very complex material in order to present it here. We don't want to imply that the narrator outside the story has been replaced by Strether, only that another level of narration has been cloned (Strether's), which allows the narrator outside the story (there must always be one) to be less evident.

These assumptions of the objective, non-commenting narrator also came under attack in literature. A pivotal book, Wayne Booth's *The Rhetorical Fiction* (Chicago: University of Chicago Press, 1961) demonstrates just how involved the so-called invisible narrators actually were.

7. Rudolf Arnheim made a more general instance of this argument in his book *Film As Art* (Berkeley: University of California Press, 1957), but he was dealing with experimental film and the whole question of modifying the image per se. We are dealing with a narrative situation rather than experimental film and will suggest that this may be done by story construction.

16

■ ■ ■ ■ ■ ■ ■

Writing the Narrative Voice

In this chapter, we look at some of the practical consequences of placing the narrative voice in the foreground. However, we need to make one warning before we go on. As we said in the last chapter, most of the traditional screenwriting rules are designed to feature the dramatic voice. Because we will be looking, instead, at the narrative voice, some of the ideas in this chapter will not only seem different, but will be a violation of those rules. This is intentional. Remember, the purpose of this book is not to ask you to adopt all these thoughts on alternative screenwriting but to make you aware of what is possible, so that you might look further. Then, if you decide to write a mainstream script, you make a conscious decision to do so.

Openings

Exposition in Mainstream Scripts

The beginning of any story must establish the tone, the relationships between the characters, and any necessary prior history (called *back story*). Exposition is traditionally handled as invisibly as possible—the action is never stopped to explain back story. This treatment of exposition is based on two concerns. You want to keep up story interest by moving forward, even when conveying past information, and you want to preserve the realism of the dramatic voice. If the convention is that characters are being inadvertently observed in their day-to-day activities (if you assume they know each other and have a common past), then the characters would have no need to explain their pasts to each other, but would simply act on them. By creating this implied commonality, you allow your audience to project the characters back in time. This gives your film a feeling of extension that goes beyond the two hours on the screen.

In practice, writing traditional exposition is very difficult precisely because it must convey information without calling attention to itself. The amount of attention you can get away with varies with which voice you are emphasizing. If you emphasize the dramatic voice (the poet speaking in the voice of the characters), the exposition has to be nearly invisible. When you use the narrative voice (the poet speaking to the audience), you can be quite explicit about the handling of exposition. In *Psycho*, for instance, we the audience have no problem with the subtitle identifying the time and place of the story, because it is superimposed over the opening panoramic shots of Phoenix that move us into Janet Leigh's hotel room. Such a series of shots is overtly narrative. They seem to be saying to us, "At 2:43 p.m. on a typically, beautiful day, Friday, December 11th in Phoenix, Arizona, two people have just finished making love in a hotel room." However, if the same title superimposition occurred over the dramatic dialogue scene between Janet Leigh and Anthony Perkins in the lobby of the Bates Motel, we would be annoyed at the authorial intrusion pulling us out of the ongoing drama.

Exposition using the dramatic voice generally comes from character exchange. When the characters are new to one another, exposition can be quite easy and natural. The custom official in *Niagara* can ask Marilyn Monroe and Joseph Cotton why they are heading to the Canadian side of the border, because we assume this is something that custom officials do. In *Melvin and Howard*, Howard Hughes can ask Melvin Dummar where he's going or what he does for a living, because it is the first time they have met. However, Galvin's drinking buddies in *The Verdict* cannot credibly ask how long he has been a drunk, because we assume they have been drinking together for a long time and have no need to ask.

Exposition may be revealed between characters who know one another by heightening the conflict between them to such an extent that the conveyed information seems less important than the subtext motivating the conflict. For instance, the angry Mickey, Galvin's ex-partner in *The Verdict*, can reveal that he has been helping Galvin when he yells at the hung-over lawyer, "I got you a good case, it's a moneymaker. You do it right and it will take care of you. But I'm through. I'm sorry, Joe, this is the end."[1] This does not feel like naked exposition because our attention goes to the subtext, the disappointment and disgust that motivates Mickey's outburst. Trying to read Mickey's rage and Galvin's reaction involves us, makes us active viewers. The dialogue has motivation; it does not merely sit there. Only incidentally do we pick up the information.

Another form of exposition is called *unreliable direct exposition*. We expect a detective story to open with a client presenting a problem to the detective. This can be as up-front as possible; the only given is that the information has to be wrong or incomplete. Since we, along with the detective, know enough to be skeptical, we are actively involved in looking for holes in the story.

We can generalize and say that, except for small amounts of exposition that occur between people who don't know one another (these scenes tend to have little dramatic interest and cannot be sustained), the trick to handling exposition is to misdirect our attention. If you develop sufficient conflict between characters, we respond to the subtext, the unspoken tension between them, and absorb expository information without noticing it. If you don't develop conflict, the dramatic voice is broken and we can almost see you the writer turning to us directly and letting us in on what we need to know, and what you have failed to dramatize.

Exposition in Alternative Scripts

Predictably, since many alternative films want to heighten the narrative voice, they don't hesitate to use blatant exposition that intentionally lets us know that we are watching a film. In *She's Gotta Have It,* we push in on Nola Darling's bed as she sits up. Initially, we may read this move as a narrative device (the filmmaker is bringing us in) leading into a dramatic scene (we expect Nola to react to someone in her room). But instead of responding to another character Nola speaks into the lens, announcing her position in the movie. "I want you to know the only reason I'm consenting to this is because I wish to clear my name, not that I care what people think but enough is enough."[2] Not only is information placed in the foreground even in this apparently dramatic mode, but the whole convention of realistic cinema is exposed by Nola's looking into the camera and speaking directly to us.

In *Blue Velvet,* the only thing we know about the hero's father, Mr. Beaumont, comes from what we infer from the montage of idealized small-town life that opens the film. Presumably, Mr. Beaumont is the personification of this innocence. The narrative voice is placed so much in the foreground, is so intent on making us see the connections it wants us to see (rather than those we infer from the action), that, as Mr. Beaumont has his stroke, the camera glides away from him and sneaks up on the insects busily fighting on the grass below. Since the insects function as symbols rather than antagonists (they didn't cause the stroke), the camera movement serves not so much to introduce conflict in the story, but to make a self-conscious metaphor by comparing the generalized small-town innocence to the brutal nature that lurks below. Because the shot is so self-conscious, we view it as a wink at us, a connection made between filmmaker and audience, at the expense of the characters in the film.

The Location of Conflict

Let's carry this idea of winking a little further. When Ben runs out of the party in *The Graduate*, the camera holds for a moment on Mrs. Robinson watching greedily from behind. She looks after Ben, not at us; if we had to draw a line to detail the tension of the scene, we would draw it from her look to Ben's departing back. The tension remains with the protagonists and antagonists who inhabit the story world.

But the tension does not have to remain embedded in the fictive world. We can shift the conflict so that it runs between the characters in the story and the narrator who frequently seems to stand in for us. *Blue Velvet* and *She's Gotta Have It* both implicate us to a greater degree than do more classic scripts. We (as opposed to a character) look down fascinated at the terrifying insects. We feel we must have maligned Nola and caused her to direct her opening outburst at us. As we will see, this has a profound effect on how we respond to the story.

(A theoretical aside. In his famous essay on deep focus, the famous French film theorist Andre Bazin praised the "ambiguity" of deep focus, which allowed the viewer to choose what he or she would look at.[3] Our instance on the narrative voice leading us would seem to violate Bazin's concerns, but we would argue that is not the case. Deep focus or not, all films organize space to lead us through the frame. The question is to what extent the viewer is conscious of being led. The assertion of the narrative voice that we are talking about implies a certain self-consciousness. These films work by, in effect, placing a dramatic voice and narrative voice in conflict with one another. The viewer must progressively decide to which he or she is giving most credence. A film whose narrative voice totally and consistently dominated the dramatic voice would seem over-determined, dramatically dead and would have no interest to us.)

Development

Focus and Build

One of the great paradoxes of dramatic writing is that even if you want to write a script that touches on issues going beyond the events of the story, you first need to make the story itself strong and clearly focused. Instead of freeing the viewer, a script that wanders all over the place is generally so hard to follow that it loses its ability to stretch and take on larger issues. Therefore, no matter what your approach, we encourage you to write with focus.

However, we suggest a broader definition of what is being focused on. The trick to being able to write the middle of a story is to deepen the conflict set up in the opening of the film. In mainstream films, this deepening is driven largely by the forward motion of the plot. However, a script might also be organized around character insight, theme, irony, recurring motif, and even childish wonder—but it is not easy.

A number of scripts start with this looser sense of organization, but then the writer, fearing the lack of a story, seems to panic and reach for melodrama. The first forty minutes of Steven Spielberg's *E.T.* are as loosely structured as any independent film, delightfully avoiding any single strong dramatic conflict, while instead concentrating on the wonder the children feel in dealing with the alien and, to a lesser extent, the problem of hiding it from their mother. A few shots of people searching the landing site with flashlights are thrown in to prepare us for the melodrama that comes later. But, the central dramatic issue is how Elliot, so awkward around his older brother's friends, finds an identity with E.T. Once the villainous adult scientists arrive, however, this issue gets lost under the mechanics of the quarantine, the operation, and the final chase. The first bicycle-flying scene, in which Elliot feels the transcendence of all human limitations, resonates with much greater richness than the second flying scene when the joy is framed in terms of kids escaping from evil adults.

Many writers consider the middle to be the hardest part to write, because it calls most directly on the resources of imagination. However you start, the trick is to carry through with the implications of the questions you've opened up. Sigmund Freud once said that his goal was to study something over and over again until it spoke for itself. This kind of unflinching, honest attention is necessary for a story to develop. Gross plot manipulation will always be a temptation for the writer seeking to keep the middle of her story alive. This must be rejected. The mechanics of drug dealing, the violence between Pakistanis and English, and the lurid details of the homosexual relationship between Omar and Johnny might all have taken over *My Beautiful Laundrette*, but they are not allowed to. By progressively unraveling the complex determination, ambition, and love that makes up Omar's character, while at the same time keeping the movie focused on the paradox of the well-to-do former colonial subjects and the poor English lower class, the film sustains and develops its extraordinary resonance and insight.

John Waters's *Polyester* (1981) plays out in the opposite direction, but is still true to the absurdity of its opening. Francine Fishpaw loses her husband to another woman, sees her son arrested for foot-stomping, and sends her pregnant daughter to a nunnery. Then, everything reverses—her children reform and she marries the dreamboat, Todd Tomorrow. When this falls apart, when her mother and Tod Tomorrow lie murdered at her feet, she can still stare up into the craning camera and yell, "We are still family." Although we feel a surprising amount of tenderness for Francine, she has not reformed and the movie is not allowed to surrender to sentimentality. By the time Waters made *Hairspray* in 1988, his edge had softened and, unlike in *Polyester*, we are invited to regard the happy ending without irony.

Meaning and Action

In the traditional script, meaning must flow from action. Characters are defined by what they do, not what they say. In an alternative script, there is greater freedom to bend the rules. In fact, such scripts frequently gain their power from proposing several competing locations for meaning. Where exactly does the meaning lie in Louis Malle's *My Dinner With Andre?* Is it purely in the talk? Or in the reaction shots? Is it in the new way that Wallace Shawn sees the city after spending the evening with Andre Gregory? Or is it in the lack of action that makes us wonder whether Wallace Shawn's insight, no matter how overwhelming, will lead to anything?

The Aristotelian notion that "action is character" becomes much more complex. What do we mean by action? Is character defined only by the capability to act (the classical notion)? Or might it be defined by the gaining of insight? Must character be at the center of film at all? Might not the organizing principle be one of theme, of the twisting of the family melodrama cliches as in *Polyester*, of the narrative voice, or of some rich amalgam of character, theme, history, and society as in *My Beautiful Laundrette?*

Closure

How We Know It's Over

The music swells, the plot resolves, the hero and heroine kiss, the lights come up, and the movie's over. After years of experience, we can pop in on an ongoing movie and know instantly if it is about to end.

There are a number of formal elements that contribute to our sense of ending. One trick in writing effective third-act scenes is to cut down the scene's opening. This pruning accelerates the rhythm and heightens the immediacy of the conflict. By this time in the movie, of course, we should be sufficiently oriented not to need to be set up.

The restorative three-act model suggests that by the beginning of the third act, most of the character conflict has been resolved. Thus, third-act scenes tend to be external, a playing out of the stakes that were raised in the second act, rather than the working through of character. Tactics are placed in the foreground. Hesitation tends to be directed toward overcoming obstacles, not scruples. We wonder how the character is going to achieve his goal, not what that goal is, or whether it is right or wrong.

Of course, we are familiar with the tying up of plot. Stop the film in the middle and try to identify all the questions raised. In most mainstream films, these questions will be quite clear-cut. If you make a list, you will find that invariably they are answered (or at least finessed) by the end of the film.

Most independents do not end with such a complete sense of closure. These open-ended films make a different demand on the viewer. Mainstream films tend to generate a great amount of moment-to-moment tension, which explains their hold on us. But once they end, the hold tends to vanish. This how-does-it-come-out style of moviemaking is an essential consequence of restorative three-act structure. If you stop a more offbeat film in the middle, it is generally not as easy to pinpoint the tension that must be resolved, because the tension tends to be less urgent while at the same time more broadly resonant. The ending in such a script does not have to resolve one monolithic flow as much as finish one element of a multistranded flow, while letting the others continue to play out in the viewer's mind.

Thus, the whole notion of story structure has to be rethought in open-ended scripts. Part of this requires displacing the location of the conflict.

The Relocation of Conflict

As we have said, in restorative three-act scripts the conflict remains almost entirely with the character and the character's particular situation. Rarely is there a cultural, social, historical, class, or gender-based element to the conflict. If the conflict exists totally within the story (i.e., totally within the control of the writer who is inventing fictional characters and giving them problems to solve), there is nothing to keep the conflict from being fully resolved. But if the conflict is designed to touch on the larger world right from the beginning, if we are asked to see the individual's problems against an on-going historical process, then we don't expect the same kind of complete resolution. In fact, if we get it, we tend to think the writer is naive for ignoring the long-term persistence of such problems in the world beyond the story.

In his excellent piece on open-endings and ideology, the Israeli Eran Preis talks about writing a script on the Lebanon invasion.[4] His lead character chooses to hide his hospitalization for paranoia, because to reveal it would mean that he would have to leave the army, which is socially unacceptable in Israel. Yet, word gets out. As he becomes increasingly ostracized in the army, he comes to see the problems of the militarized Israeli society. The film ends with him stripping off his army uniform and standing in the road as the tanks drive off. All we know is that he is no longer in the army. How he will live in the society that he no longer trusts, and that no longer trusts him, remains unresolved.

Maintaining enough resolution to satisfy, while still keeping the story open, is very tricky. Generally, the immediate dramatic problem has to be solved, so it must be posed in such a way that the larger issues still ring. In a mainstream script, these issues, because they exist completely in the world of the story, are clearly resolved. We feel comfortable in guessing that, in *Wall Street*, Bud will get out of jail and that his father will remain proud of him. The Gekkos of the world will be written off as bad guys. There won't be an analysis of American society or any suggestion that Gekko represents something that we all might share. By contrast, although the character in Preis's film has solved the problem of whether he will remain in the army, we have no idea how he will deal with his society in the future. The question of how to live with Israel's current militant response to a long and impotent history cannot be so easily answered.

In Godard's *Vivre Sa Vie*, the character Nana insists that she is responsible. A prostitute by choice, she falls in love and wishes to leave the business. But before she can, her pimp, inexplicably, seeks to trade her for money. The exchange is made, but the money is not what was promised and Nana is killed, by accident, in the ensuing gun fight. The film ends.

The arbitrary randomness of Nana's death makes for a powerful and appropriate ending for this film. However, the very arbitrariness would be a disaster in a more mainstream script, because it does not answer such questions as, What motivated the killing? Who were the other guys? Why weren't they set up earlier in the story? These would be fair questions, because mainstream scripts are based on clear-cut principles of causality and clear expectations set up in the first act.

If we want to deal with randomness and lack of simple causality, we must establish these elements at the beginning of our film and we must not raise expectations of answers in the first act (unless we are planning to subvert these expectations). It is not enough to declare that the world doesn't make sense any more, we must incorporate this breakdown of order into the questions raised by the structure itself. For instance, the script of *Platoon* fails to chart the arbitrary lunacy of Vietnam (although there are some brilliant moments in which the filmmaking depicts this), because its structure—a clear villain in this most morally ambiguous war and an avenger who is able to take his revenge—is so old-fashioned and comforting. This dislocation must take place in the way the story is told, the way the narration is asserted.

Nana's claim "I am responsible" raises the whole question of our freedom of will in a mass society; the filmmaker's intervention and explicit foregrounding of the narrative voice raises the question of the freedom of the characters from the narrating agency. This has a profound effect on how we understand stories. The form, the way the story is told, becomes as important (or more important) than the story. In effect, an equation is being made—the society that gives shape to our lives acts, in some way, like a narrator acts toward a character. Society educates us, presents us with choices, and determines what we fight against.

Narration, whether overt or not, defines a similar range of choices for the characters contained within its story. If, as in a mainstream script, the narration is not acknowledged, then the characters are given the illusion of being free while we, as onlookers, know exactly what they have to face up to. This displacement leaves us protected, entertained, but never implicated by the film. If, however, the narration is foregrounded as it is in *Vivre Sa Vie* (and, as discussed earlier, in *Vertigo*), then we have to pay attention to it. Where is it coming from, we have to ask. Is it coming from a direct extension of our wish to have a story? Is it in part an expression of our own desires? Thus, the conflict extends from the story world out to us. Rather than being left unscathed by the story, we are forced to question our desire to look on and enjoy.

Conclusion

The mainstream script tends to use structure as the invisible narrator of the story. This structure provides organization and meaning as though it evolved logically from the characters and the situations of the story. The alternative script tends to foreground structure as the voice of the self-conscious narrator organizing the material. With this change, the location of meaning tends to shift from being fully contained within the fictive world to running between the fictive world and the narrator.

This shift allows us to rethink how we can actually use structure. If the narrative voice is in the foreground, then exposition, typically rendered invisible in a mainstream script, can become an expression of the narrator's presence. Development can be broader, apparent not only in how the characters act, but in their insights and perceptions. Closure can become much more open-ended. In this chapter, we have only touched the surface of available options. But by identifying the location of the conflict and by figuring out exactly what you want to say, you can use structure as an expressive form, not a predetermined given.

References

1. David Mamet, *The Verdict* (Twentieth Century-Fox, 1982), p. 6.
2. Spike Lee, *She's Gotta Have It* (New York: Simon & Schuster, 1987), p. 279.
3. "The Evolution of the Language of Cinema" in *What Is Cinema?* (Berkeley: University of California Press, 1968).
4. Erian Preis, "Not Such a Happy Ending," *Journal of Film and Video* 42, No. 3 (Fall 1990) pp. 18, 23.

17

■ ■ ■ ■ ■ ■ ■

Rewriting

Of course, once we subject the mainstream rules to scrutiny, we are left without a map upon which we can depend. By what standards do we critique our own work? How do we get ourselves out of trouble? What guides our rewrites? We don't want to minimize how difficult it is to work without guidance. Models *do* provide an important framework. For instance, in her book *How to Make a Good Script Great*, Linda Seger offers a very good checklist of what each act should accomplish. "What kinds of action points are within my script? Barriers? Complications? Reversals? Where do they occur, and how often?"[1] are a few of the questions she asks about Act Two. These questions are very helpful to a writer.

However, we feel that checking your script against a list of questions does not address the fundamental issue. It presumes that the questions are universally right and that the rules are more important than the life or urgency we hope will be created by your script itself. Anyone who has read amateur scripts will bear witness to this misappropriation of values. Most amateur scripts contain every one of the prescribed act breaks and many would pass the checklist for act accomplishments, yet most of them are absolutely dead.

Screenplays fail not because they break the rules, but because the writer has failed to imagine and see clearly. Screenplays fail because they lack urgency and life. The reason we talk about rules at all is because no one can directly teach you (much less talk about) how to imagine and how to generate urgency and life, especially in a book. We don't pretend to be able to do so. All we ask is that you don't substitute preconceived models for the apparently formless chaos that, at some point, is a component of all truly creative projects. Time consuming or not, any screenplay that has life has to be invented from the ground up and has to discover its own rules.

So how do you rewrite? Beyond everything else, you seek to recapture the impulse that brought you to your particular script in the first place. Where do you get this impulse? Anywhere and everywhere. It depends on you, but it must be there. This is so critical, that many books on fiction-writing dedicate whole chapters to it. For instance, R. V. Cassill in his excellent book, *Writing Fiction*, worries about students getting sidetracked by sensational melodramatic subjects that have nothing to do with their own experience:

> I never quite understood why students should waste their time
> and mine on efforts so far off the right track. Sometimes I guessed
> that they might be afraid to discover how little of their own
> experience they had actually possessed, how little of their own
> lives they had grasped. . . . But the choice of becoming a writer is
> the choice to face some fears, including the fear of being a hollow
> or a dull person with nothing to say.[2]

Harsh words, but true. If you don't command the emotional resources to respond, to worry, to be obsessive over your experience, you will find it very difficult to write.

We are not making the old argument that you should write only about what you know. While this may (or may not) be useful in fiction writing, it would unduly limit the scope of your scriptwriting because film requires a larger audience than does fiction. Rather, we are saying write only about things you feel passionate about, things you haven't fully worked out, things you don't mind going back to, again and again. Get words down on paper that express these feelings. Anything. An image, a scene, a moment of characterization, of blocking, of sound, of conflict that embodies the story you want to tell.

Only when you put down such a concrete moment have you truly started to write. But once you have, you already have something greater than any abstract knowledge of structure will ever give you. You can continue to go back to that moment to recapture the impulse that brought you to your story in the first place. Eventually, as your story line grows clearer, you may want to replace this initial moment with another that seems to come closer to what you are after. But that doesn't matter. You have started. And now you can build from there.

How do you do that? By trial and error. There is no other way. By going forward until you get lost. By going back to where it works, rekindling your ideas, recapturing your thread, and going forward again. This process of keeping the whole story in front of you is no easy task. Many writers use a bulletin board covered with scene cards to remind them of how the story is moving. Others write paragraphs summarizing the development of plot, theme, and character. Use whatever works, but learn the technique of stepping back from your story and seeing it in its totality.

Most writers will tell you that developing the middle of a story is the hardest part. Here again, we urge you not to worry about abstractions like complications, barriers, and reversals, but rather to go back to your initial impulse. The reason the middle is so difficult is because you've taken your original story idea as far as you can imagine and now you have to go even further. You might be working out of character. In that case, try to identify what you have only hinted at but not fully explored. What are the rough edges? The dark sides? The unspoken or misunderstood motivations? How can the character be pushed so these are uncovered and the fullness of characterization be revealed? You might work thematically. In that case, try to identify what are you really trying to get at? What ambiguity or confusion in the situation has not yet been examined? What contradictions are there to be explored? What things are always assumed, but never examined? Suck everything you possibility can out of your material.

As you gain more experience, there will be much less trial-and-error. You will come up with possible solutions and quickly play them out in your head to see if they will work for you. However, even as do, you want to be careful. Writing is not like learning to tune a car—once learned, then many times repeated. To write well, you must go through the feeling of learning to write all over again each time you start a new script. You must discover for yourself why the strategies you decide to use work for your particular story.

Taking Suggestions

You should feel as confident about rejecting suggestions as you are in accepting them. A writer must have the ego, the toughness, to stand up and say, "This is my idea." Otherwise, your script becomes an amalgam of all the responses to it. However, it is very important to learn to listen to suggestions. This requires getting over the natural defensiveness we all feel when we are criticized, in addition to understanding how to decipher someone else's ideas.

Any criticism you can get is worth having. Note exactly what your reader is having difficulty with and pay particular attention to how the objections and suggestions are phrased. It is useful to write down the exact wording. If several readers object to the same thing, make sure you look at it closely. Don't bother responding (otherwise, readers will start critiquing your comments rather than your script). Rather, study the suggestions when you are alone.

However, unless your critic is another writer whom you respect, never take suggestions at face value. The reason that we respond the way we do is frequently deeply embedded in the structure and development of the script. In most cases, it is very difficult for an untrained reader (and even a trained reader won't know the script the way you do) to take into account the implications of making a change. Instead of taking your critics' suggestions at face value, try to use them to figure out exactly what isn't working.

Frequently, you will find that you have inadvertently set up a line of expectation twenty pages before the scene your reader is talking about, and that is what needs to be changed. Or an earlier moment, that may be perfectly clear to you, is read as something entirely different, which affects all that comes after it.

Once you make your corrections, it is tempting to go back to readers and ask them if your fix of the earlier scene helps the problem, but in most cases you will be disappointed. Rather than showing them the earlier scene, you might want to ask your critics to read the whole script again. If you have made the right prior adjustments, they may come to the identical scene they complained about before and remark on how much better it is this time.

Sample Exercises

We have purposely kept this chapter general because we don't want to inadvertently propose a series of rules to replace those we are asking you to reconsider. We will, however, end with some sample exercises. These exercises are designed not so much to help you solve specific problems as much as they are to help you to regard your work from varying perspectives. Once again, we believe that you get stuck when your vision fails. If you can see anew, you can discover solutions on your own.

■ ■ ■   Closing Distance: Write Out Subtext

The mechanics of screenwriting can seem quite clumsy. You may find yourself so concerned with visualizing and blocking, that you forget what is going on with your characters. If you are writing a character-driven script, you want to avoid such loss of internal life. One solution is to use a stream-of-consciousness style to write the flow of your character's thoughts under each piece of action or line of dialogue. Compare this to what is actually going on. You may discover several things:

1. Your character has no thoughts or thoughts of no particular urgency. In this case, ask yourself, What is the point of the scene? If it doesn't have a dramatic function, if it doesn't cost the character something, cut it.
2. The thoughts are a mere rehash of the dialogue. You've got no subtext and the scene will probably be dead. Remember, characters need not know exactly why they are speaking or their reasons may contradict the viewer's sense of their motivation. However, there must be some skew between dialogue and

thought. Consider pushing the conflict harder to give your
character reasons not to speak everything on her mind.

3. The thoughts don't correspond to the actions that are supposed
to express them. This is not as much of a problem as it may
seem, because it means you know what the scene is about, but
you haven't visualized it successfully. Try to imagine your character
free of anything governing her actions except her thoughts. Let
them move her. Use the camera to underscore this movement;
reveal a sense of motivation to the viewer, without exposing it to
other characters in the scene.

Sometimes, it is useful to start writing the character's stream of
consciousness from scratch. Write only the progression of the point-of-view
character's thoughts against the dialogue of the other characters. Only after you
have the line of the thoughts written down do you want to write the dialogue
that goes with them.

■ ■ ■ Gaining Distance: Shift the Point-of-View Character

Sometimes writers have the opposite problem—they are too close to
a character. In a character-driven story, most often you will be writing from the
perspective of a point-of-view character. Try arbitrarily reversing this. Write the
scene from a totally different perspective. Use this new perspective to see your
original point-of-view character from the outside. This technique is useful
because writers frequently get so close to their point-of-view characters, that
the characters cease to exist in the concrete world. But we will be seeing them
on the screen. What will they be doing? How do they react and how are they
reacted to? How will their thoughts be communicated or suppressed?

■ ■ ■ Gaining Even More Distance: Write a Totally Unreliable Scene

Do you want us to be with the character at a particular moment? Do
you want us to understand that you approve of what the character is doing?
This closeness can be harder than it looks, because all writers have a tendency
to fall in love with their characters. When this happens, viewers tend to check
out. Who cares about a paragon of virtue—now someone who only appears to
be a paragon, that's interesting.

One way to avoid falling in love with your characters is to artificially
distance yourself. Add some irony to the scene; have other characters contest

your character; let your character do something you don't feel all that happy about. Establishing distance can be enormously freeing, because by implicitly telling your viewers that you don't stand behind everything your character does, you don't fall into the trap of trying to present yourself.

■ ■ ■   Easing Exposition: Rewrite an Early Scene Like a Late Scene

Expository scenes are very difficult to bring to life. After several rewrites, it becomes difficult to sort out what is the bare minimum of information that must be communicated to make the script work. Since the line of the script may have changed through your rewrites, you may be carrying much more expository weight than is needed.

One solution is to strip the scene of any expository function. Cut down the beginning of the scene and write the whole scene with the economy of a later scene. Assume we know enough to follow the scene. Now go back and identify exactly what information you need to communicate. Frequently, you will find that by stripping down the scene, you have so increased its dramatic urgency that it becomes easier to add the now limited expository information.

■ ■ ■   Reshaping: Shift the Story Frame

Imagine your script starting on page 10 or page 20. Consider what this does for your story. Even if you don't make these cuts, you may find that a great deal of information in the beginning of your script can be trimmed down.

Now look at the end of your script. Have you gone far enough? Have you truly squeezed everything out of the story? Sometimes, after you've finished a draft, the whole window of the story can be adjusted to take in more of the story and less of the setup.

■ ■ ■   Visualizing: Write with Dialogue Crossed Out

You may want a scene to be stagy or talky. For instance, *Stranger Than Paradise* is structured in single-shot scenes with the camera looking in (as opposed to being in) on the action. By its very refusal to yield more insight into the characters through camera placement and cutting, this style becomes an expression of the material, insensate, physical world that denies us the romantic release of penetration into character.

However, when you want to bring the camera inside your story, your staging should reveal the fundamental tension of each scene. The best way to make sure you are doing this is to cross out the dialogue so that you can't read its content (although you are still aware of its placement). Reading just the stage directions, you should still be able to identify the scene's basic dramatic movement, the dominant character, and the beat where the scene turns.

■ ■ ■   Giving the Scene Some Breathing Room: Rewrite with an Opposite Outcome

One of the great (and true) cliches of realistic narrative writing is that you want to create scenes that have the possibility of coming out in at least two different ways and you want to sustain such a possibility for as long as you can. This balancing of choices allows the viewer to participate in the drama by constantly weighing and rethinking the possible outcome.

Try rewriting a scene and intentionally reversing the outcome. If you have written a scene in which the outcome is determined too early, you will have to do a great deal of rewriting to reverse it. Once you do, go back and, with the minimum of changes, restore the original direction of your ending. You will find that the tension now sustains itself to the end of the scene.

Such a technique is also useful for characters written as all dark (evil). Try reversing them and see what dimension emerges. Use this dimension throughout the scene.

■ ■ ■   Taking the Curse Off: Write with Overt Reasons, Not to Explain

Sometimes writers, more often than not sensitive writers, cannot resist the opportunity of having the characters explain exactly what they feel. The explanations may even be extended to include little essays on the theme. We see no problem with this if there are conflicting viewpoints presented with equal authorial authority. As long as the viewer has to work to synthesize meaning, multiple voices can only contribute to the richness of the script.[3] Think how resonant the contrasting perspectives of Omar and Johnny are in *My Beautiful Laundrette*.

However, you want to avoid head-on, reliable exegeses in which you tell us exactly what you think about the situation. Such commentary is impossible to play, causing actors to use the term *taking the curse off* when they find a way to diminish the obviousness of these lines.

The solution is simple. Find an overt reason in the scene that keeps the character from explaining. A man who tells a woman that he desires her but is afraid of losing her is a lot less interesting (to us and to her) than the man who avoids such a confession because he knows that is precisely what would doom him.

■ ■ ■   Breaking Out of the Narrow Mind-Set: Ask a Whole Group to Rewrite Your Scene

It takes considerable courage to have a class or workshop rewrite your scene, but it can prove to be very worthwhile. You are not looking for answers. Rather, you want to break out of the narrow mind-set with which you have approached the scene, by seeing in just how many directions it might actually go. You won't believe what people will discover in a scene that you felt you've already thought through.

Conclusion

Writing beyond the rules requires that you approach any given rule with skepticism and that you don't use it until you are satisfied that it works for you. The difficulty with such an approach is that you have no authority, no place to go for guidance. We suggest that you learn to look at the strength of your own impulse for guidance and that you build from that through trial and error. While this is more frightening than working with a preconceived model, it encourages you to do the real exploration necessary to write material that is truly original and alive.

References

1. Linda Seger, *Making a Good Script Great* (New York: Dodd, Mead, 1987), p. 58.
2. R. V. Cassill, *Writing Fiction* (New York: Prentice Hall, 1975), pp. 11–12.
3. See M. M. Bakhtin, "Discourse in the Novel" in *The Dialogic Imagi-nation: Four Essays* (Austin: University of Texas Press, 1985), pp. 259–422.

18

■ ■ ■ ■ ■ ■ ■ ■

Personal
Scriptwriting—
The Edge

William Goldman, in his amusing book about screenwriting, *Adventures in the Screen Trade*, advises that new screenwriters realize that an excellent screenplay is a well-structured screenplay, but no one knows what constitutes a successful screenplay.[1] An entire world of difference exists between these two desirable adjectives—excellent and successful. Many elements beyond your control determine whether your screenplay is excellent *and* successful. Agents, producers, directors, and, above all, actors, influence the outcome of your screenplay.

If Goldman's proscription is dire, it certainly isn't overly dramatic. Screenwriting is not akin to a lottery, but time is pushing it in that direction. As successful screenwriters are paid more and more for their screenplays, the risk factor in production suggests an increasingly conservative attitude toward screenplays and screenwriters. Film is already (given its economic structure) the most conservative of the arts!

Does this mean that the screenwriter must study and write for the market? Only partially. The search by studios for the successful screenplay is more urgent than ever. Therefore, screenwriters, more than ever before, will have to strive to differentiate themselves from the rest of the marketplace.

All producers expect well-structured screenplays. But as producers read with an eye on emulating the latest great success at the box office, you have to capture their interest by writing something different. In the end, the only source of inspiration is screenplays that are different. This is the reason for the meteoric rise of Spike Lee and John Patrick Shanley. As a writer, you have a choice—to imitate, as do so many others in the marketplace, or to innovate. We suggest that you innovate. If you do, you'll have a better opportunity for excellence and success. This means that you have to move your screenplay beyond structure. It also means you take on a more personal form of storytelling.

In this chapter, we reiterate screen story conventions and how to write against those conventions. We look at form, character, language, and tone, and highlight narrative strategies that yield fresh options. We also highlight how the other arts provide sources of options to strengthen your screen story. We want to stress that there is no strictly technical solution to writing a successful screenplay. They are a mix of technical form, good story, characters by whom you are fascinated, and a deep interest on your part to invite the audience to stay with your characters for two hours. During these two hours, you want the audience to feel pain and pleasure, and at the end of the experience, you want them to leave stimulated or exhausted. You want the audience to think and to feel, and, in doing so, to experience a level of satisfaction for having spent those two hours with your story.

If this stimulation is missing, you have failed. If it is present, you have worked a small miracle, given the distractions of modern life. You will have convinced, hopefully, a large paying group to suspend their sense of the present and enter the world you've created. After two hours of escape into your world, they've been entertained, stimulated, and may leave not quite the same as when they entered. This change may last twenty seconds or twenty years. This is the extent of your influence.

Your Story

Whatever the source for your screen story, whatever your motivation for writing the story, it has to reach an audience or it remains incomplete. Unlike a novel that can be published modestly, or a play that can be produced locally, a film requires an infrastructure for production, distribution, and exhibition. Consequently, the economics of production preclude the production of the vast majority of screenplays. With producers, distributors, and exhibitors all eyeing audiences to determine what will sell, screenwriters are constantly pressed to do this as well. The results are screenplays that are strongly influenced by current issues—social, political, economic. Almost any personality or event that has significantly captured the public's interest, even for an instant, merits screen consideration.

Your story, however, doesn't have to be a direct rendering of such an event. The perspective you choose, along with everything else, is up to you. This is where your individuality can yield an interesting angle. This is where you begin to apply the range of narrative strategies that best suits your story. This is where your life experience helps you coax an unusual perspective from your story.

This individualism explains the powerful moral fervor of the scripts of Paul Schrader. Whether the subject is Jesus Christ *(The Last Temptation of Christ)*, a high-priced male prostitute *(American Gigolo)*, or pornography *(Hardcore)*, Schrader's perspective makes his screenplays intense, probing, and unpredictable. He's made the subject his own. However we feel about his treatment of the subject, the films differ dramatically from other screenplays about similar subject matter.

Turning to another writer, one who grew up in Hollywood, Blake Edwards, we notice that whatever the subject matter or genre, Edwards's screenplays are, first and foremost, entertaining. His feeling for keeping his audience blunts the intensity of his films about sexual identity *(Victor, Victoria)* and middle-age crises *(10)*, but the subject matter is as serious as that of Schrader's scripts. Edwards, above all, wants to entertain, so he uses the situation comedy, rather than the melodrama, to provide entertainment values that are much stronger than those in a Schrader screenplay.

The key point, here, is that these two screenwriters are serious, but their priorities and approaches differ from one another. Both are successful and individualistic. The best approach to your story is the approach that respects your individuality and seeks to differentiate your story from those about the same subject.

Approaches to Structure

The respect paid to structure in contemporary, produced screenplays grows every day. Respectfully, structure has become Hollywood's eleventh commandment. Challenge to the structural model has been tempting only to those who are established in the industry. No studio is going to tell Woody Allen or Spike Lee that it will not finance his next film. Allen's and Lee's pattern of experimentation marks the route of Fellini and Bergman. Having reached their audience, these writer-directors want to experiment. The result is that they often challenge our notions of structure and allude to what structure can be.

We are not suggesting that you should rail and rebel against structure gurus, Syd Field or Bob McKee. But, we are saying that audiences today are very media-wise and they tire of repetition. You can help your career and foster your creativity by varying your structural approach.

Structural options begin to develop once you have a main character, a premise, and story form (the genre). Immediately, you face two issues—at what point will your audience enter the story and, if you sense a possible ending, what is the end point or climax?

Whether you opt for a three-act structure depends on how open-ended you want your story to be. If you see a story with a resolution, a three-act structure is called for. However, if you don't find a resolution necessary or interesting, you may opt for a two-act structure. If you do, realize that this choice has implications for every other element in your screenplay. To make a two-act screenplay work, you need gripping characters with whom we won't mind spending time. Since there is less action, particularly rising action, in the two-act approach, your audience will demand more from your dialogue as well as from your characters. The conflict that doesn't happen visually must be manifested in the language.

The decrease in action also has implications for the number of plot points and the number of plot-oriented devices you employ (i.e., reversals and surprise). Because the amount of plot is lessened in the two-act approach, there will be less need for reversals and surprises. The audience's involvement will come from its involvement with your characters not with your plot.

If you *do* choose the three-act structure, there remain many structural options available to you. Rather than writing within the genre context, you can challenge or alter a primary genre motif. A recent example is the Coen brothers' *Raising Arizona*. The main character (Nicolas Cage) isn't driven by material success like the classic gangster. He is a man who is driven by love of his wife. She wants a baby, so he steals a baby for her. His sweetness is an element that is foreign to the main character in the gangster genre, whose transgressions are carried out to get ahead materially in society. Yet, *Raising Arizona* remains, at least partially, a gangster film.

Another option available to the writer is to mix genres. This approach is rapidly becoming an industry standard. The mix of science fiction and gangster genres is the most popular. But the most unusual of combinations have proved successful. Certainly audiences have found mixed genre films to be an appealing novelty.

The issue for you, whether you alter a motif or mix genres, is, does it improve your story? This is a critical question. If you alter a motif or mix genres for novelty's sake, the benefit to your story remains superficial. If, on the other hand, the mix helps reach another level of meaning that makes your story more credible and revealing, then the structural shift has served you well.

The protagonist-antagonist mix is a power struggle of considerable force in the melodrama. *Kramer vs. Kramer* is an example in which both protagonist and antagonist were members of the same family—husband and wife. This same approach is taken in *Music Box*, but this film has a twist. In *Music Box*, daughter and father are protagonist–antagonist, but the daughter doesn't know it. In fact, for the majority of the screen story she is the lawyer for her father. Only at the end of Act Three does she face the truth about her father and his Nazi past. This twist of bringing protagonist and antagonist close together within the melodrama, lends a force to the story that would not be present if this choice hadn't been employed by a screenwriter such as Joe Eszterhas. It also helps create the background story of the film.

The key is that the motif shift brings us into the story in a deeper way than if the same story were presented with the daughter, father, and the father's lawyer. In *The Music Box*, the motif shift adds an additional layer of meaning to the melodrama.

If we look at Errol Morris's mixed-genre film, *The Thin Blue Line*, the use of the dramatic form of the police story, together with the investigative documentary, makes the film both realistic and stylized. The artifice of the drama makes the viewer ask the question, "Am I being manipulated or did this really happen?" The viewer is invited to consider who is manipulating whom. Consequently, *The Thin Blue Line*, in using a mixed-genre approach to structure, makes the central theme of the documentary come alive for the viewer. Who are we to believe? Randall, his accuser, the police, or the filmmakers?

Remember that the strength of challenging a motif or a mixed-genre approach lies in what the narrative strategy adds to your story. Does it make the story deeper? Does the approach give us new insights about your main character? Does the approach help sidestep audience expectations? If it does, you are on your way to writing a unique screen story.

Approaches to Character

Perhaps the most important decision you make about your screenplay is the identity of your main character. You must then ask yourself why you have chosen this person to tell your story. The appropriateness and flexibility of your main character can't be overestimated. Not only does the audience enter the story through that character, they also relate to the story to the degree in which they become involved (positively or negatively) with that character.

Your decision about character has many implications about the nature of the other characters, as well as the degree of plot in your story. The specificity of your character—the socio-economic, regional, cultural, political, and psychological qualities of that character—affects the nature of the dialogue.

Real Drama and Unreal Life

At the baseline, your character has to convince us of her credibility. This doesn't necessarily mean you need to take a slice-of-life approach to the nature of the character. Indeed, too literal a view of realism yields an unrealistic character in dramatic terms. To put it simply, drama and real life are distant cousins; they are not synonymous. Whether we view drama as exaggerated life situations or real life as drama taking place with long stretches of filler between dramatic incidents isn't as important as not mistaking one for the other.

Screenwriters have to use compression, coincidence, and conflict in order to create dramatic situations, which are the meat and potatoes of audience expectations. We experience the long stretches of filler in our lives. We won't pay to see more of the same thing; we want drama.

So your characters have to be credible. But in order to be credible to the audience, they have to get involved in events and with other characters far beyond what might be called credible. This contradiction is willingly overcome if you fascinate us and convince us to suspend our sense of realism in order to enter, with your character, into your screen story.

The Role of Dilemma

When George (Bob Hoskins), the main character in Neil Jordan and David Leland's *Mona Lisa*, returns from seven years in prison, he finds that his wife has thrown him out and his mobster boss, for whom he suffered imprisonment, is disinterested in him. George's dilemma is that he is free, but he feels betrayed by his two principal sources of support—his wife and his boss. How George deals with this dilemma is the subject of the balance of the film. The fact that George is both violent and tender adds dimension to this gangster film centered in London.

The dilemma serves to bring us very quickly into the story and to see George as disadvantaged. In spite of his being a gangster, his callous rejection by his wife and the corporate style of gangster life seem to justify George's outbursts. He yearns for life as it was.

The dilemma helps us identify with George. Once this identification has taken place, we are ready to follow George through the story, hoping that he will be able to resolve his problem.

Whether the dilemma is coincidental, as it is in John Cassavetes's *Gloria*, or logical, as in *Mona Lisa*, the role of the dilemma is to bring us into the story quickly and get us to identify with the main character.

The Role of Charisma

Whether one describes the main character as appealing or charming, main characters also need charisma. The sense of energy that the character displays may develop out of a sense of commitment or out of an intensity that may be sexual, aggressive, or both. It is valuable to the writer when the main character isn't likable, but the character does have to attract the viewer, he has to be charismatic.

While dilemma gets us involved with your character, charisma keeps us involved. In William Inge's *Splendor in the Grass*, the main character's intensity is sexual. In John Steinbeck's *Viva Zapata*, the character's intensity is political. In Elia Kazan's *America, America*, the character's intensity is born out of a will to survive. In each case, the main character has an honesty as well as an intensity that shows the audience his vulnerability. The result is that we remain involved, throughout the screen story, with each of these characters.

The Tradition of Nonconformity

In North America, nonconformity as a philosophy of living has always had appeal. This is not lost on screenwriters who often will position the main character so he appears to be a nonconformist.

Whether we view the country singer, portrayed by Robert Duvall in Horton Foote's *Tender Mercies*, as a stranger to the community or as a man with an unconventional vocation, he doesn't quite fit into the community. He is an outsider. So too, are Pelle, in Billie August's *Pelle the Conqueror*, and Bishop Pike, in Walon Green's *The Wild Bunch*.

It is useful to the writer to create an additional layer of conflict when the main character's position is that of the nonconformist. Nola, in Spike Lee's *She's Gotta Have It*, and Brie Daniels, in Judy and David Lewis's *Klute*, both pursue behavior that is nonconforming.

The fact that North American culture has always embraced the nonconformist does much to explain the popularity of the antihero, the cowboy, and the gangster. The usefulness of nonconformity in behavior and appearance is dramatic and appealing. Indeed, the writing tradition suggests that the use of a nonconformist as your main character enhances his appeal.

Character Vs. Plot

An issue you will continually face has to do with the primacy of character over plot or the plot over character—the foreground-background dilemma. As we mentioned, stories are enhanced by having both foreground and background. However, there are particular stories and genres that need more of one than the other. Adventure films, farce, satire, and musicals do not need complex characters, but they do need elaborate plots. Other genres, such as the melodrama and *film noir*, depend on the complexity of the characters. Consequently, the screen time spent with characterization, rather than plot in melodrama and *film noir*, is much greater.

When the background story takes precedence over the foreground story, such as in Sam Shepard's *Fool for Love*, character becomes everything and the plot, the foreground story, withers in importance. In the extreme case of background story primacy, such as John Patrick Shanley's *Moonstruck*, the plot can be described in two lines.

In these cases, where the background story is prevalent, the nature of the character, the role of charisma, as well as dilemma, become even more important. The consequence is a reliance on character.

Implied in the reliance on character is the increased reliance on dialogue. Your dialogue in background stories has to be exceptionally charged and appealing to compensate for the simpler plot. The audience's need for stimulation is no less in the strong background story than it is in the foreground screen story. You should keep in mind the tradeoff between plot and character. What does your story need? Does it need more of one than the other?

Character Types

The Marginal Character

As mentioned earlier, audiences find the outsider appealing as a main character, the sense of mystery and surprise she brings to your story is useful. But marginality only works when it interacts with the larger society or with mainstream ideas. If Nola in *She's Gotta Have It* didn't flirt with the idea of a life with one of her three men, there would be no personal conflict and, consequently, no story.

Mozart may be a musical genius in Peter Shaffer's *Amadeus*, but his manners and behavior are far below the expectations of the Viennese court in which he seeks fame and fortune. He is an outsider seeking to breach the social order and his failure leads to his death.

Whether your main characters are prostitutes, pimps, or princes, the marginalized position in which they find themselves comes alive when you create dramatic situations in which margin and center clash in terms of characters.

The Mad Character

An extreme example of a marginal character is a mad character. Whether madness is the subject matter of the story, as in Ken Loach's *Family Life*, or the posture taken by the character to meet the world, as in Julius Epstein's *Reuben, Reuben*, the mad character places the viewer in a challenging position. The mad character is not charismatic, but the opposite. This character pushes us away to reflect on his plight and the reasons for it.

Often, the writer will use the mad character to comment on significant relationships or on society. Robert Klane uses mad behavior and mad characters to comment on society. His screenplays for *Where's Poppa?* and *Weekend at Bernie's* use humor to make the mad behavior more palatable. Essentially, the behavior of the mad character remains irrational, but, the fact that he experiences humiliation causes us to feel sympathy for this character.

The benefit of using a mad character is the distance between the character and the audience. This distance allows the viewer to reflect upon events. In this sense, the mad character is useful in the same way the ironic character is useful.

One last point. Because of the extreme behavior of the mad character, the writer has a volatile unpredictability that can be useful to rouse the feelings of the viewers beyond the usual experience. Bo Goldman uses this powerful quality in *One Flew Over the Cuckoo's Nest* and *Shoot the Moon*.

The Victim

In many ways, the mad character is the ultimate victim. But many other screen stories present the main character as a victim, without the overlay of madness. The screwball comedy, *film noir*, the horror film, the satire, the melodrama, the war film, and the situation comedy can all present the main character as a victim. Who can forget Felix in Neil Simon's *The Odd Couple?*

The benefit of using this position for the main character is the inherent conflict of the position. If the character is being exploited by a situation or a person, we can readily hope he will not only survive but also overcome his dilemma. It's the old story of rooting for the underdog.

There are stories where the character is being victimized by himself. The main character in Roger Simon and Paul Mazursky's *Enemies, A Love Story* needn't go on acting like the victim, but a mixture of living in the past and fearing the present maintains his position as a victim.

As long as you can avoid a position in which the character accepts being a victim, the main character as victim is useful to you. Just as the marginal character needs the center to rail against, the victim needs to struggle against the oppressor. As long as the character struggles, we hope for the best and fear for the worst, a useful position for the writer to have us in.

The Hero

The natural position for the main character is the hero. This is probably the easiest character with which to work. The hero is attractive, has charisma, and, by virtue of the dilemma in which you place the character, the struggle of the character can be easily presented as heroic. We are not suggesting that this is the position most useful for your screenplay. Rather, we suggest that the presentation of the main character as a hero needn't mean James Bond or Josie Wales. It does mean that the behavior of Rory, in *Inside Moves*, in his decision to make something of his life rather than remain a victim, is a heroic act. Rory is a hero, in spite of his passivity as a character. Regina's decision to go against her mother, in Lillian Hellman's *The Little Foxes*, makes Regina a hero.

In order to make the main character a hero, even a passive character, you need a plot that suggests the many barriers to heroic action. You also need an antagonist who is so formidable that the behavior of a Rory or a Regina will seem heroic.

Heroic action does not need superhuman effort. From a writer's perspective, this option needs only proper positioning of the character and plotting of the story. The main character as a hero probably offers you the strongest formula for identification, but to be credible, it challenges you to create a story that, on a personal level, seems like the climb up Mt. Everest; it's tough, but worth the try.

Your Attitude to Character

Your attitude toward the character is the most important decision you'll make for your screenplay. You don't have to love your character, but you should be fascinated by him, so fascinated that exploring the facets of that person is very real for you. If the character grips you, your audience should follow readily.

There are a variety of positions that help you set up your character so that conflict flows more readily. The marginal character and the mad character are positioned to fight the values of the center, the society. This struggle brings us into their stories. The victim and the hero are more readily viewed as characters with whom we can easily identify. Again, the situation in which they find themselves is a conflict, therefore we can enter their story quickly.

Seduction and Scriptwriting

There is another dimension to your work with character. It is not enough to make us care about your character. It is not enough that you grip us with your character. If your screenplay is to succeed we have to live through a relationship with all its ups and downs with your main character. To be more specific, we suggest that most successful screenplays tend to acknowledge a special relationship between you, the writer, and the viewer. We intentionally call this relationship between writer and audience *seduction and scriptwriting*. The hyperbolic term "seduction" is used to focus your attention on the devices you use to involve us in your screen story. To capture our attention, we suggest that you involve us in an intense relationship with your main character and that in the course of the screen story, we in the audience have to live through an emotional relationship with that screen story. The relationship needs many of the satisfactions of intense personal relationships. We need to love and hate and to resolve the state of the relationship. Our contention is that without this level of intensity, structure, plotting, and character, elegant language will not be enough to link us to the screen story.

To illustrate what we mean, we will look at five screen stories dealing with the same story. Essentially we want to illustrate why *Wyatt Earp* (1994), the Lawrence Kasdan and Dan Gordon version of the Wyatt Earp story failed. We contend that it failed because of its failure to establish a deep relationship with the main character, Wyatt Earp. By looking at four other versions, we will show how important it is for the writer to create and maintain an intense relationship between us and the main character.

The four other versions of the Wyatt Earp story are *Tombstone* (1994), written by Kevin Jarre, *Hour of the Gun* (1967), written by Edward Anhalt, *The Gunfight at the O.K. Corral* (1957), by Leon Uris, and *My Darling Clementine* (1947), by Samuel G. Engel. All five share the following elements:

1. Wyatt Earp is the central character.
2. He is the sheriff of Tombstone, Arizona.
3. He was formerly the sheriff of Dodge City, Kansas, where he earned a reputation as a lawman.
4. He worked closely with his brothers, Virgil and Morgan, as both sheriff and deputy.
5. He struck up a friendship with Doc Holliday, a tubercular gunfighter who was a gambler and former dentist from the East.
6. Tombstone is a tough frontier town. The cowboys, including the Clantons, the McLowerys, Curly Bill, and Johnny Ringo, were the dominant outlaw force in the territory.
7. The famous gunfight at the O.K. Corral is fought in Tombstone. The Earps and Doc Holliday fought against the Clantons and the McLowerys.
8. As a consequence of the gunfight, Morgan Earp is assassinated.
9. Wyatt Earp wreaks revenge on the cowboys by destroying those who stood against him, and Doc Holliday continues to help.
10. Earp himself, although he believes in his family, is a man with rough edges. He functions well as a lawman because he is as ruthless as the cowboys.

11.   All the Earp stories focus on the 1880 period when he is sheriff of Tombstone.

These are the story elements of all five screen versions. Each of them works with the historical record, some more literally than others. The two versions that attempt the greatest verisimilitude—Anhalt's *Hour of the Gun* and Kasdan and Gordon's *Wyatt Earp*—are the weakest screenplays.

The Anhalt version opens with the actual gunfight at the O.K. Corral and focuses on its aftermath. It's not quite docu-drama but the historical events themselves are the focus of this version.

The Gordon-Kasdan version covers forty years in Earp's life, beginning with him as an adolescent and ending with him in middle age. The events of the O.K. Corral gunfight occur shortly after the midpoint, although the preparations open the film. The goal here seems to be to look at Earp the man while dismantling Earp the legend. The three other versions each take a particular dramatic approach to the story.

In typical John Ford fashion, Samuel G. Engel's script for *My Darling Clementine* (1947) approaches the story as a struggle of two families, the Earps and the Clantons. The Earps represent family values—loyalty, responsibility and morality—while the Clantons, although loyal to one another, are cattle thieves and murderers, who kill James Earp at the beginning of the story. The gunfight at the O.K. Corral becomes the ritual that purges Tombstone of its immoral element and establishes the primacy of the Earp family values as American, as a source of strength of the individual, Wyatt Earp.

The next version is Leon Uris's *Gunfight at the O.K. Corral*. This version, as with *My Darling Clementine*, takes place principally in Tombstone and focuses on the evolution of the friendship of Wyatt Earp and Doc Holliday. Although Holliday is important in all the versions, no single version focuses on him as much. Indeed, the friendship supersedes the antagonists, whether they are the Clantons, Curly Bill, or Johnny Ringo. Friendship and personal sacrifice are all that count in this version.

The final version, Kevin Jarre's *Tombstone*, focuses on Wyatt Earp as a man with material ambitions for himself and his family. Those ambitions take him to Tombstone and away from the law. But in *Tombstone*, the power of the cowboys is such that they stand in the way of his material climb. He takes up the law to protect what he views as his material well-being. The cowboys are so relentless and vengeful that all those who stand in their way become their targets; they force the confrontation with the Earps. (In this version, Wyatt is deputized by Virgil in order to fight as a lawman at the O.K. Corral.) Doc Holliday, his friend, fights as well. Only the assassination of Morgan forces Wyatt to eliminate the cowboys. He uses all means and his ruthlessness is necessary for his survival. In the end he has lost the very thing he came to Tombstone for: prosperity.

In the most successful versions—*My Darling Clementine* and *Tombstone*—there is a natural progression in our relationship with the main character. Each film begins with a clear articulation of the goal of the main character—prosperity for the family. In *My Darling Clementine*, it involves a cattle drive. In *Tombstone*, it involves buying into a gambling emporium/saloon.

In each version, a bully taunts the ordinary citizens of Tombstone, and in each case the objectionable person is easily overcome by Earp. The consequence is that Earp is a highly desirable person for the position of sheriff. In *My Darling Clementine*, he accepts; in *Tombstone*, he does not. In each film, we see Earp struggle to maintain his position in Tombstone as either lawman or businessman. And in each case, a clear antagonist(s) emerges to position himself against Earp. In both films that character is Ike Clanton (although Curly Bill and Johnny Ringo are more prominent co-antagonists in *Tombstone*). Our point here is that the clarity and persistence and the cruelty of the antagonist(s) in *My Darling Clementine* and *Tombstone* draw us closer to the main character, Wyatt Earp.

Another dimension of our relationship with Wyatt Earp is to see his vulnerability in a love relationship. In *My Darling Clementine*, it is Earp's unrequited love for Clementine that makes him seem vulnerable. In *Tombstone*, it is his attraction to Josie, the actress, that makes him vulnerable. We know he doesn't take up with Josie because of his existing relationship with the prostitute Mattie. Out of loyalty, in this version, he does not take up with Josie. Consequently, in both these versions, Earp seems a man incapable of finding love. The loss ennobles his sense of responsibility to his family and to Mattie.

Finally, there are the concepts of family and friendship. Earp works closely with his brothers, and in both versions he is strongly supported by an alter ego, the educated, articulate killer Doc Holliday. In *My Darling Clementine*, Doc dies in the gunfight. In *Tombstone*, he fights on with Earp against the cowboys after the famous gunfight. In the latter version, Earp is present at the sanitarium when Holliday is near death. Although much is made of family, it is the friendship and its dignity that emotionalizes both *My Darling Clementine* and *Tombstone* (as it did in *Gunfight at the O.K. Corral*); it's as much the mystery of the attraction of opposites as the commitment and importance of friendship in the midst of so hostile an environment as Tombstone. The friendship humanizes and serves to ennoble the notion of friendship and in this case, its object, Wyatt Earp.

Returning for the moment to the concept of family, this issue is much more powerful in *My Darling Clementine* where it is two families, the Earps and the Clantons, who sum up the struggle of good against evil in Tombstone.

Consequently, family is very important in *My Darling Clementine* and it too serves to root and ennoble the Wyatt Earp character.

We turn now to the flaws in the Gordon–Kasdan version, which essentially come down to our lack of involvement with the main character. This version fails for the reasons that the Jarre and Engel versions succeed.

First, the issue of the main character's goal. In the Engel and Jarre versions, we learn the goal of the main character right away. This is not the case in the Gordon–Kasdan version where we first see the young Earp trying to run off to war. For the first hour of the film we understand him as a character struggling between what he wants to do and what his father wants him to do. He experiences disappointments and tragedy (the loss of his first wife), but we never do know what his goal is. We have to assume that he is a character without a clear goal, an ambivalent character, rather than a character who wants material success for his family, as the Earp character does at the outset of *My Darling Clementine* and *Tombstone*.

A second problem in the Gordon–Kasdan script is that there is no clear antagonist. The Clantons, the McLowerys, Curly Bill, and Johnny Ringo are present in Tombstone, but we never understand the antipathy of the Earps toward them nor do we understand what they are fighting about. It is as if Gordon and Kasdan are so concerned with debunking the myth of Wyatt Earp that they make him his own antagonist. The consequence is that we do not understand Wyatt Earp in his struggle. We watch as observers on the sidelines rather than as identified participants in his struggle.

And what of Wyatt Earp the lover-in-waiting of *My Darling Clementine* and *Tombstone*? That is not the Wyatt Earp we meet in the Gordon–Kasdan version. Instead, we find a Wyatt Earp who never recovers from the loss of his first wife—he takes up with a prostitute, Mattie, and simultaneously begins to sleep with the actress Josie. Instead of Earp, the vulnerable male, here we have Earp, the selfish male. Instead of caring, he seems cruel. Instead of vulnerable, he is cold and calculating. This is not a character we want to be involved with.

Turning to the issues of family and friendship, we find a similar Earp. In the Gordon–Kasdan version as in the other, he does work with his brothers. However, the brothers' wives constantly complain that Wyatt runs their lives and eventually ruins them. In this version Wyatt Earp is in a constant power struggle for control of his family. This is hardly the ideal Earp family portrayed in Engel's *My Darling Clementine*. As with Wyatt, the unrequited lover, here Wyatt the family man is unattractive.

This leaves only the issue of his friendship with Doc Holliday as a source of audience empathy for Earp. There is friendship here, but it's a case of too little, too late. Earp seems so impervious to feeling that the empathetic Holliday appears marginal and pathetic. Given Holliday's fragility, the friendship says more about the Holliday character. Consequently, it does not help our relationship with the Earp character as it does in the more successful versions.

At all levels, the Gordon–Kasdan version of the Wyatt Earp character deflects us from an active involvement and empathy with the character. Without that intense relationship with Wyatt Earp, the screen story fails. Without the writer seeking and cultivating a special relationship between the main character and the audience, screen stories fail. To succeed, the audience needs that special relationship, and writers can cultivate that relationship by understanding the dramatic means to achieve it.

How to Make Your Script Your Own

If the narrative strategy you've employed takes advantage of your character choice and your structural choice surprises and delights the viewer, all that remains to making the script your own is to infuse it with details that mean something to you and with language that allows your emotions to speak. This may sound optimistic, but it isn't. What we are saying is that having a good feeling for the structural choice and character type that best suits your story isn't quite enough to make it unique. You have to be willing to invest more feeling in the story.

This effort is akin to the mechanical adjustment you can make to alter a character who is a stereotype. Move away from the idealistic professor who is curious about everything, to the idealistic professor who follows up his curiosity with action, and you've got Indiana Jones. But it isn't until Jeffrey Baum begins to probe Jones's conflicting relationship with his father that we begin to understand Jones's quick frustration and misunderstanding in his relationships. This move humanizes Jones and makes the third film in the series, *Indiana Jones and the Last Crusade*, seem fresher. Jones is now far from a stereotype.

This is the sort of creative metamorphosis that makes the story seem new and appealing. This is the path Alvin Sergeant follows in *Julia*, and Sam Shepard and Wim Wenders follow in *Paris, Texas*. It's the path Julius Epstein has followed from *Casablanca* to *Reuben, Reuben*.

Screenwriting and the Other Arts

Screenwriters are storytellers who write stories for film. Some make a great deal of money, but get very little respect from their peers. Most make very little money and get very little respect from their peers. It has always been perplexing, but that's the way it is. Nevertheless, writing talents such as Clifford Odets, Sam Raphaelson, Preston Sturges, and Harold

Pinter have been attracted to the form. The works of Billy Wilder, Joseph L. Mankiewicz, and Ben Hecht remain vital and artful, especially from today's vantage point.

Just as other industries compartmentalize function, so, too, do the arts. A screenwriter is no longer a writer from a community of storytellers. She is a screenwriter. It would be timely for the screenwriter to reconsider her linkages with other communicative and popular arts. We have much to learn from playwrights, novelists, and journalists, just as they have something to learn from us. Whether their interests are social action or a good laugh, we share our interest in capturing our audience. They, and the screenwriter, live in a world of ideas.

Screenwriters can strengthen their foreground stories by telling them clearly and quickly, as journalists do, who have to maintain reader interest to the end of the story. At any point, a reader can set down a newspaper. Screenwriters can learn a lot from the strength the playwright brings to the background story. Character and language are all the playwright employs to keep his audience. Consequently, these elements have to be amusing, stimulating, and must compensate for the relative loss in action the stage suffers relative to film. Screenwriters can benefit from the use of stronger background stories. They can be emboldened by the structural experiments of writers such as Ann Beattie *(Picturing Will)* and Don DeLillo *(Libra)*. These structural experiments add layers of meaning to the content of the work, just as the structural experiments of screenwriters such as Stanley Kubrick and Spike Lee add meaning to their work.

Screenwriters and the Market

In *Broadcast News*, James L. Brooks begins the film with three small vignettes about the three characters of the story as adolescents. After this prologue, the film shifts to the time period of the film, some fifteen years later. Brooks's point is that characters come from somewhere and go somewhere. They have regional, cultural, sexual, and behavioral differences. The same can be said for writers. Unfortunately, if you were to watch all the films released in any three-month period, you'd hardly know it. You'd think they all grew up a ten-minute drive from Universal Studios, were all the same sex, and were born minutes apart.

Our point, here, is that you are the only you there is, and your script will be better if it reflects your individuality, rather than what you think is selling today. This isn't a particularly radical thought. If you look at cinematographers and directors, notice how many come from Australia, England, The Netherlands, and Germany. Hollywood has always sought out talent wherever it was available. The only thing North American writers have going for them is their ease at writing colloquial English. This will change, as English becomes more and more widespread and will end the North American writer's monopoly on screenwriting. Unless, of course, we start writing better scripts.

Ann Beattie, Richard Ford, Baharati Mukherjee, and Margaret Atwood are all exceptional world-class novelists. Playwrights such as Sam Shepard and Neil Simon have also made their mark around the world. North America has fine storytellers. Will the art of screenwriting follow suit? It will when screenwriters tell stronger, more personal stories. To compete in the fickle entertainment market, screenwriters have to be as innovative as our novelists and playwrights.

We hope you will be.

We know you can be.

References

1. William Goldman, *Adventures in the Screen Trade* (New York: Warner Books, 1983).

19

∎ ∎ ∎ ∎ ∎ ∎ ∎ ∎

Personal Scriptwriting—
Beyond the Edge

Up to this point, we have been discussing scripts for feature length, theatrical films written in standard screenplay form so that others might direct them. However, with the growth of alternative sources of funding and the low-tech production opportunities afforded by Hi8 video, super-16 or even Fisher Price Pixelvision, we are seeing an explosion of productions of varying lengths, intended for a wide range of audiences, many of them written to be directed by the writer herself. Although some of these are so personal that they are elaborate home movies, others have demonstrated new ways to speak from experience and, in so doing, have redefined our notion of the possibilities of the personal script.

In addition to raising questions of screenwriting technique, these alternative, self-made forms have served as vehicles for underrepresented peoples to express a voice perhaps otherwise denied them. Many times, their expression unites directing and writing, suggesting that the way we see and the stories we use to organize our seeing have to be developed together. Thus many of these films open up story structures to provide opportunities to explore moments of visualization and rhythm that can be prepared for, but not directly expressed, through writing alone. Working through distribution channels such as *Deep Dish TV* and *Women Make Movies*, women, historically minimally employed as mainstream writers and directors, have transformed low-tech video into an expressive form in its own right, while *Third World Newsreel* has provided distribution to emerging writers-directors of color.

We would like to conclude *Alternative Scriptwriting* with a brief consideration of a few short films, paying particular attention to their development of new narrative languages that serve as expression of voices not traditionally heard.

But we cannot do this without considering once more the power and the problems associated with working close to personal experience. As we have said before, one of the central premises of this book has been to encourage writing out of the self, because that is where the deepest possibilities for self-expression and originality lie. But, as writing teachers, we see everyday examples of what can get created under the notion of the personal—highly self-involved stories whose authors write with the same blindness that cripples their characters. The approach to the personal we are talking about must find a way to counter this by requiring both immediacy and reflection. Without the immediacy, our work will have neither heart nor drive. However, without the reflection, our work risks being only an immature self-justification of the particular limitations that bedevil our life. To break out of this, we must find some way to look with clarity at the very personal experience from which we are writing.

Seeing Oneself

Undigested, our lives, our personal perceptions, our experiences communicate nothing. Without any prior, extratextual interest in the author, we cannot expect our audience to care. That which is purely personal is, by definition, inherently uninteresting to others.

Although this is not true of textbooks in fiction writing, most texts on screenwriting warn against this personal writing for exactly this reason—in a medium that needs to reach millions of viewers, it is assumed we cannot find something in the details of our lives that is sufficiently broad. Screenplay texts stress conceptual issues such as structure, act breaks, and even external conceptions of character as a means of separating writers from the personal, of concentrating on communication practices rather than the extraction of meaning from that we know best. They do this for a number of reasons, of which two are important to us here. The first is that mainstream film, almost by definition, substitutes the broad and the general for the individual. The second is that while it is possible to guide writers by making general statements about structure in a textbook, it is not possible to discuss how to make meaningful and universal the individual experiences that make up our lives and that we seek to transform into story. While we will provide some examples, we have no illusions we can do that here.

Being aware of the danger must not keep us from working out of our own sense of the world, because without doing so, we have little true investment in our work. We must learn, however, that while we fully embrace our experience, we also must stand outside and understand what the viewer might make of it. The central issue here is not one of technique but of courage and honesty in looking at ourselves. We all have areas of darkness where our motivations are not clear or our self-perceptions serve to hide our disappointments. This can be rich and powerful stuff, but it can also be terrifying to examine. But we cannot write about these areas without honest self-awareness.

Characters may in fact never escape this trap of self-delusion, but we as writers cannot let ourselves fall in. We must push our characters to the point where they either must see or be lost.

Peel and _Molly's Pilgrim_   We will start as we did in Chapters 2 and 3 by comparing a traditional short film with an alternative short.

In _Molly's Pilgrim_[1] a young woman and recent Russian-Jewish immigrant is teased by her schoolmates because of her accent and her misunderstanding of American culture. Assigned to make a pilgrim doll for Thanksgiving, she brings in instead a doll dressed in a Russian folk costume. Her class and her teacher laugh at her misunderstanding of how a pilgrim should look until Molly explains that she has come to America to seek freedom and that makes her a pilgrim also. The teacher, realizing her mistake, connects the Thanksgiving feast to the Jewish Festival of the Tabernacle, and Molly's classmates come to accept her as one of their own.

Jane Campion's _Peel_[2] is much more difficult to summarize. A man, his sister and his son, driving back from viewing a piece of land, fight, pull off the road, and, although their alliances change, continue to fight. The film ends with the son jumping on the car's roof as the sister sulks inside and the brother sits dejectedly on the rear bumper.

On one level, looking at these films together is unfair because _Molly's Pilgrim_ is designed for a young adult audience while _Peel_ is not. Yet, _Molly's Pilgrim_ is valuable to us because it illustrates in a short form some of the elements we have talked about as characteristic of mainstream film—problems are shown to belong to individuals, not to society at large; when individuals overcome the problems, the problems vanish; stories have a clear beginning, middle, and end that shape experience in a satisfying way; the individual voice of the filmmaker is concealed behind the working-out of the story; the implied perspective of the filmmaker regards the class's ultimate acceptance of Molly as right and proper, as does the viewer; this eventual acceptance is set up as the correct answer in the beginning and the story serves to bring us to its realization.

We can see the clarity of this design by considering the way _Molly's Pilgrim_ begins. Molly stares at a music box that we read as representing her Russian past. Her mother enters and begins to speak Russian before Molly interrupts her, asking her mother to speak only in English. The two-part split represented by the music box and by speaking English resolves at the end of the story when Molly has both her Russian pilgrim and her English friends.

Peel works on totally different terms. The character tension develops first between the man and his son because the son refuses to stop throwing an orange peel out the window and then, after the son has been sent off to gather the discarded peel, it shifts to the man and his sister. The text of the argument is trivial—the sister is angry that she has gone on this expedition with the brother because she will miss a favorite television program. The argument appears continuous, without end, and seems to conceal more than it reveals. Finally, an added element of tension that drives the story is the threat from the cars that are whizzing past on the highway.

Let's look at conflict a little closer. In a mainstream film, the main characters are thought to be in a transitory state—playing out the story is designed to bring them to resolution. If the conflict does not resolve, the characters will remain undefined and the film will not appear to be over. (Think, for instance, of how vague the character of Rick in *Casablanca* would be if the film ended before he made his final decision about Ilsa.) Thus, conflict functions as an obstacle for resolution; it must be transcended for the story to end.

As the character moves to resolution, several things tend to happen. First, the subtext emerges and in most cases is confronted head-on. This is part of what gives many mainstream films a "self-help" feel—i.e., confronting feelings leads to overcoming them. Thus, the class's recognition of how unfairly they have misjudged Molly in rejecting her pilgrim is a necessary precursor to accepting her in the end.

Second, a lurking potential for resolution set up earlier in the story becomes activated. Molly initially is rejected by classmates who represent a spectrum of attitudes from hostility to just going along with the group. When the story resolves, the classmate who has been most tentative in rejecting Molly is now the one who first hugs her, not the classmate who has been most hostile. By introducing a range of characters, the potential for change in some of them has been set up right from the beginning.

In *Peel*, however, the text of the argument is about nothing that is intrinsically important, and the sub-text seems to imply a whole history of specific irritations rather than one global conflict that can be overcome. Nothing deeper than the surface conflict is even engaged; there is no suggestion that something might be overcome. Arguments cannot be transcended as they are in mainstream films, because arguments and a kind of low-grade tension are precisely what define character and the experience of life itself. Thus, the argument in *Peel* provides a kind of centrifugal force, a sense of what makes families spin apart.

But stop. Anyone who has seen student films or read student stories knows about this centrifugal force. At a certain age and with a certain mindset, young writers and filmmakers always construct a world in which everything falls apart. Anxiety is glorified, despair celebrated. Stories end with suicides or lonely walks in the woods; they do not recognize the needs that work to hold us together. If this is what we mean by personal filmmaking, then why should anyone be interested?

It is not. It is precisely the perspective that the writer gains by being able to look back on her experience that provides an answer to this.

Recognizing the limitations of presenting disintegration as an easy way out, Campion proves a contrasting centripetal force by dramatizing the cost of the tension driving this family apart and in so doing brings a perspective to its disintegration. The boy, confronted with his aunt sitting motionless behind the wheel and his father, head in hand, on the rear bumper, stares into both of their mute faces, looking for similarities, apparently seeking to connect their faces with his own. The shots that Campion gives us go beyond the boy's individual point of view to represent a more general meditation on commonality and difference.

As the boy touches the faces, the camera frames them with great tenderness, caressing them in such a way as to suggest it is seeking a connection between father and aunt, and the reverse shot of the boy. At this moment, although the conflict does not end, we see, directly expressed by the narrator, the forces that keep us from spinning entirely apart. Conflict is not transcended, definition is not static. Rather life is seen as a movement between forces of disintegration and the need for cohesion.

Finally, *Peel* is not a work in which we can separate script from final film. The dialogue is minimal and hardly consequential; there is not a clear and readable progression of beats that serves to bring us into character, nor is the action focused to provide revelation. The quality of shots in which we examine the faces at the end could not really be anticipated in writing. All this is not to negate the importance of the writing or the design of the piece, but to reposition it. Although achieved without a traditional script or relationship between writer and director, we are still witnessing a masterful act of storytelling that has been constructed to allow shots to resonant far beyond their literal meaning.

Sink or Swim   Su Friedrich's *Sink or Swim*[3] is structured in twenty-six sections, each of which is introduced with a short title. The titles begin with the letter "z" and work through the alphabet in reverse order, "Zygote," "Y Chromosome," "X Chromosome," "Witness," etc. Over them, a young girl's voice narrates the story of a woman we come to regard as the central character. Gradually, the narrated story focuses on the relationship between this woman and her father. We learn of its precariousness, the cruel tenderness that marked their dealings with one another (after she learns to swim by being thrown into a pool, she and her father celebrate their enjoyment of swimming together before her father frightens her by impossible tales of water moccasins lurking in the lake), the hurt the woman feels when her father leaves her mother, and later when her father sends the woman home early after an abortive vacation in Mexico. Struggling with subsequent unsatisfactory contacts with her father, the woman finally is able to declare herself and begin to live her own life.

Told this way, the story sounds as specific and private as the stories of many of our friends. It is so personal that our reaction might be to think, "What a difficult situation living with a father like that, but we all have our problems and we can only listen to so much that does not directly concern us." Friedrich counters this by finding moments of broader resonance that make the actual narrative less important than what she sets against it. This narrative space is created by various formal strategies that serve to modulate the distance with which we regard the story.

The voice-over itself is stylized in a number of ways. Using another character to narrate the woman's story suggests a distance that could not be achieved if the woman narrated on her own. The effect is almost that of the close-in, third person narrator used by Henry James. For much of the film, we are so close we feel as though the story is being narrated by the woman herself, then suddenly something shifts and we become aware of the narrator who stands between us and the woman. Sometimes the film uses its greater narrative distance for irony, as in the passage where the girl tells us that the woman looked up her father's work to see what he had written at the time of the divorce. "She discovered that two of the articles written that year involve the study of kinship systems." No comment. No reaction. The girl does not probe the woman's mind and we are left to fill in the irony for her. At other times, we move in very close and the sudden collapse of distance is very powerful, as in the section where we watch the woman type a letter to her father without any comment from the girl narrator. The effect of this movement constantly makes us consider our position relative to the woman character. Sometimes we see it as purely her story; at other times we are pulled back and invited to consider more broadly the marks a parent leaves on a child.

Making the narrator a young girl contrasts with the controlled, at times formal, diction of the voice-overs. It adds a sense of longing to the film, a sense of a simplicity that seeks to speak directly but that cannot. We tie this blockage to the woman's difficulty in speaking about her father. Using the reverse alphabet serves to organize the story around language, providing another way to extend the story beyond the events it describes. Language itself is seen as a way for the woman to come to terms with her father.

Finally, individual sections use a wide variety of narrative techniques including a recounting of myths, spoken and sung nursery rhymes, Schubert *lieder*, and a letter.

The images themselves are as diverse as the narrative style. Some are almost literal, such as the roller-coaster ride that plays against her father's taking the woman to a terrifying movie. But most function to open a space between voice-over and image. For instance, after the title "Kinship," we hear a scratchy recording of Schubert's song "Gretchen am Spinnrad," music that we later learn evokes her mother's love for her father. We see images from a plane window, then we move to a deserted landscape, then to the same landscape seen from a car, then to women in a shower, then to strangely floating birds, then circle back to the women embracing in the shower, back to the desert, then to women drying themselves and laughing in the shower, and finally to baked, cracked desert soil. There is no way to summarize all this communicates except to note that this moment, which we will retrospectively come to regard as the moment when the woman's father left her mother, is associated with a more generalized feeling of space, of the ramifications of sexual identity, and a kind of parched dryness that transforms a specific personal event into a celebration of much greater beauty and meaning.

Daughter Rite   Michelle Citron's 1978 *Daughter Rite*,[4] a personal hybrid documentary/fiction, intercuts Citron's processed home movies of her childhood under voice-over meditations on her mother, with a series of acted improvisations based on the background of Citron and her sister.

We identify the voice-over with the filmmaker. "I started this film when I was 28," is the first thing she tells us. She goes on to explain that 28 was her mother's age when the filmmaker was born and connects her own need to make the film with this coinciding of their ages.

The voice-over meditations are written and delivered with no irony or narrative distance and, considered alone, they are a bit too complete in their understanding of the mother. Within these sections, little challenges the voice-over. Although the filmmaker describes her mother's actions, we have no basis for seeing them except as the narrator instructs us to. We do not pick up on any inadvertent slips or contradictions that betray the authority of the narrative perspective.

We can relate this to our discussion about the tension between the narrative and dramatic voice in Chapter 15. If the narrative voice so dominates a film that it makes other readings difficult, we would say the film is "overdetermined" or without "air." Another way to talk about this is to say that such a film provides the viewer no opportunity to work within the context of the film. We can take it or leave it, but we cannot engage it.

The particular power of the fictional forms we have been discussing is that by balancing narrative voice with dramatic voice, they allow us to hear what the narrative voice is declaring while at the same time, by considering our engagement with the dramatic voice, we can challenge and read behind the narrative voice. If *Daughter Rite* remains overdetermined, this tension would be denied it.

This is where the use of the improvised footage comes in. In these scenes, we are privy to a great deal more than the voice-over gives us. While sharing great intimacy with the filmmaker, the sister's take on the mother is much more forgiving. At times, the sister seems naive relative to the filmmaker, but at other times, she acts to expose sides of the filmmaker we do not get in the voice-over. We have to weigh the contrasting perspectives.

Here again, we see playing out a tension of the immediately personal with its prejudices and short-sightedness, expressed in the voice-over, against the more considered personal, which uses constructed dramatized sequences to imply a multiplicity of perspectives that the single voice-over could not convey. Our sense of the meaning of the film lies in the space between these two presentational styles.

Family Gathering   While *Daughter Rite* is dynamic in its effect on the audience, the structure of the film remains the same throughout. Lise Yasui's *Family Gathering*[5] (1989) changes right before our eyes. This leads us to another generalization about personal filmmaking—that one of the ways to start from the personal and move to the more universal is through the introduction of elements that are outside the writer's control.

Family Gathering is a study of the filmmaker's grandfather, a survivor of the American internment camps for citizens of Japanese descent during World War II. About halfway through the film, and about halfway through the filmmaker's progress of making the film, the filmmaker learns that her grandfather's death was actually a suicide that came as a direct result of his experience in the internment camp, a family secret that she has not known.

At this point, the filmmaker's unraveling of the grandfather's story stops. The issue abruptly becomes one that affects the making of the film itself. Confronted with this new knowledge, can the filmmaker go on and complete the film? Does she want to document her discovery of this family secret? Or is it too great a violation of her family's history, which should not be exposed?

The viewer feels strangely ambivalent, sympathizing with the filmmaker's dilemma while at the same time wanting the story to move to completion. Eventually it does. But now we watch the film differently.

Before, although we had been told that the filmmaker was attempting to reconstruct a past that she did not know, her authority still carried us along. Now the whole dramatic structure of the piece functions to reveal just how little control the filmmaker actually has and how affected she is by the rawness of what she has discovered. The acute personal nature of her story is given an extra resonance because we witness the immediacy of history's impact on an individual's life and understand that as much as we try to define ourselves on our own terms, there are also forces greater than we can control that cause us to discover ourselves as we react to them.

   Nice Colored Girls   Sometimes the tension between history and the individual is played out more explicitly. Tracey Moffatt's film *Nice Colored Girls*[6] (1987) follows four story lines—in contemporary Sydney, aboriginal women pick up a guy in a dance club and ply him with drinks; a voice reads an account of the first British landing on Australian shores; a black-and-white picture of that landing is shown hanging on a wall while performances of the actions depicted in the readings are played out against it; and an aboriginal woman standing on a beach stares into the camera.

   The Sydney scene is edited without synch sound. Instead, we are given what looks to be subtitled documentary comments by the aboriginal women about their experiences picking up men they mockingly refer to as "captains."

   The irony of the piece is generated by the resonance of this reversal—the present-day captains are powerless against the aboriginal natives. However, the juxtaposition of the landing account against the contemporary scene adds an additional twist to this shifting of power. The Western settlers believe they have brought control and civility to this wild land. But the film cuts back a number of times to the woman on the beach staring into the camera with a force that denies anyone's domination. This, combined with the Sydney scenes, makes us listen more closely to the reading of the landing account and, as we do, we realize that in each encounter described, the English sailors are really acting on the dictates of the aboriginal women. While this does not deny the history of Western colonization, it suggests a much more complex dynamic of power than that traditionally presented.

Summary

   We have ended *Alternative Scriptwriting* by looking at a different notion of writing than that discussed in the earlier chapters. We present this for two reasons. The first is that these works demand serious attention in their own right. These pieces, along with many others not described here, have contributed to a new visual and narrative expression by people not traditionally in control of media. The second is that these pieces all suggest means of exploring the tension between the narrative and dramatic voice that writers, no matter what their genre, may learn from and use.

   Although these works are not written in standard screenplay form, are usually designed to be directed only by the writer, and are not feature length, they are logical extensions of the concerns of this book in their intensely personal nature. They provide examples of solving the problem that confronts all independent writers, which is how to embrace our own experience while at the same time gaining sufficient perspective on it to make it significant beyond the facts of our life. This taking what is ours and learning to make it over so it resonants for others is the ultimate and most important thing we hope you take from this book.

References

1. Distributed by Phoenix Learning Resources, 2349 Chaffee Drive, St. Louis, MO 63146 (800) 221-1274.
2. Distributed by Women Make Movies, 462 Broadway, Suite 501, New York, NY 10013 (212) 925-0606.
3. Ibid.
4. Ibid.
5. Distributed by National Asian-American Telecommunications Association, 346 9th Street, 2nd Floor, San Francisco, CA 94103 (415) 863-0814.
6. Distributed by Women Make Movies, 462 Broadway, Suite 501, New York, NY 10013 (212) 925-0606.

Index